Razia Sultanova is Research Fellow of the Faculty of Asian and Middle Eastern Studies, University of Cambridge.

To the memory of my grandmothers
Fatima and Maftuha

from SHAMANISM to SUFISM

Women, Islam and Culture in Central Asia

RAZIA SULTANOVA

I.B. TAURIS

LONDON · NEW YORK

New paperback edition first published in 2014 by I.B.Tauris & Co. Ltd
London • New York
Reprinted 2015
www.ibtauris.com

First published in hardback in 2011 by I.B.Tauris & Co. Ltd

ISBN: 978 1 78076 687 4

A full CIP record for this book is available from the British Library
A full CIP record is available from the Library of Congress

Library of Congress Catalog Card Number: available

Contents

List of Illustrations

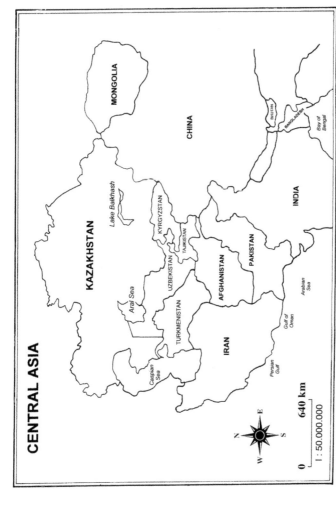

Map 1. Central Asia

Acknowledgements

I would like to credit AHRC for a generous three-year grant (2004–07) for the preparation of my monograph, SOAS and Cambridge Central Asia Forum, University of Cambridge for financial support on the last stage of my book's publication. Further acknowledgements go to James Piscatori, Lester Crook, Iradj Bagherzade, Veronica Doubleday, Irving Wardle, Youseff Azemoun, Philippa Vaughan, Annemarie Schimmel, Shusha Guppy, Montu Saxena, Almut Hintze, Rahim Ashirmuhammad Sultan, Galia Abuzar Sadreddin, Sultana Al-Quaiti, Sultan Ghalib Al-Quaiti, Vsevolod Timohim, Umida Muhammedrahimova, Erkin Agzamov, my friends Lesley Hall, Cheryl Tobler, Patricia Bater, Proika Semyonova, my husband Hamid Ismailov, and children Rano and Daniyar for their help during the final stage of the manuscript's publication.

Preface

In 1989, when I was asked by a Russian publisher in Moscow, where I lived and worked at the Union of Soviet Composers, to write 'something' about music and religion in Uzbekistan I travelled to the Ferghana Valley, the poorest and also the most religious area at that time, where I felt rather puzzled. How could I research such a topic in our ancient lands, when the study of religion was forbidden and the amalgam of 'music and religion' said not to exist? According to the Soviet account at that time, all Soviet republics, including Uzbekistan, were populated exclusively by 'atheists'. Not only the relationship between music and religion, but the very presence of such a phenomenon as Islam was under question. I remembered myself that in the early 1980s several of our relatives from Andijan, which is in the Ferghana Valley, were excluded from the Communist Party just because they had buried one of the family members in a traditional Muslim way.

After several weeks of fieldwork in and around the same Andijan, I discovered that, in fact, the area was deeply involved in musical religious activity performed by women, each village having its own female representatives. It transpired that the whole Ferghana Valley area harboured the most interesting, intensive and varied forms of religious rituals, none of which had previously had any opportunity of being mentioned in any official papers, research projects, books or articles. I felt just like Columbus discovering America.

I must mention that after speaking to these women, and having reassured them that I was not going to give away their secrets, I was allowed to join their rituals, to make recordings and take interviews. But there was a long way to go. I still had no idea how I could approach the many hours of recordings to examine this heritage. There were several questions to be answered.

How was it that this whole phenomenon had gone unnoticed, deliberately or naturally, for a whole century, without being acknowledged by researchers, folklorists, or the media? Could these rituals be categorised as a musical phenomenon, as their status was not that of a musical performance but an integral part of daily life? How could one recognise such performances within the long-standing tradition of 'liturgical music' (a term accepted in Islamic music study) if, as forms of religious service, they were interwoven with the routine of everyday life? Should they count as a 'musical phenomenon' at all, consisting as they do of vocal recitation without any instruments? Should they be classified simply as recital of poetry?

I had some practical questions for myself too: how in the late 1980s could I conduct research into this rich unknown material, and speak up about the amazing, all-female rituals of religious nature, when female members of local communities were still involved in them? What should be the focus in studying these rituals? What was the right angle from which to scrutinise them? Should I look at this phenomenon as an insider, as a person for whom the Ferghana Valley was a native place, or as an outsider for whom the rituals were just another example of live music performed in local communities with limited access for outsiders? Eventually, having looked through other research and having found many interesting sources to help me to approach these recordings, I was convinced that what I had found there and then in Uzbekistan was a unique genre of religious ritual based on poetry and music, or, more precisely, Sufi poetry and music, which had undergone development deep underground. For centuries scholars and historians studied those questions focusing only on male involvement leaving behind its overshadowed female face. Therefore this book is a long journey to Central Asian culture, religions, and music-making traditions performed in female communities. Pre-Islamic religious practices and mainly Shamanism as well as Islamic Sufism are the main stops on that journey and women are the main heroines.

1

Historical Overview

1. EARLY RELIGIOUS PRACTICES AND BELIEFS

At the dawn of Central Asian civilisation the sun shone above the mountains, steppes, and valleys. The sun was considered to be a god and people worshipped it every single day. The sun was pre-eminent and everyone knew that life depended on it. The sun was the centre of attention and crowds of pagans knelt down at its appearance, setting rituals for its honour. The sun would set and yet return, and people would celebrate this again and again. Prayers and hymns were sung to please the divinity at sunrise.

Sun-worshipping rituals developed into other rituals and people celebrated every important event with singing and dancing.

The sun was associated with different aspects of the culture of the universe, and sunlight was praised from dawn to dusk. Central Asian people considered the sun to be their God... Fire, as sun's reflection, was also worshipped, creating the basis for Zoroastrianism.[1] It also features in many other belief systems, including Central Asian Tengrianism,[2] Manichaeism,[3] and Shamanism.

The questions we investigate in this book are: How are all these religious practices reflected today in Central Asian culture and music? Where one can find their traces? Who performs these rites?

As in the past, female gatherings in Central Asia area relate to the system of celebrations based predominantly on Islam but also on the solar/lunar calendar or on different religious beliefs, such as Manichaeism, Tengrianism, and Zoroastrianism. Women celebrate the most famous events like *Navruz* (pre-Islamic New Year celebration) with singing, to the accompaniment of *doira* (frame drum) or clapping, featuring solo, duet, or chorus singing which are based on repetitive forms of blessings, greetings, or jokes. Ceremonial singing is built on simple melodic patterns, short metrical and rhythmical structures that date back to the time when singing was intended to protect, and to deflect the power of spells and the evil eye. The music-making process in general is associated with the nature of the universe.

According to scholars, at the very beginning of human history the sky was mythologically associated with the 'mother goddess', the giver of life, representing all time and space. Myths accounted for planetary cycles, marking days, nights, months, and years of unending time. So, in general, spiritual practices were based on local beliefs that god is a woman. Mythical and cosmological views developed in Central Asia were associated with the motion of the solar system – the sun, moon, planets, comets, and so on. In ancient times nomads of the Great Steppes of Central Asia believed in a god of the Sky called Tengri.[4] This faith was based on the belief that Tengri created everything in the world from chaos and oceans.[5] Tengri had two halves: the male and the female – Tengri Umai. Tengri Umai lived on the top of the mountain Sumera, in the upper sky near the milky mountain lake Sutkol. From the foot of Tengri Umai was born the goddess Ot-Ona (mother-fire), who resides in the fireplace of every house, being responsible for meals and warmth.[6]

Central Asian peoples believe that fire is sacred. In Zoroastrian belief an Indo-Iranian cosmological figure, Anahita (Aredvi Sura Anahita in the Avestan language), was the goddess of water and rain. Associated with fertility, healing, and wisdom, she looked after the well-being of women, promoting fertility, safe childbirth, and making the life of women a little easier. In the area of Khorezm (west of Uzbekistan), Anahita became known as Ambar-Ona, whose power comes from the Amu Darya River. Female Shamans still invoke her name for the success of healing rituals. At *Navruz*, songs are performed in her honour during the preparation of the sacred meal Sumalyak (Photo 1).[7]

In the Boisun area, in the southern part of Uzbekistan, the story of *Bibi-Seshanba* (Lady Tuesday) is still widely popular today. The female goddess *Bibi-Seshanba* is believed to be the protector of all women in the world. She is praised, and her help is invoked where women are gathered together. At these gatherings the women sit on the floor around a table-cloth set for lunch, light candles, burning off the *isrik* (dried herb healing treatment).

All appeals are made to the goddess in collective prayers and singing, in the dark, smoky room. The ritual proceeds slowly, and begins with prayers said aloud and the singing of devotional poetry – this is the main part of the ceremony. This is followed by confessions in which every participant joins in, and discussion across the room. The full ritual is performed on a Tuesday,

Photo 1: *Navruz* ritual – making Ser-Malyak

which, as we shall see, is appropriate. The very name of the ritual means an appeal to Mother-Mushkul Kushod, 'the lady who solves problems'.

The roots of this tradition lie in the distant past when Turkic people believed in Mother Umay, a Turkic goddess. Later, these beliefs were transformed into the Islamic cults of Mother Aysha, the wife of the Prophet Mohammad, and of Mother Fatima, his daughter. Their image as protectors of fertility and patronesses of women became extremely popular with Islamic women.

2. ISLAM IN CENTRAL ASIA

The Muslims first entered Central Asia in the middle of the seventh century during their conquest of Persia. The local peoples of Mawarannahr, as the Arabs called this place between the two rivers Amu Darya and Syr Darya, were unable to defend their land against the Khilafah because of internal divisions and the lack of strong indigenous leadership. Nevertheless, for a long period, the Muslims were unable to conquer the territory, and the process was completed only in the eighth century. An important role in the conquest was played by the Arabian military leader Qutaybah ibn Muslim (killed in 718). Arabs were highly motivated not just by the desire to spread Islamic ideology but by the wish to annex new territories with rich resources.[8]

The new way of life brought by the Muslims spread throughout the region. In the ensuing centuries native cultures were replaced or transformed as Islam moulded the people into a single community – the Islamic umma. However, the destiny of Central Asia as an Islamic region was firmly established in 750 by the victory of the Khilafah (Caliph Abu'l-Abbas) over Chinese armies in a battle at Talas River. Under Islamic rule, Central Asia was, for centuries, an important centre of culture and trade. The language of government, literature, and commerce – originally Persian – was replaced by Arabic. Mawarannahr continued to be an important political player in regional affairs. During the height of the Abbasid Caliphate in the eighth and the ninth centuries, Central Asia and Mawarannahr experienced a blossoming, and Bukhara became one of the leading centres of learning, culture, and art in the Muslim world, its magnificence rivalling contemporaneous cultural centres such as Baghdad, Cairo, and Cordoba. Some of the greatest historians, scientists, and geographers in the history of Islamic culture were natives of the region. One should mention here that Imam Muhammad ibn Isma'il al-Bukhari (810–70), the author of *Sahih al-Bukhari* (or: *Al-Djami al-Sahih*) (The True Collection of Sayings and Actions of the Prophet Muhammad), which is considered to be the most reliable and important code of hadiths – the second most important source in Islam after the Holy Qur'an – was born in Bukhara, the fourth holiest place in Islam after Mecca, Medina, and Jerusalem. The names of al-Khakim Abu Abdallah Muhammad ibn Ali al-Tirmizi (ninth century), Burhan al-Din Marginani (twelfth century), Abu Nasr al-Farabi (d. 950), Abu Ali ibn Sina (Avicenna, d. 1037), Abu Raihan Muhammad al-Biruni (d. 1048), Mirza Ulughbek (killed in 1449), and others were well known not just in the Islamic world, bringing fame to the area and generating respect across the world.

Many scientific achievements at this time had a great impact on European science.[9] Avicenna's *Canon of Medicine*, translated into Latin in the twelfth century by Gerhard von Cremona, was for centuries the predominant medical book in all European universities. Words like 'algebra' and 'algorithm' are rooted in the Islamic history of Central Asia, being references to the name of Muhammad ibn Musa al-Khorezmi (eighth century) and his work *Al-Kitab al-muhtasar fi hisab al-jabr va-l-mukabala* (The Brief Book on Accounting Algebra and Mukabala).

There is an opinion that Central Asia entered a 'golden age' at the time of Amir Temur, who was also known as Tamerlaine the Great (1370–1405), when Samarkand became the centre of political, scientific, and cultural life. There, Amir Temur gathered architects, craftsmen, builders, musicians, singers, and dancers from all the neighbouring countries that had been conquered by him. Cultural life was a mix of many different ethnic–national traditions, and it flourished spectacularly well. Architectural marvels from that epoch can still be seen today – the splendid mosque Bibi-khanum, Shahi-Zinda, Registan Square in Samarkand, Aq-Saray palace in Shahrisabz, and the magnificent shrine of Saint Ahmad Yassavi in Turkestan. Temur the Great celebrated each of his victories, diplomatic successes, and family events (especially weddings) splendidly, with music, poetry, and dances. Hundreds of thousands of people took part in the festivals and holidays, which took place in Samarkand and Shahrisabz. Splendidly-decorated city arches and pavilions were especially built for the celebrations, some of which continued for as long as three months. Singers, actors, dancers, circus acrobats, fighters, hunters, horsemen, and thousands of musicians all took part, providing contact with various neighbouring countries and historical-cultural territories such as India, China, Eastern Turkestan (today Kashghar in Northwestern China), Turkey, and Iran. No wonder, then, that, as the historian of Temur's life and epoch, Sharaf ad-Din Yazdi wrote in his book *Zafar-name* (The Book of Victories), the musicians and singers played and sang to (according to the original text) 'yusuns of Turks and ayalghu of Moghols, rools (rasm) of Chinese and qaida-yi Arabs, tariqa-yi Persians and tartib-i Ajam' (Persian tunes, Arabic melodies, Mongol vocal styles, Turkish customs, Chinese singing rules, and Altai metres).[10]

Women also took part in these celebrations as musicians, singers, and dancers.

The main form of gathering was known as majlis. These 'feasts' or 'meetings' brought together poets, musicians, scholars, artists, and other people from the intellectual community; even some members of the ruling (shah's) family played instruments at the assembly. That epoch continued for some time after Amir Temur died, as his most wonderful heritage during the period of the Temurids. The great poet and founder of classic Turkic and Uzbek literature Alisher Navoiy (1441–1501) was not only one of the viziers of the Temurid ruler Husain Baiqara (d. 1506), but also a great poet who participated in the court's entertainment life. Navoiy liked music very much and involved himself from time to time with performance and music compositions, creating pieces in the genres of *Naqsh* and *Peshrav*. At the courts, benefactors such as Alisher Navoiy created artistic dynasties that continued for generations. The British Museum has a collection of magnificent manuscripts with miniatures produced by those who were working for him.

While the Age of Enlightenment was progressing through Europe, Islamic Central Asia entered a period of long deep stagnation crisis in its development (which, according to some scholars, had started in the sixteenth century), engendered by many serious causes, such as trans-regional and international economic routs; and it was torn apart by self-destructive wars, ideological paralysis, and economic problems.

3. CENTRAL ASIA UNDER RUSSIAN AND SOVIET RULE

Tsarist troops invaded Central Asia in the second part of the nineteenth century as a part of the 'Great Game', whereby both Russia and the British Empire were intent on securing part of the southern frontier for economic, social, political, and strategic purposes. The Russian conquest of Central Asia in the nineteenth century was easily accomplished owing to tribal or clan warfare. During the colonisation of Central Asia, Russian forces confronted resistance by members of the Sufi orders rather than opposition from local feudal lords, the state apparatus or the armies of local rulers. Nonetheless, at that time, the Russians were mere intruders and did not overtly attempt to transform Islam in Central Asia: for the most part, they ignored Islam and focused on expansion. Tsarist Russia did not exert much power, money, or time in what is modern-day Uzbekistan, and generally did not interfere with the Muslims or Islamic observance.[11]

However, Islam in Central Asia *was* affected by Russian colonisation. A reformist movement called *Jadidiya* (*jadid* means new in Arabic), which initially started in Russian Muslim regions, especially in Povolj'e (Kazan and Ufa) and Krym, and also in Turkey, spread among young Islamic intellectuals in Bukhara, Samarkand, Tashkent, and other cities of Russian Turkestan. They argued for political, economic, and social progress, for reforming Islam and Islamic lands according to modern civilisation. The names of Mahmudhodja Behbudi, Abdurauf Fitrat, Munavvar Qori, and others are still remembered in Central Asia.[12]

In 1917, the Communist authorities of the Soviet Union inherited Central Asia from the old Tsarist Empire, which had collapsed during the First World War. In spite of the political turmoil existing within the former Tsarist Empire, heightened by the civil war that followed, the newly created Communist regime did not allow the Central Asian region to escape its clutches. It became clear to the Muslims of Central Asia that the Bolsheviks had no intention of granting Muslim independence, even though the Muslims, and particularly Jadids, initially supported the Bolshevik Revolution.

The Communists viewed Islam, like any other religion, as 'the opium of the people'. It was treated with hostility and suspicion, and the Muslims of the Soviet Union were subjected to countless secularisation campaigns. Initially, Bolsheviks adopted a policy of assimilation that was passive enough to preserve the archaic form of Islam and Islamic culture, but which soon took a more aggressive stance against Islam. The acceptance by Central Asian Muslim groups of certain socialist ideas did not imply any change in the orientation of their campaign. It was simply the revolutionary aspect of the Russian socialist movements that attracted them, not Marxist doctrine. Muslim freedom fighters, called *Basmachi* (robbers), fought alongside the White Russians in the civil war against the Bolsheviks, fought largely on Muslim soil. By 1920, Russian troops had stormed the Islamic citadels of Central Asia and present-day Uzbekistan, Bukhara and Khiva, and transformed them into People's Soviet Republics. They also tried to replace the region's Islamic identity and loyalty with ethnically created republics.

In 1924, the Turkestan Autonomous Soviet Socialistic Republic, Bukhara and Khorezm People's Soviet Republics were carved up by the then Commissar of Nationalities, Joseph Stalin. Over a period of time, five ethnic republics were created, Uzbekistan and Turkmenistan in 1924, Tajikistan in 1929, and Kazakhstan and Kyrgyzstan in 1936. Shirin Akiner notes that, 'These republics were entirely new state formations with no basis in historic nation-states. They were created not in response to popular demand, but at Moscow's behest.'[13]

The Soviets had clear political reasons for creating what were formerly known as Turkestan and Bukhara and Khorezm, into five new republics. The first was based upon a clear policy of divide and rule. Moscow did not want the creation of an 'Islamic Turkestan' to be a singular republic within the Union of Soviet Socialist Republics (USSR). Moscow was particularly virulent in quashing all forms of Islamic identity that existed in the region, and sought its replacement with attempts to form loyalties to the newly-created republics and to Marxist ideology.

Martha Brill Olcott has argued that 'Stalin drew the map of Soviet Central Asia not with an eye to consolidating the natural regions, but rather for the purpose of reducing the prospects for regional unity. Five separate republics were formed, creating national units for ethnic communities that had yet to think of themselves as distinct nationalities. Moreover, boundaries were set to insure the presence of large irredentist populations in each republic.'[14]

The Muslims of Central Asia were thus subjected to living within the Soviet Union under an authority and an assumed identity to which they did not adhere. The emphasis which the Soviets placed upon 'ethnicity' was formulated to channel the allegiance of the Muslims towards the newly created republics, while their Islamic identity was viciously suppressed.[15]

It is interesting to see what happened to the Islamic and traditional identity of Central Asian people during the 1930s, the time of the 'cultural revolution' when the Soviets were enthusiastically creating a new Soviet ideal.

4. 'LAND PLOUGHED BY CULTURAL REVOLUTION'

The cultural situation in the Central Asian republics during the 1930s was as complex and controversial as in many other regions of the former Soviet Union. The introduction of a new alphabet was accompanied by a revolutionary upheaval in culture and the arts, creating tension between new things found to be in the spirit of the time and old ones rejected as obsolete. The latter were mostly seen in the system of cultural traditions. The new cultural policy favoured mass art on a large scale, in keeping with modern life, 'taken out of the narrow national confines and opened to boundless internationalism'. That was achieved by encouraging amateur art – large companies of amateur musicians, sometimes reinforced with a few professionals, performing new genres. It should be noted that the oriental world of Central Asian republics was, at that time, particularly rich in professional music of ancient oral tradition with a whole constellation of great names representing its splendour.

How did that new socialistic art emerge and evolve against the background of highly developed traditional culture? The only sources available on the subject are press reports and reviews which bear witness to the processes and events of those years.

The slogans of the new cultural revolution in Central Asia were far-reaching. Here is a report by A. Bender entitled *Musicians of the Great October*: 'Chopin and Beethoven will be heard from the states of our factories' and collective farms' clubs, they will be given a new sound and inspire our socialist Beethovens, Tchaikovskys, and Mussorgskys. Where only yesterday all was obscurity and ignorance, where vicious exploitation and colonial plunder suffocated all talents, magnificent self-taught musicians of the Great October are flourishing in the land ploughed over by the great revolution.'[16]

The epithets 'obscurity, ignorance, suffocated talents', so arrogantly applied by the reporter to a millennium-old culture, seem all the more misplaced when we think of the many illustrious names which stood in those years for the best achievements in the Asian oral artistic tradition. Music researchers noted at the time: 'great love of poetry, music, and other arts among the working people of Uzbekistan. Nearly each home has (popular folk instruments) *tanbur*, *dutar*, and *nai*. The Uzbek people highly esteem their poets and prose writers, also their singers, particularly with high voices.'[17]

Great popularity was enjoyed by leading musicians, such as Maqam singer Domulla Khalim Ibadov, or mullah Tuychi Tashmuhamedov, a connoisseur and performer of traditional music, widely known far beyond our Central Asian republics. Another celebrated name was Hoji Abdulaziz Rasulov, a singer and *dutar* player from Samarkand, who had visited Mecca and studied the music of Iran, Arabia, India, and Afghanistan. Shorakhim Shoumarov, a singer loved in Ferghana and Tashkent, was invited to Bukhara by its last Emir Alimkhan (1910–20). Another voice much valued in Bukhara belonged to Levi Babakhanov, who was recorded by the Riga Gramophone Company before the 1917 October Revolution.

The best-known Maqam singer in Khorezm was Madraim Jakubov (also called Sherozi). His reputation was so great that the best way to gather people for any purpose was, they say, for the royal herald to call out, 'All go to Nurlibay (the former palace of the Khiva Khan) to hear Sherozi sing his songs.'[18] Kyrgyzia also had its own flourishing school of singers and other performers: the singer-poet (*akyn*) Toktogul Satylganov and his followers are well remembered to this day.

The history of oriental music of that time would not be complete without mentioning the glorious contribution of the Turkmen masters Shukhur-Baqshi, Mollanepes Sari-Baqshi, Tourli-ogli, and Targmamed Sukhunkuliyev. Kazakhstan – the land of the legendary singer Korkut-Ata – treasures the names of Ykhlas Dukenov and Makar Sultanaliyev. The republic's west rang with the fame of Kurmangazi Daulekterey and Dina Nurpeisova, the east with that of Tattimbet and Dayrabay. That nation gave birth to the great akyn Jamboul Jabayev, a spontaneous improviser, who created a wealth of poetry and music during his 99 years.

But the many names representing Central Asian traditional culture helped little in getting it official recognition. On the contrary, traditional art, as something belonging to the old world, was judged critically, and rejected in shame. The Communist Party's cultural policy was set in the speeches of its leaders, such as the First Secretary of the Uzbekistan Communist Party's Central Committee, Akmal Ikramov: 'The average collective farmer is beginning to feel that old Uzbek music is not satisfactory. It was created many years ago when the Uzbek working people were doubly oppressed by the Khans and Beks and by the yoke of Russian imperialism, so that the leading motifs in Uzbek music were lamentation, wailing, and tears. That no longer meets the needs of our day.'[19] Such a primitive sociological approach towards culture and the arts was the hallmark of the time.

The cultural revolution of that period was an active attempt to create a new culture in the region, based on a complete rejection of the old one. 'The culture we are developing is in principle, in form, and in content different from the pre-revolution Kazakh culture,' to quote the republic's Communist Party press.[20]

Cultural reforms were seen as a vehicle for new ideas and a new way of life. 'Cultural work with the masses is not an end in itself,' wrote cultural ideologues, 'but a means to organise and edify young people including the Young Communists, a means to reach the principal goals set before us by the Party and Comrade Stalin.'[21] The utilitarian attitude towards culture was not concealed, but flaunted in a form sometimes driven to the absurd: 'Cultural work should arm collective farmers in their struggle for a successful spring sowing, in the organising of weeding, and in the campaign for good crops.'[22] Further, 'It should increase the class vigilance of the working masses and help expose the class enemies and their agents – defeated, but not yet completely crushed, the still lurking remnants of the Bai and Kulak classes (feudal lords and rich farmers).'[23]

Thus, step by step, a new socialist culture was instilled and the old one ousted. Part of the programme was 'a wide network of mass amateur art clubs – choirs, drama groups, and music companies – with a view of turning them eventually into collective fans' theatres'.[24] The result was a booming mass amateur movement encouraged and patronised from above. Amateur theatricals cropped up everywhere, reported in upbeat press reviews. 'On the initiative of the Tashkent city council's cultural department, weekend performances by Tashkent workers' clubs are organised in the city park. For the first time ever amateur art finds its way to the professional stage. Special note should be taken of the Kafanov factory club which performed on 13 June. Their programme included the play *Pougachenok*, directed by Noskov-Stakhov, also other drama and music productions, an agitpop brigade, and a brass band...' wrote the leading Uzbek paper,[25] echoed by a Kazakh journal: 'A fine amateur music club has been set up in the Stalin district of the Karaganda region.'[26]

Gradually, standardised mass art was set up on a large scale in forms previously unheard of. In his report to the 18th Congress of the Communist Party, Stalin mentioned a rise in the number of amateur clubs between 1933 and 1939, from 61,000 to 95,600.[27] That was followed by a triumphant report in the Kazakh Communist Party journal: 'From the cultural development point of view the 1934–38 period was a true cultural revolution. The number of clubs has risen in Kazakhstan to 4,119 by 1938.'[28]

To a superficial observer, the region's culture had really undergone substantial changes: within a short time, new artistic forms had sprung up to express new content in keeping with the time. But how had that been achieved? To what extent was that art new in reality? Who were the performers obeying the Communist Party orders in the newly recruited armies of amateur artists? Let us analyse, for instance, the way amateur orchestras were set up. The traditional folk instruments were meant to play in unison, each improvising in turn. Music was never fixed in writing, but existed in the artist's memory. The basic melody was readily recognised and therefore had no need of musical notation. Its further dynamic development depended on the skill and taste of the performer, who was highly sensitive to the response of the audience. New improvisations were produced for more sophisticated listeners; the culmination of the piece – the so-called *Awj* – was played with extra care, and so on. Such was the system of oral, unwritten, oriental monodic improvised music.

Those original characteristics were then distorted, the ancient refined manner of solo improvisation was standardised to suit European ideas of polyphonic orchestra sound. It was done crudely and awkwardly, as witnessed by one of the conductors: 'We had to overcome the folk musicians' solo traditions...to tune all the instruments to a single orchestra pitch, and to get all its members, used to creative improvisations, to play in a similar manner. Each had to be taught anew even those pieces he had known before.'[29]

11

In that way, amateur orchestras 'stormed' the unfamiliar technique, often without proper command of their instruments. Commenting on the first women's *dutar* ensemble founded in Uzbekistan in 1939, the leading Uzbek musicologist Ilyas Akbarov remarked: 'Most of the girls had a very vague idea of their instruments' technique.'[30] Moreover, by their nature, the folk instruments had a soft chamber sound which was not suited to the new repertoire. So, the instruments were modernised to get them closer to the European look and sound. The need for such a revamping is still hotly debated, but remember that the first step in that direction was taken during the 1930s. Another barrier then breached by the new type of music was the use of written notation previously unknown to oriental musicians. 'A most radical shock for the monodic oral tradition was to start playing with sheet music. It was a kind of aural and psychological revolution for both musicians and their listeners,' writes N.G. Melik-Shahnazarova.[31]

Other genres were easier to adapt. As to songs, the old tradition of textual contamination made it particularly convenient to set new words to old melodies. 'For the coming tenth anniversary of the Turkmen republic the central commission for the celebrations will hold a contest for the best mass song. Ten prizes are offered. The texts are to reflect the main themes of socialist construction,' announced the Turkmen press.[32] And the required songs came forth: verses about 'The Factory' glorifying free collective labour with the 'Omonyor' refrain were set to the old Uzbek song of that name; the melody 'Omonyor III' was used for the verses 'Salute the Kremlin'.[33] The lively songs of the Koshuk, Lapar and Yalla genres were chosen for new texts, along with instrumental dance tunes and Ufar melodies from *Maqams* suitable for 'singing glory'.[34]

A similar process of creating new songs was followed by each choir or ensemble. Radio Tashkent set up a folk ensemble of musicians drawn from all over Uzbekistan. 'The traditional folk songs are not the only ones making up the ensemble's repertoire, there are also new ones about building collective farms, factories and plants, about the new free and happy life. The songs on the themes of the day are composed by the members of the ensemble. The most popular ones are "The Song of the Factory", "The October Dawn", "Our Epoch", and many others.'[35]

New songs to familiar old melodies adorned the programmes of concerts and contests of folk art. This, as well as folk orchestras, was the sign of new times, of 'reshaping the old way of life'. New conditions demanded an adaptation of that most venerated ancient Asian genre – the art of improviser-poets. The Turkmen *Baqshi* was now singing of heroic labour, new great names, and new ideas. A modest tune like *Layale*, limited formerly to everyday themes, was now used for grandiose modern subjects. Here is a new text to one of the girls' layales:

Sow your fields, collective farm!
Manure them well, collective farm!
Uproot the Bai and Kulaks
And burn them up, collective farm!
Girls, sing a song
Of a gallant rider
Who fights with glory
For his land.[36]

The well-known song about a happy Kazakh mother by a Kazakh *akyn* (i.e. singer-poet) glorified the Stalin era.

Lovely flowers on the rug
Made by mother's skilled hands...
You'll be, my baby, a mighty man,
The flowers are for you.
The steppe is singing songs for you,
Stalin, radiant like the sun, is holding out to you
Golden keys to a happy life.[37]

That song, made up of traditional images and phrases, illustrates very well the ease with which new names entered the familiar patterns. A Kazakh improviser-poet usually freely adapts a stock of pre-set motifs to fit any current situation. He is ready on the spur of the moment, in any circumstances, to pay homage to the victorious hero, or to salute the central figure of the feast, be it an old man celebrating his jubilee, or newlyweds, or a newborn baby, or just any hospitable host. A true singer can do that, effortlessly fitting any important name in his story, from the village elder to a khan or emir. With an ease characteristic of improvisational art, any ruler can be honoured, and from the 1930s that was, naturally, Stalin. That is the explanation for lines like these:

We treasure our honour and our hoards,
We'll cut our foes to pieces with swords,
We'll fight in the sun, in the rain, in the snow,
Till at last we make all our enemies go,

That at the victory Stalin should touch
His hand in contentment to his moustache.[38]

Jamboul Jabayev, the author of the above lines, merits special attention. This Kazakh *akyn* was born in 1846 and created many epic poems in the Aytys, Tolgau, and Ornau genres – rich in form and colourful language. Jamboul enjoyed nationwide renown and was named 'the patriarch of folk poets'. In 1938, he was elected deputy of Kazakhstan's Supreme Soviet (parliament). He had won his fame long before the revolution, but the new events, the changing life, found response in his chants, adding new facets to his work. That included, of course, homage to Stalin:

Sleep, my little one, Kazakh baby-boy,
You're safe in good hands.
Stalin looks out the window.
He sees all our land,
He sees you, little one,
He loves you, little one,
The whole country cares for you,
My warm little pet.[39]

After Stalin's death, Jamboul was accused of 'creative contradictions' and 'ideological and artistic weakness'. His reputation was reassessed. What can we make of Jamboul's art after all these years? Was it genuine and sincere? Or was he merely fawning to the Communist Party elite? Research into the contemporary press throws some light on the questions.

The newspapers and magazines of the 1930s reveal that *akyns* were given literary secretaries, or consultants, who were supposed to document the singers' improvisations. Moreover, there is evidence that the *akyns'* texts were 'edited' and the poets were urged to learn the corrected versions for future use. Even should the authors reject the corrections, their written texts continued to have an independent existence, with accents shifted in such a way as to make the poetry 'a product of the time'. It was admitted by some researchers that some of the editors added whole stanzas to Jamboul's original texts in the personality cult vein. 'I find the attitude towards folk poets far from deferential. Their work is often glossed over. Translators of Jamboul sometimes make fourteen lines out of his four...' wrote the folklore scholar T. Vladimirsky in 1939.[40] Because of this cavalier treatment, Jamboul himself felt highly responsible about his mission as a popular *akyn*. 'When I sang about myself', he said, 'I also sang about my people...and my songs flew above our Jatys like free birds.'[41]

So what was the effect of the 1930s on the cultural situation in Central Asia? The new genres fostered among amateurs have long been represented as 'art of the new time' alternative to the national artistic tradition of the region. True enough, in their external form, the mass amateur performances seemed very different from meditative oriental art. Ostensibly, the aim of creating a new art that differed from the national, regional, types had been achieved. But a more careful look at the content of amateur music of the 1930s reveals another picture: through the veneer of 'new' amateur forms we distinguish the inimitable features of Asian folklore with its unmistakable colour and flavour. No doubt, national art was used as a basis for some new artistic forms. But how could that new socialist culture emerge at all without the ancient traditional one that had existed for centuries in the land 'ploughed over by the great revolution'?

The Soviet Union attempted to challenge Islam intellectually with Marxist dogma and suppressed any public manifestation of Islam. Throughout the history of the Soviet Union and its dealings with Islam and the people of Central Asia, outright repression through to cooption were the mechanisms employed by the state. Although Soviet officials had previously confiscated religious property and either arrested or exiled mullahs, placed them under strict government control or forced them out of their religious positions (my own grandfather-in-law was shot dead in a Stalinist prison in 1939), that policy was relaxed during the Second World War to keep up the morale of the army and the people, since millions of Muslims were fighting on the Soviet side. In 1944, the Spiritual Board of Muslims of Central Asia and Kazakhstan was created, thus allowing registered clerics to worship within the constraints of state-sponsored Islam. The Soviet Union, as the state, sought to bring in certain aspects of Islam and tried to incorporate them within the state's structure. This leads to a Soviet 'official Islam', sanctioned and acceptable to the regime, and an 'underground Islam', which sought to keep alive pre-Soviet Islamic ideas and practices.

Soon after the end of the war Stalin's attacks on religion resumed under the excuse of 'fighting cosmopolitanism', and new waves of arrests of national intelligentsia began to take place.

The real boost to Islamic aspirations followed Uzbekistan's independence in 1991, though political Islam has become one of the most contradictory and complicated problems of modern Uzbekistan and the whole of Central Asia. Civil war in Tajikistan (1994–97) and militant incursions into Kyrgyzstan and Uzbekistan (1999–2000) are the indicators of that difficulty.

Uzbek life demonstrates the strong influence of Islam up to the present day. Like most Sunni peoples, the people of Uzbekistan have inherited and followed Islam in every aspect of their lifestyle, family norms, legal system and culture. The real boost to Islamic aspirations carried Uzbekistan's independence in 1991, though the authorities, fearing the upheaval of radical Islam, started implementing their policy of repression under the banner of fighting fundamentalism. Out of nearly 5,000 newly opened mosques, at the time of writing, almost two-thirds have been closed or converted into sports halls or other public facilities. Thousands of Islamic figures have been arrested and imprisoned. This harsh policy towards Islam caused another wave of Islamic radicalisation, with incursions of Islamic guerrillas to the southern parts of Uzbekistan.

On the other hand, the authorities could no longer deny Islam as a new source of people's identity. They tried to make strong and clear separation between traditional or 'enlightened' Islam, which is supported by the state and considered as key national value, and fundamentalist Islam, which has to be dismissed from the country.[42]

2

Shamanism in Nomadic Culture

5. THEORY AND PRACTICE

Shamanism probably developed in the Stone Age (possible the Palaeolithic era) and was known to all people in the early stages of their history. It has often been declared that originally, in deep antiquity, anyone was able to Shamanise.[43]

Without going into the existing theories on Shamanism, I would like to draw reader's attention to the most important elements of this practice, by considering the following questions: Who is a Shaman? How does a Shaman communicate with spirit? How is Shamanism connected to Islam? How popular is Shamanism among women? What is the role of music in Shamanic rituals? Those questions are addressed below.

Examining the present rich variety of forms of Shamanism in Central Asia, numerous scholars mentioned that 'in Central Asian culture Shamanism was an essential part of religious beliefs'.[44] Based on cults of ancestors, stones, mountains, and the earth goddess Otukan, Shamanism was shared by the Uzbeks of the Oxus delta, and the Mongols and Turkmen.[45] Nineteenth-century Russian ethnographers reported the presence of Shaman-sorcerers and exorcists in Tajikistan, who employed human skulls drums, smoke, and animal blood in their rituals.[46] Similarly, the Uzbek and Kazakh Shamans, until the nineteenth century, had beaten sacred drums and were adept at divination and healing. Among the Kazakhs these specialists were known as *Baqshi*. They were said to have been able to communicate with *jinns* (spirits, in Arabic), who acted as their familiars, helping them to cure illness, foretell the future, and combat the malicious influence of evil spirits.[47]

The Turkmen also had Shamanistic beliefs, several of which persist in Afghan Turkestan. Among the Kirghiz and Uighur, Shamans were also known as Baqshi. While curing illness and foretelling the future, they used to beat drums, enter into trances, and invoke Allah, Adam, Noah, and other members of the 'Biblical-Qoranic pantheon'.[48] Ancient Turks called Shamans *Kam*. They are first mentioned in the *Tan'shu*, Chinese manuscripts of the tenth century, which refer to Hakass and their *Kams* (Shamans). Some evidence of Central Asian Shamanism is displayed in *Kutadgu Bilig* by Yusuf Hos Hajib (eleventh century) and the *Dictionary of Turkic Dialects* by Mahmud Kashgari (eleventh century).[49]

Today, in Ferghana Valley, Shamans are mostly women. Shamanic rituals there take place during daylight hours, not in the dark as in Kazakh or Turkmen cases. In Ferghana Valley, Shamans are called baqshy, parihan, (*Pary* – a spirit, *hondan* – to read), or falbin (*fal* – a destiny, *bin* – to see). Also they could be called taib (*tabib* in Arabic) or kinanchi (the person taking evil from a patient). The predominant tool for Shamanic healing rituals is a frame drum.[50]

According to the study of Shamanism, the term 'Shaman' is derived from the Tungus-Ewenki (the ethnicity living in the forests north and east of Lake Baikal in Siberia, speaking Altaic language) word saman or vaman,[51] meaning a magician, healer, priest, mystic, poet, and performer of miracles, or a Shaman as 'one who uses specific techniques of ecstasy'.[52] These techniques include music, rhythmic dancing, seclusion, and, most frequently, *Zikir* (i.e. *Zikr*) – the repetition of mystical formulae.[53] Therefore, the most distinguished features of Shaman should be: 'unique ritual paraphernalia, a specialised mystical language, and operational procedures such as working for a fee'.[54] It is a common picture to see that a Shaman 'begins to pronounce his incantations and, holding a drum, strikes it forcefully against the ground'.[55]

6. HOW TO BECOME A SHAMAN?

In studying Shamanism as an important phenomenon in Central Asian culture, we cannot avoid the usual question related to the origin of such experience: how to become a Shaman. What precedes a Shaman's training? By what means did the Shaman grasp the secrets of their complicated skills?

It has often been declared that originally, in deep antiquity, anyone was able to Shamanise.[56] However, the situation has changed these days. It seems difficult to imagine that the novice Shaman could begin practising without first undergoing an apprenticeship from an experienced master (Photos 2 and 3). Nonetheless, ethnographers have gathered little

Photo 2: Healing Shamanic ritual with sweets sharing (Surkhandarya district, Uzbekistan)

Photo 3: Magic fire ritual – purification prior to *Navruz*

information confirming the existence of a 'school' of Shamans. In Siberia, among the Buryat, the novice would be taught by an experienced master: the Nenets, also, appeared to have a kind of Shamanic 'school'. In the latter half of the nineteenth century, among the Nenets, an adolescent would be 'abducted' and taken to the family of a Shaman-teacher. Here he would be taught to handle the drum, 'dissemble, perform tricks, recite incomprehensible words, howl like all the animals, imitate the hissing of the snake, mimic, in sound, the ambling of the bear through brushwood and the scurrying of the squirrel along branches'. And among the Selkup, 'a Shaman who agreed to teach (a beginner) would often remain in the tent of the young Shaman's family and live there a certain time, less commonly taking the pupil to his home.'[57]

However, among many peoples, no traditions of direct teaching have been found. For example, the Nganasan 'oppose the view that a Shaman school exists, or that the Shaman is taught by anyone'. According to the Nganasan, the Shaman is supposed to do what the spirits and gods tell him.[58]

Central Asian Shamans also made do without teaching. How can the absence of a Shamanic 'schools' be explained? Perhaps this teaching takes place in strict secrecy? No, quite simply, the 'school' is not the only, compulsory form of learning. Knowledge necessary to a Shaman can be gained independently. The ideas regarding the organisation of the world and the spirits have been known by the entire communities, and each member of the Shaman's tribe interested in the subject would be well informed on the details of the Shamanic rites. As for the skills, these come with practice. Kharuzin himself stressed this fact. 'The actual instruction involved not only mastering the ritual but also developing the essential qualities of the Shaman,' he wrote. A person who is willing to become a Shaman 'will develop and perfect these qualities during a preparatory period. He will strive to increase the number and clarity of his visions and dreams, have more frequent attacks, and place himself in a stimulated state.'[59]

The novice Shaman seeks solitude. Away from the eyes of others, he tries his power in singing and in the art of mastering the drum. The Shamans of the Tajiks and Uzbeks stayed at home for forty days in ritual isolation. Alone with himself, the Shaman learned his new role. Not only did he learn to sing and perform the ritual, but most especially he developed the ability to fall into ecstasy and to contemplate the spirits. He was expected to master the technique of self-hypnosis, and this was done by continual practice. The training of the Shaman did not end with the preparatory period. According to the ethnographer G.D. Verbov, one night was usually sufficient for the future Shaman to learn the basic technique, but many years were needed to achieve mastery.

7. WOMEN AND SHAMANISM IN CENTRAL ASIA

The question of women's role in Shamanism in Central Asia deserves special attention. Female Shamanism in the area has had a long development and is still popular today.

The presence of female Shamans in Central Asia was documented at the beginning of the twentieth century as a phenomenon 'under the sound of the drum and the singing of the Shamaness'.[60] Female Shamans, like men, have also been through the 'rites of initiation' where spirits have given them the right to Shamanise.

Very often, women became Shamans at a mature age. As Basilov noticed, 'The good many Uzbek Shamanesses underwent the 'Shamanic illness' well after marriage, already having one to three children'.[61] There are some special reasons for female participation in Shamanism. As the scholar and expert on Shamanism, Vladimir Basilov, assumed: 'Belief in spirits, in saints, or simply in certain supernatural forces continues to attract to Shamans people, chiefly women, who are troubled with illness of a child or their own ailments. Sometimes those whom modern medicine has not been able to help will go to Shamans. They reason: Why not try my luck, just in case? And like hundreds of years ago, a homemade lantern for the sprits will be lit and the drum will sound.'[62]

The social separation of male and female members of community prescribed by Islam, particularly Sunni Islam, is undoubtedly another reason for the wide spread of female Shamanism in Central Asia, where only female Shamans can assist women.

According to Basilov's reports, Shamanism is most deeply entrenched among the people of Central Asia and Kazakhstan. Describing a visit to the 80-year-old Kazakh Shamaness, Balbike-baksy (Southern Kazakhstan), Basilov mentioned that she told him 'how she cures patients by playing on the kobuz and summoning the Muslim saints and spirits, the peri. At times she puts aside the kobuz and takes up a knife.' Recounting the names of the saints, she touches the patient's body with the knife. If the illness is grave, it is necessary to perform a *Zikr*; and those attending the ritual, along with the Shamaness, shout the names of Allah or phrases such as 'There is no God but Allah!'

Traditional forms of Shamanism are preserved among the Tajiks and Uzbeks. Their Shamanism has long been distinguished by great diversity. Male and female Shamans have different helping spirits, and different healing and fortune-telling practices. Instead of the drum (or sometimes additionally), a lash, a sieve, a wooden serving spoon, a staff, a mirror, and a cup with water are used as ritual objects.[63]

Another example was documented in Uzbekistan where Basilov met another Shamaness on many occasions. Describing the meeting in 1983 in southern Uzbekistan, the Shamaness 'called her pari spirits by playing the drum and looked at the open pages of a book – the Birthday of Ker-Ogly, a folk epic (*dastan*). The spirits also aspired her to sing. After we became better acquainted she took up the drum and in high strong voice sang a song praising the scientists of the Academy of Science. "you see, my pari send you greetings", she said.'[64]

Female presence in Shamanic rituals affect even the province of fashion! According to Basilov: 'The spirits are also favourably disposed to modern fashion. I recall the village women talking about a twenty-year-old girl who had become a Shamanesss: Her dress is short, and her shoes are high-heeled, And she wears lip-stick!... the girl was dressing as the spirits commanded.'[65]

We can further see that the female role in both religious practices developed in similar way. When Shamanism was declining, women took it up. As we will see below, the same happened in Sufism: when male leadership was banned by Soviet policy, women took over and preserved that knowledge for new generations.

8. EPIC FORMS: KYRGYZ HEROIC MANAS

Epic forms played an important role in Central Asian culture, where the Kyrgyz are the most ancient people of the area. An exclusive place in their cultural heritage is held by the heroic epic Manas, which is the chronicle and encyclopaedia of the Kyrgyz people, consisting of over one million lines. According to Jirmundskyi, Manas is longer than any other of the world epics. Sayakbay Karalaev's version of Manas, for example, is twenty times as long as the Iliad and the Odyssey together, five times Shah-name, and two-and-a-half times as long as the Mahabharata.[66]

Manas is also Kyrgyz sacred wisdom, which marks every state and family event from Independence Day to every single domestic celebration.

As with all these examples of heroic epics, the place of Manas in Kyrgyz mentality could be described in the following words of Karl Reichl: 'In the performance of heroic epics tribal and cultural origins are explored and hence the primary function of epic is not entertainment but the search for ethnic and cultural identity.'[67] Despite its huge size, every Kyrgyz knows the main plot of Manas, can name all the main characters, and describe the most important episodes. It is impossible to meet any Kyrgyz who is unfamiliar with the most imaginative lines from the epic or who cannot recite some of them by heart.

As a rule, every single Manaschi would say that it was not a teacher who taught him Manas, but the spirit. This phenomenon of esoteric knowledge transmission is widespread among Turkic-speaking people.[68]

According to Rahmatulin: 'the legend of spiritual contact is something special about Manas himself, as it brings the image of Manas to the highest accomplishment and prestige.'[69] There is a widespread opinion that becoming a Manaschi is possible only when there has been a dream about it. Probably, such a dream makes a performer more confident in his talents and his destiny.[70]

For example, Manas performer Saparbek Kasmambet, listening to famous Manaschi including Sayakbay Karalaev from early childhood, absorbed the best forms of its performance. Today he is a bard-improviser and a storyteller. When he was 12 years old he went through a severe illness, dreaming about Manas every night, hearing voices and sounds of battle and war. His mother told stories about that difficult time. Once Saparbek woke up in the night claiming the horses of Manas were surrounding their house. He wanted to get out of the house but his mother, seeing he was ill and feverish, would not let him go. When she went out in the morning, to her surprise she found that the grass around the house had been trampled by horses – in a village where there were none! To get the boy out of trouble his mother slaughtered a goat to appease the spirits. Soon he recovered, and after that he began to perform Manas, as his mission had been approved by the spirits. However, as he jokes himself, his voice is not deep and strong, but high and weak like a goat's. If his mother had had enough money to slaughter a lamb, he would sound like a real singer!

Everyone can tell fairytales, claim the Kyrgyz, but only professionals can tell them as an artistic performance. Kyrgyz consider that Manas belongs to the genre style *jomok* (the narrative of the past). It is not only heroic genre images that are represented in Manas: there are laments (*Koshok*); songs of complaint (*Armans*); a statement of a will (*Kereez*); educational songs (*Sanaat Nasiyat*); descriptions of rites of passage (weddings, engagements, feasts, mourning, burial); episodes of land division; tales of moving from one land to another; and so on.

The epic Manas is considered to be an art of syncretism reminiscent of the theatre, with the remarkable singing of an inspired performer, his emotional excitement, his rich gestures, his body movements.

'Within centuries the Manas epic played a role of education book-novel influencing the audience as a play, as a staged performance, screen, reflecting historical events from the past of the nation.'[71] The vital force of Manas is reflected in its poetry echoing sounds of people and nature's cry penetrating earth and sky:

> There was a great cry!
> The people cried!
> Weeping trees were crying!
> The grass was crying!
> Tears came out of the ground!
> Mourned the earth!
> There came a black day
> Days and nights the dog of Manas
> Kumayuk was whining!
> The cry went on days and nights.[72]

Manas is performed only by men. Women also work on old Kyrgyz epics, for the purpose of healing and entertainment.[73] Usually, they use their own preferred style for epic performance. One remarkable Kyrgyz female musician who works on the old epic style today is Roza Amanova. Coming from a traditional musical background (her mother Chonmurun kyzy Marjankul was a famous singer), Roza sings little-known genres, but her powerful voice captures you and the sounds stay with you for a long time. Her performance recreating the centuries-old epic Kurmanbek (the national hero of the sixteenth–seventeenth century) could, owing to its universal content, be of widespread interest today.[74]

Kyrgyz epics and songs are moving and impressive. The world-famous Kyrgyz writer Tchingiz Aitmatov, in his novel *Jamilia* spoke of the tender, penetrating, yearning loneliness expressed in Kyrgyz songs, when the voice wavers and rings out with increasing power. These songs are able to evoke everything – mountains, steppes, grass, clouds, rivers, and people's feelings.[75]

9. SHAMANISM AND ISLAM

Islam in Central Asia was no different from other world religions from the point of its social functions. However, in the history of the area, Islam as the form of social conscience fostered wide growth in the humanities, philosophy, logic, linguistics, literature, and the arts. From the seventh to the eleventh centuries, Samarkand, Bukhara, Urgench, and other cities became centres of science and culture.

In early medieval times in Central Asia, social–political forms of Islam faced strong resistance from local populations struggling against Islamic ideology and feudal despotism. The historian Narshahi wrote about that time: 'Every time people of Bukhara were converted into Islam they soon gave up again.'[76] All resistance was developed on theoretical issues of pre-Islamic religions of Central Asia like Zoroastrianism, Manichaeism, and others. This could possibly explain the wide development of numerous Sufi orders within Central Asia as resistance against Islamic dogma and belief.[77]

Islam and Shamanism in Central Asia are contrasting phenomena: Islam is a mass religion whereas Shamanism is represented only by rare individuals, and was present in those lands which Islam conquered in the seventh century. Shamanism is usually associated with 'marginal hunting cultures' based on agriculture and animal herding, which lack the complex technical and social organisation of Islamic civilisation.[78] Shamanism is represented by individual, personal communication with the spirits whereas Islam and Sufism are meant to be communal, mass association with God.

Indeed, Shamanic beliefs in Central Asia have shown a remarkable ability to persist alongside major religious traditions, from Islam's point of view, Shamanic traditional tolerance for *adat* (from the Arabic for customary practices) has enabled it to accommodate Shamanism as well as other indigenous cultural practices and beliefs.[79] The main Shamanic attributes are represented by the upper and lower worlds. We may trace the development of the community priesthood from Shamanism. In southern Siberia, this process led to differentiate Shamans into 'black' and 'white' (where 'black' Shamans were servant of evil spirits and 'white' of good spirits), relating to the idea of the 'lower' and 'upper' worlds, though 'the greater' Shamans Shamanised to both.[80]

The figure of the prophet, familiar to virtually every religion in the world, is also connected with Shamanism. In the prophet – chosen by god, who proclaims to the people revelations heard from the deity itself (or an angel) – it is not hard to recognise the Shaman, divested of ritual guise. The legend of Muhammad's ascent into the sky riding a fantastic beast, from which he was shown heaven and hell, could be also of a Shamanic nature.[81]

Islam had a well-organised clergy and enjoyed the support of the authorities. All of them tried to do away with Shamanism. In Orthodox Islam,

Shamanic beliefs in good and evil spirits are seen as *bid'at* (superstition) and even *hurofat* (heresy) and were therefore prohibited. However, in everyday life, many of those beliefs were adopted in a culturally disguised forms and therefore in an 'Islamised' way (i.e. adjusted to Islamic practices). In Central Asia, Shamanism took on a Muslim cast. Conflicts between mullahs and Shamans remained, but became a 'professional competition' rather than a collision of different ideologies. In their outlook, Shamans did not differ from other orthodox Muslims. When beginning a rituals, Shamans appealed first to Allah, then to the various Muslim saints, and only afterwards to their helping spirits, who were considered a kind of genie (*jinn*), so often mentioned in the Qur'an.[82]

A typical synthesis between Shamanism and Islam can be observed in Uzbekistan where Uzbek Shamans began a seance by singing:

For this undertaking of mine – *bismilla,*
For all of my undertakings – *bismilla,*
I lie down, I get up – *bismilla,*
I set out on the journey – *bismilla.*

Bismilla is a shortened form of the Muslim formula *Busmillakhi-r-rakhmani-r-rakhim* (in the name of Allah, the merciful, the good). It is to be uttered before beginning any undertaking, the Shamans of the other Central Asia people also began their rituals singing with similar phrases.[83]

So, one can see that Shamanism employs divine forces for practical purpose: to heal, to solve a problem, and so on, when Sufism focuses on mystical union with no practical profit other than spiritual personification.

Shamanism employs a spiritualist/medium. A sage establishes a direct line of connection with the spirits without any mediators. This means stronger links, a go-between for the physical and spiritual realms, having prophetic and healing powers, seeking therapeutic and curing effects for people. As mentioned above, no teachers are involved in a Shaman's training, only spirits.

Sufism, a mystical development within Islam, is based on a different technique: on a well-established teaching system with 'ladder' structured development related to the idea of spiritual perfection following a master's instructions. This is called Usto-Shogird. As we will see below, all professional schools in Islamic civilisation are founded in this way, acknowledging the influence of the teacher and all previous contributors.

As shown, pre-Islamic religious practices have been integrated deeply with local traditional culture and art. Shamanism appeared in many forms of esoteric practices, and still does. However, the present religion, Islam, having a long association with culture and art, has produced many fundamental links with music, and this is the subject of the chapters that follow.

3

Sufism in Central Asia

10. HISTORICAL DEVELOPMENT

Our understanding of Islam in Central Asia would not be complete without considering the Islamic teaching called Sufism. The word Sufism (originally *tasavvuf*) is, according to one widespread explanation, probably derived from the Arabic *suf* (wool; hence *sufi*, a person wearing an ascetic's woollen garment), denoting Islamic mysticism. Although outside movements have had some influence on Sufi terminology, Sufism is definitely rooted in Islam itself. During the early years of Islam's development (under the Prophet Muhammad, and later Abu Bakr, Omar, Usman, and Ali) the rule of law did not exist, and a source for the solution of every single problem occurring in social life had to be found somewhere. The Holy Qur'an, as the revelation of Allah, was the first book used in this way, and the Hadith – the sayings and actions of the Prophet Muhammad – were added later. The profession of Muhaddith – collector and interpreter of the Hadiths – was developed at that time, and was close to the role of the contemporary lawyer.[84] As the Muhaddith would make adjustments from time to time, according to his ability, to suit the government's situation rather than considering the needs of society, compulsory law was soon established. Each Muhaddith had to follow, in his own life, prescriptions as set down in the Hadith. As the French scholar L. Massinion has pointed out, to follow Hadith meant to follow in every single step of private life the lifestyle of the founder of Islam, Prophet Muhammad – that is, an ascetic lifestyle full of trembling admiration for Allah.

This ascetic development within the Muhaddith is considered to be the embryo of Sufism. Consequently, within the first century of Islam, for every Muslim believer, the image of God (Allah) appeared mixed with threats and admonishments concerning every single step of his life. Allah warned everyone that there was no escape from consequences, and that every single matter would be questioned in the next world. At a time of internecine strife, when everyone was involved in a struggle for power, fear of the Day of Judgement dominated, leading to the rejection of enjoyment in this world for the sake of future life in the next.

The constant thoughts of Allah, the sense of the eyes of the Almighty watching you everywhere, and the readiness to sacrifice all enjoyment in this life for the pleasure of life in another world all contributed to the exaltation and excitement which are the foundation of the mystical dimension of Sufism.[85]

One of the first recognised Sufis, al-Hasan al-Basri (642–728), preached a rejection of the world and courageously criticised those in power when he felt that they were not conducting themselves according to the ethical standards of Islam. A second figure, Rabi'ah al-Adaviyah (d. 801), culti-vated the attainment of mystical union with God through the love of God. A third, and controversial, mystic, al-Hallaj (857–922), lived as a wandering preacher, who gathered around him a large number of disciples. Such was al-Hallaj's sense of the intimate presence of God that he sometimes appeared to be identifying himself with God. He is reported to have made a famous statement *Ana-l-Haqq!* (I am the Truth!), which caused such outrage that he was imprisoned for eight years, and in 922 executed in a horrible man-ner. Al-Hallaj's death illustrates, in an extreme way, the tensions that would characterise the relationship between Sufi mysticism and the Islamic legal authorities. It was only in the twelfth and thirteenth centuries that orders or *Tariqahs* emerged, which were stable enough to continue after the death of the founder. This continuity was achieved through the current master nominating a successor who would lead the order after his death. Thus, the origins of these orders could be traced through a chain of masters.

The three regions principally associated with Sufism are Central Asia, Mesopotamia (Iran and Iraq), and North Africa. In Central Asia a num-ber of major Sufi orders emerged between the twelfth and seventeenth centuries. The earliest of these, Yassaviya, was founded in the region now known as Turkestan and played a major role in spreading Islam among the nomadic Turkic tribes of Central Asia.[86] Possibly deriving from Yassaviya is the Bektashiyya order, which spread in Turkey. According to tradition, Hajj Bektash, the founder of Bektashiyya, originally belonged to the Yassaviya order. Another Central Asian order is Chishtiyya. The origins of this order are uncertain, although the founder is generally believed to be Mu'in al-Din Chishti (*c.* 1142–1236), a native of Sijistan. The order gradually spreads into India where it remains today as the largest and most important Sufi order.

Mawlaviyya traces its origins to the famous Turkish mystic and poet al-Rumi (1207–73). The order's name comes from the Arabic word *Mawlana* (our master), a title given to al-Rumi by the order. Mawlana was born in Balkh (nowadays northern Afghanistan) and later moved to the Turkish town of Konya, the home of the famous 'whirling dervishes'.

Kubraviyya was founded by Najm ad-din Kubra (1145–1221), a famous Sufi from Khorezm (nowadays Uzbekistan), and a pupil of Abu Najib Suhrawardi. Qadiriyya is also rooted in Central Asia, being founded by Abd al-Qadir Gilani (Djilani, 1077–1166). The Naqshbandis is possibly the most famous and widespread Sufi order nowadays. Founded by Baha ad-din Naqshband (d. 1389), based on the theory and practice of Yassaviya and the previous mystic school of Khajagon in a village near Bukhara in modern-day Uzbekistan, the order gradually spread eastwards into India and westwards into Turkey.

Before describing specifics and differences of some major *Tariqahs* let us examine the common principles and practices that unite them under the name of Sufism. The Sufi path leading to God and the higher mysteries of the human 'self' is based on the doctrine of stations (*maqamat*) and 'states' (*hal* or *ahwal*), which retains its importance for the Muslim mysteries, and is considered to be the cornerstone of Sufism. It may therefore serve as an apt introduction to the fundamental points.

The Way (the form of mystical perfection) suggests at least three different stages: *Shariah, Tariqah,* and *Haqiqah. Shariah* means to follow the public law. After learning Shariah one can reach the *Tariqah* (the Way, hence its second meaning as a Sufi order). This term *Tariqah* appeared in the ninth century representing not only the image of the Journey but also the image of the traveller and his stations (*Maqams*), which are essential for Sufism.

Maqams (stations) of the *Tariqah* (way) are:

Tawbah	–	confession
Wara	–	circumspection
Zuhd	–	temperance
Faqr	–	poverty
Sabr	–	tolerance
Tawakkul	–	hope, prospect of God.[87]

Maqams (stations) are stable, but there are other sudden outpourings of divine grace which are *Hal* (or plural: *Ahwal*), that is, instant states of the soul. They could be different, introducing various emotional feelings and sentiments:

Qurb	–	closeness
Muhabba	–	love
Hauf	–	fear
Raja	–	hope
Shawq	–	passion
Uns	–	friendship
Itmanina	–	peace of mind
Mushahada	–	contemplation
Yaqin	–	confidence.

After achieving all of these states, the traveller approaches the last stage, which is *Haqiqat,* meaning the 'true being'.[88] The culmination is that Sufis can sometimes feel so close to God that they lose the sense of their own self-identity and feel themselves to be completely absorbed into God. This, in fact, is the goal or *Haqiqat* of the Sufi. Through following a series of devotional practices, which lead to higher levels of ecstasy, Sufis aspire to realise a condition in which they are in direct communion with God. Ultimately, the individual human personality passes away and the Sufi feels his soul absorbed into God.

Sufis strive to 'constantly be aware of God's presence', stressing 'contemplation over action', spiritual development over legalism. Popular participation in Sufi gatherings and support for various types of *Tariqahs*

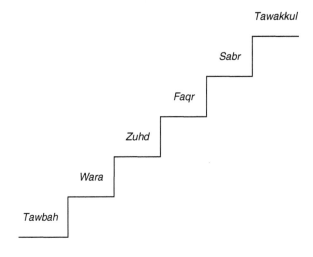

Figure 1: *Maqams* of *Tariqah*

remains high throughout the Muslim world, emphasising communal activities such as *Zikr* (also known as *Dhikr*). Sufism depends on emotion and imagination in the divine–human relationship. Sufism is unrelated to the Sunni/Shii split, schools of jurisprudence, social class, gender, geography, or family connections. It is closely associated with both popular religion and orthodox expression of Islamic teachings. It has been both opposed and supported by the state. Sufi rituals consist of the recitation of prayers, poems, and selections from the Qur'an, and methodical repetitions of divine names (*Zikr*) or Qur'anic formulas, such as Shahadah. In communal gatherings, Sufis perform *Zikr* aloud, often with musical accompaniment. The specific structure and format of the daily devotional exercises and activities were set by each order's founders as a distinct spiritual path. The founder was the spiritual guide for all followers, who swore a special oath of obedience to him as their teacher, their Sheikh (or Sheikh). The record of the transmission of the rituals was preserved in a formal chain of spiritual descent (*silsilah*) extending back to the founder and then usually to Muhammad. Leadership was passed down either within a family line or on the basis of spiritual seniority within the *Tariqah* (order). The typical initiation rite transmits a blessing (*Tarakah*) to the disciple, transforming his or her soul.[89]

So the main features of Sufism are: regular community meetings for religious purposes; a clear hierarchy within a constant number of members of the congregation, which is supposed to have a leader (Sheikh, Pir, or Imam) and his subordinates, and to include two or three generations; the presence of a succession, called *silsilah*, aimed at the transmission of sacred knowledge from older to younger members of the congregation; and the performance of *Zikr* (remembrance of God), an act of devotion during and after a prayer.

11. MAIN *TARIQAHS* OF CENTRAL ASIA: NAQSHBANDIYYA, KUBRAVIYYA, YASSAVIYA, AND QADIRIYYA

Naqshbandiyya

Naqshbandi (**Naqshbandiyya**) is one of the major Sufi orders (*Tariqah*) of Islam. Formed at the end of the fourteenth century in the holy city of Bukhara, and based on the theories and practices of the previous orders (Yassaviya, Khajagon), the order is considered by some as 'sober', and known for its silent *Zikr/Zikr* (remembrance of God) rather than the vocalised forms of *Zikr* common in other orders.

The *Naqshbandi* order is also notable as it is the only Sufi order to trace its spiritual lineage (*silsilah*) to the Prophet Muhammad through Abu Bakr, the first caliph. In contrast, most other *Tariqahs* trace their lineage to Ali ibn Abu Talib, the prophet's son-in-law and fourth caliph. The word *Naqshbandi* is Persian, taken from the name of the founder of the order, Baha ad-din Naqshband Bukhari. Some have said that the translation means 'related to the image-maker'; some consider it to mean 'pattern maker' rather than 'image maker', and interpret *Naqshbandi* to mean 'reformer of patterns'; others consider it to mean 'way of the chain' or 'golden chain'.[90]

This is the chain from Prophet Muhammad to Baha ad-din Naqshband Bukhari:

Prophet Muhammad – Abu Bakr Siddiq – Salman the Persian, – Qasim ibn Muhammad ibn Abu Bakr, – Ja'far al-Sadiq, – Bayazid Bistami, – Abul-Hassan Kharaqani, – Bu Ali al-Farmadi, – Yusuf Hamadani, – Abul Abbas al-Khadr, – Abdul Khaliq Gijduwani, – Arif al-Reogri, – Mahmood al-Injir al-Faghnawi, – Ali- Ar-Ramitani, – Muhammad Baba as-Samasi, – Sayyid Amir Kulal, and, the last one, Baha ad-din Naqshband Bukhari – namesake founder of the Naqshbandi order in Bukhara.

From here, the order branches into several sub-orders. One of the most important and widespread is the *Naqshbandi-Mujaddadi* branch founded by Ahmad Sirhindi. The chain between Baha ad-din Naqshbandi and *Ahmad Sirhindi* continues as below:

Alauddin al-Bukhari al-Attar, – Yaqub al-Charkhi, – Ubaydullah al-Ahrar, – Muhammad Az-Zahid Wali, – Muhammad Darwish, – Khawaja al-Akmangi, – Muhammad al-Baqi Billah, – Ahmad Sirhindi.

There are several existing branches of Naqshbandiyya in India, Pakistan, Turkey and Cyprus, and one in Uzbekistan, each with its own Sheikhs and *silsilahs*. There are 11 main principles of Naqshbandiyya first stated by Abdul Holiq Gijduwani:

1) **Conscious Breathing** (*Hosh dar dam*). This means, according to Abdul Khaliq al-Gijdwani, that 'the wise seeker must safeguard his breath from heedlessness, coming in and going out, thereby keeping his heart always in the Divine Presence; and he must revive his breath with worship and servitude and dispatch this worship to His Lord full of life, for every

breath which is inhaled and exhaled with Presence is alive and connected with the Divine Presence. Every breath inhaled and exhaled with heedlessness is dead, disconnected from the Divine Presence.'

Ubaidullah al-Ahrar said, 'The most important mission for the seeker in this Order is to safeguard his breath, and he who cannot safeguard his breath, it would be said of him, "he lost himself."'

Sheikh Naqshband said, 'This Order is built on breath. So it is a must for everyone to safeguard his breath in the time of his inhalation and exhalation and further, to safeguard his breath in the interval between the inhalation and exhalation.'[91]

2) **Observe Your Steps** (*Nazar bar qadam*). This means that the seeker must keep his eyes on his feet while walking. Wherever he is about to place his feet, his eyes must be there. He is not allowed to cast his glance here or there, to look right or left or in front of him, because unnecessary sights will veil the heart. This is why Sufi saints do not allow their followers, who have purified their hearts through constant *Zikr*, to look elsewhere other than at their feet. Their hearts are like mirrors, easily receiving and reflecting every image.

Lowering the gaze is also a sign of humility – proud and arrogant people never look at their feet. It is also an indication that one is following the footsteps of the Prophet, who never used to look right or left when he walked, but used to look only at his feet, moving steadfastly towards his destination. Sheikh Naqshband said, 'If we look at the mistakes of our friends, we will be left friendless, because no one is perfect.'[92]

3) **Journey Homeward** (*Safar dar watan*). This means to travel to one's homeland. It indicates that the seeker travels from the world of creation to the world of the Creator. It is related that the Prophet said, 'I am going to my Lord, from one state to a better state and from one station to a higher station.'

The *Naqshbandi* divides that travel into two categories. The first is external journeying and the second is internal journeying. External travel is from one land to another searching for a perfect guide to take and direct you to your destination. This enables you to move to the second category, the internal journey. Seekers, once they have found a perfect guide, are forbidden to go on another external journey. The second category is internal journeying. Internal journeying requires the seeker to reject his lowly manners and embrace a higher form, to cast out of his heart all worldly desires. He will be lifted from a state of uncleanliness to a state of purity.[93]

4) **Solitude in the Crowd** (*Khilwat dar anjuman*). *Khilwat* means seclusion. It signifies to be outward with people while remaining inward with God. Seclusion also is divided into external seclusion and internal seclusion. External seclusion requires the seeker to seclude himself in a private place away from other people. Staying there by himself, he concentrates and meditates on the remembrance of God. This leads to the second category, internal seclusion. Internal seclusion means seclusion among people. Therein the heart of the seeker must be present with his Lord and absent from His creations while remaining physically present among them.

It is said, 'The seeker will be so deeply involved in the silent *Zikr* in his heart that, even if he enters a crowd of people, he will not hear their voices.' This is the highest state of seclusion, and is considered the true seclusion, as mentioned in the Holy Qur'an: *Men whom neither business nor profit distract from the recollection of God* [24:37]. Sheikh Naqshband emphasised the goodness of gatherings when he said: *Tariqatuna as-suhbat wa-l-khairu fil-jamiyyat* (Our Way is Companionship, and Goodness is in the Gathering).[94]

5) **Essential Remembrance** (*Yad kard*). The meaning of *Yad* is *Zikr*. The meaning of *kard* is 'do', that is, the essence of *Zikr*. The seeker must make *Zikr* by negation and affirmation on his tongue until he reaches the state of contemplation in his heart.

That state will be achieved by reciting every day the negation (*La ilaha* – no Gods) and affirmation (*Il allah* – but Allah) on the tongue, between 5,000 and 10,000 times, removing from his heart the elements that tarnish and rust it. This daily *Zikr* will bring the seeker into the perfect presence of Allah. The *Zikr* by negation and affirmation, in the manner of the *Naqshbandi* Sufi masters, demands that the seeker close his eyes, close his mouth, clench his teeth, glue his tongue to the roof of his mouth, and hold his breath.[95]

6) **Returning** (*Baz gasht*). This is a state in which the seeker, who makes *Zikr* by negation and affirmation, and comes to understand the Holy Prophet's phrase, *ilahi anta maqsusdi wa ridaka matlubi* (O my God, You are my Goal and Your Good Pleasure is my Aim). The recitation of this phrase will increase in the seeker the awareness of the Oneness of God, until he reaches the state in which the existence of all creation vanishes from his eyes. All that he sees, wherever he looks, is the Absolute One. As Bayazid said: 'When I reached Him I saw that His remembering of me preceded my remembrance of Him.'[96]

7) **Attentiveness** (*Nigah dasht*). *Nigah* means sight. It means that the seeker must watch his heart and safeguard it by preventing bad thoughts from entering. It is acknowledged in the Naqshbandiyya that for a seeker to safeguard his heart from bad inclinations for fifteen minutes is a great achievement. For this he would be considered a real Sufi. One Sufi Sheikh said, 'Because I safeguarded my heart for ten nights, my heart has safeguarded me for twenty years.'[97]

8) **Recollection** (*Yada dasht*). This means that the performer of *Zikr* safeguards his heart with negation and affirmation in every breath without leaving the Presence of Allah.

9) **Awareness of Time** (*Wuquf zamani*). This means to watch one's composure and check one's tendency to heedlessness. The seeker must know how much time he has spent in moving towards spiritual maturity and must recognise at what place he has arrived in his journey towards the Divine Presence. Ya'qub al-Charkhi recounted that his Sheikh, Ala'uddin al-Attar said, 'In the state of depression you must recite *istighfar* (asking forgiveness) excessively, and in the state of elation, praise of Allah excessively.' And he said, 'To take into consideration these two states, contraction and expansion, is the meaning of *wuquf zamani*.' Sheikh Naqshband explained that state by saying, 'You have to evaluate how you spend every moment: with Presence or in Negligence.'[98]

10) **Awareness of Numbers** (*Wuquf àdadi*). This means that the seeker who is reciting *Zikr* must observe the exact number of repetitions entailing the silent *Zikr* of the heart. To keep an account of the *Zikr* is not for the sake of the account itself, but is for the sake of securing the heart from bad thoughts and to cause it to concentrate more in the effort to achieve the repetition prescribed by the Sheikh as quickly as possible. Sheikh Naqshband said, 'Observance of the numbers in *Zikr* is the first step in the state of acquiring Heavenly Knowledge (*ilm ul-ladunni*).'[99]

11) **Awareness of the Heart** (*Wuquf qalbi*). This means to direct the heart of the seeker towards the Divine Presence, where he will see nothing other than his Beloved One. It means to experience His Manifestation in all states. Ubaidullah al-Ahrar said, 'The state of Awareness of the Heart is the state of being present in the Divine Presence in such a way that you cannot look to anyone other than Him.'[100]

One of the most popular sentences belonging to the Naqshbandiyya is 'Heart to Beloved and hands to business' (*Dil ba Yar va dast ba kar*), which reflects the main social basis of the order (e.g. traders and artisans in urban areas of Central Asia) and demonstrates the balance between spiritual and practical components.

All together, the 11 main principles of Naqshbandiyya Sufi order were:

1) Conscious Breathing (*Hosh dar dam*)
2) Observe Your Steps (*Nazar bar qadam*)
3) Journey Homeward (*Safar dar watan*)
4) Solitude in the Crowd (*Khilwat dar anjuman*)
5) Essential Remembrance (*Yad kard*)
6) Returning (*Baz gasht*)
7) Attentiveness (*Nigah dasht*)
8) Recollection (*Yada dasht*)
9) Awareness of Time (*Wuquf zamani*)
10) Awareness of Numbers (*Wuquf àdadi*)
11) Awareness of the Heart (*Wuquf qalbi*).

Kubraviyya

Sheikh Najm ad-din Kubra, a famous representative of Sufism in Central Asia, was a scholar who left behind him a rich legacy in the many sciences. His teachings, called *Kubravia* or *Zahabia* (golden teaching) have had a great impact on the spiritual life not only in Khorezm, but in the entire Islamic world. Najm ad-din Kubra was a connoisseur of souls. In his view, man is a microcosm (*olami sugro*) that has all the properties of a macrocosm (*olami kubro*). In the process of spiritual perfection, a teacher (Pir, Sheikh, murshid) should lead his apprentice (*Murid*) through the ten stages of *Tariqah* (*Tawba, Zuhd, Tawakkul, Qanoat, Uzlat, Tavajjuh, Sabr, Murokaba, Zikr, Rizo*)[101] to the truth, Allah.

Najm ad-din Kubra emphasises the theory of *latif* (tenderness), according to which space consists of a glass house, which is surrounded by consciousness, feelings, the spirit, and the body. Through special exercises, a seeker must feel and see the centre, which is the result of a change in the conditions, forms and colours. Kubra states that the spiritual condition of a seeker must pass through three shapes: circle, ellipse and point. The circle is the universe, the ellipse is the image of the world, and the point is the centre (*wahdat*) of the universe. Awareness of that fact is a reflection of the divine essence of peace. This pattern (circle – ellipse – point) is in constant motion, and has some colour, which depends on the distance from the centre. Every religion or ideology contributes to the theory a colour of their understanding. The theory of colour exists in almost all Sufi *Tariqahs*. It is typical for Yassaviya, Bektashiyya, and Kubraviyya.

Kubraviyya colours progress as follows: white-yellow-blue-blue-green-red-black. The seven colours are associated with the seven states of the murid's spirit: white – Islam, yellow – *iman* (conscience), blue – *ahawan* (gift), blue – *imtinan* (faith), green – *iman* (full faith), red – *irfan* (knowledge), black – *hayrat, hayajan* (surprise, admiration).[102]

Each colour symbolises something. White for many people symbolises purity, innocence, honesty. For Najm ad-din Kubra this colour is a symbol of purification. Only after the through cleanliness and honesty can the murid embark on the road of *Tariqah*.

Yellow, unlike white, is not valued by many people. For Najm ad-din Kubra this colour symbolises a heightened sense of love for God at the beginning of life in the name of God.

Blue is the colour of the sky and the sea, marking the cold Arctic light and the shadows of the east – infinity and eternity. In Kubraviyya it symbolises a gift, the dedication of a new life to good, to the understanding and purification of sins, to the transition from everyday life to spiritual development. Blue is also the colour of dreams, tenderness, warmth, water. Najm ad-din Kubra places it after *tawba* on the path of faith, the exemption from impure thought and deeds, transition from *harom* (abstinence from what is prohibited by God) to the pure *halol*.

Green is a symbol of awakening life, recovery, new growth, the colour of grass and leaves. In Kubraviyya it is the colour of faith, the state of the murid when his soul is fully absorbed by genuine faith in God.

Red has, on the one hand, a sense of protection, symbolising fertility, beauty, joy, love, and on the other hand, revenge, hatred, war, bloodshed. For the Kubraviyya red clothing is not quite the same as a separation of the spirit from the body, but a call to take care of the soul, spiritual awareness of the world.

Black for many people means darkness, misery, grief, and is the colour of mourning, death, mystery, the underworld, and so on. For Najm ad-din Kubra black reflects our approach to the goal of the threshold of the divine world. A special place in the theory of Kubra includes colourlessness, which symbolises the achievement of the goal of *haqiqat* – true unification with the divine world, the truth. Development of the theory of 'colour' of the soul (according to Kubra) is called *Tayawwun*.[103]

We shall examine the poetic and musical applications of this theory later in the book.

Yassaviya

Hodja Ahmad Yassavi (also spelled Khoja Ahmad Yassavi or Ahmed Yesevi) was born in Sayram (now in South Kazakhstan) and died in 1166 at Yasi, Turkestan (nowadays in South Kazakhstan). He was a Turkic poet and a Sufi, an early mystic who exerted a powerful influence on the development of mystical orders throughout the Turkic-speaking world.

Very little is known about his life, but legends indicate that his father Ibrahim died when the boy was young, and his family moved to Yasi (today called Turkestan). There he became a disciple of Arslan Baba. After the death of the latter, Ahmed Yassavi moved to Bukhara and followed his studies with the Sufi Yusuf Hamadani (d. 1140). Later, he made the city of Yasi into the major centre of learning for the Kazakh steppes, and then at the age of 63 retired to a life of contemplation. He dug himself an underground cell where he spent the rest of his life.

A mausoleum was later built on the site of his grave by Timur the Great. The Yassaviya *Tariqah*, which he founded continued to be influential for several centuries afterwards, with the Yassavi Sayyid Ata Sheikhs holding prominent positions at the court of Bukhara into the nineteenth century.

There are ten Adabs or rules of behaviour in Yassaviya:

1) Nobody should be respected more than the murid's Master.
2) The murid or seeker should be clever enough to understand the hints and symbols of his Master.
3) The murid should accept whatever his Master says or does without challenge.
4) The murid should seek *Riza* (acceptance) of the Master.
5) Be honest and faithful, do not give way to doubt.
6) Be ultimately loyal to the Master.
7) Be ready to give up everything for the sake of the Master.
8) Keep the secrets of the Master and don't reveal them.
9) Follow what is advised by the Master.
10) The murid should be ready to give his life for the sake of the Master and for the union with Allah.[104]

There are main eight *Maqams* or stations on the way to perfection according to this Sufi order:

1) *Maqam* of *Tawba* or repentant people, whose Master is Prophet Adam.

2) *Maqam* of *Ilm* or knowledgeable people, whose Master is Prophet Hidhr (Iliya).

3) *Maqam* of *Zuhd* or people of temperance, with Master Prophet Isa (Jesus).

4) *Maqam* of *Sabr* or patient people, with Master Prophet Ayyub (Jove).

5) *Maqam* of *Riza* or people of acceptance, with Master Prophet Musa, (Moses).

6) *Maqam* of *Shukr* or people of thankfulness, with Master Prophet Nuh (Noah).

7) *Maqam* of *Mahabba* or people of love, with Master Prophet Ibrohim (Abraham).

8) *Maqam* of *Urfan* or enlightened people, with their Master Prophet Muhammad.[105]

Qadiriyya

The Qadiriyya order, widespread in Egypt, Turkey, and India, has a strongly instituted system of *Zikr, wird, hidhb,* which are in use among different communities. Qadiriyya uses *Zikr*, prayers, liturgies, and different invocations. Its founder 'Abd al-Qadir was regarded as the founder of a system involving rites and practices, or as a worker of miracles. He eventually became the most popular saint in Islam. Women in the Khlot and Tlik practise the cult of 'Abd al-Qadir most ardently. They come to the *khalwa* or a place for meditation for all sorts of reasons, to satisfy their loves and hates in all the acts of their existence'.[106] Their ceremonies always terminate with the words, 'Thus spoke Mawlây 'Abd al-Qadir' or 'O Mawlây 'Abd al-Qadir' – the same is found in Central Asia.

According to the description of Muhammad 'Alî al-Sanusî (1785–1859) in his *Manhal al-rawi al-ra'iq*, the *Zikr* of the Qadiri takes place with participants sitting in a circle. It should be accompanied at the start by the prayer *Jalâ Allâh wa 'azamâtihi* (the glory of God and His majesty). During this prayer, the breath is suppressed and purified, one sits cross-legged then one speaks the name of God, prolonging it for a time, and extending it with an emphatic pronunciation (*tafkhîm*) until the breath is cut off, making the words *'Azamât al-Haqq* (the majesty of the true) while exhaling the breath. One continues in that way until the heart is relaxed and the Divine Light is revealed. Then one continues with the *Zikr* of absorption (*fanâ'*) and remaining (*baqâ'*) in God, ascribed to Sheikh Sîdî 'Abd al-Qâdir. That consists of sitting as described, turning the face towards the right shoulder and saying *Ha*, turning the face toward to the left, saying *Hû*, then lowering the head and expending the breath while saying *Hayy*, repeating this without stopping. I have witnessed the same ritual in the Ferghana Valley in Uzbekistan.

It is well known that Qadiriyya *Zikr* in different parts of the world has different rules. So, Shia Sufi orders in Pakistan used to have their own musical performance, *ta'ziyya*, with wide use of musical instruments and a well-developed process of *Zikr* performance. But in Central Asia today one can find only the shadow of previous Qadiri rituals, which are expressed in the rare rites of retired participants.

12. *ZIKR* IN THE FERGHANA VALLEY: MALE SOCIETY

The traces of Qadiri Sufi *Zikr* in Ferghana Valley are found today in the Namanghan area. In 1992, I was interviewing Hodji Hofiz Niyazov (Niyazov) (born 1912) who is reputed to be one of the last local Sufi Sheikhs. His Qadiri branch has diminished now and most participants are old men. At that time, they used sometimes to perform *Zikr* inside the local mosque, named Hamid-Han Qory, near the Zarkent market. As Hodji Hofiz Niyazov said, the leader of the entire branch of the Qadiriyya Sufi order of Ferghana Valley, Muhiddin Qory, lived at that time in Andijan. His position as the head of Tariqati-Qadyri (Tarîqat-i Qadirî) is supposed to have been acquired by right of succession. Hodji Hofiz Niyazov himself provides the *Zikrs* in one of the nearby villages on the outskirts of Namanghan. He recalled that at the beginning of the twentieth century there were about a hundred *silsilah* of the Qadiriyya order in the whole neighbourhood. A thousand people met together for *Zikrs* on the bank of the river Syr Darya, singing, whirling, and spinning round under the open night sky. Large clouds of dust would billow up to the sky. Now there are only shadows alternating with the echo of the rich incantation, and a small group of old members remaining.

Both places – inside or outside the mosque – were acceptable for performing the Qadiri *Zikr* in this area. But after the Soviets came to these lands it was prohibited. Ironically, by allowing a place for social meetings, a local culture club, the Soviets provided for *Zikrs* in the heart of the community. Being a place of little importance to the main population of local dwellers it was safe to provide the *Zikrs* there hidden from public view.

Usually they started the *Zikr* in the evening after night prayer (*khufta*), about 9–10 o'clock. They sat in a circle in the main room of the club and for a long time repeated sentences of *Shahada*: lo ilaha illalloh. After a number of repetitions it slowly became shortened to the main word *Allâh*. The leader of the meeting (Hodji Hofiz Niyazov) started to repeat it with the rest of the people, as a soloist, and in dialogue with a chorus. It became faster and faster and finally alternated with other words: *Huw-Wa* (name of God), even singing by chorus. The Sheikh rose up and started to move round in the circle waving white scarves/kerchiefs. All the participants followed him, continuing to shout *Huw-Wa*.

A hundred repetitions of *Huw-Wa* are necessary to reach the end of this stage. Qadirî *Zikr* should include exactly 13 stages devoted to the Prophet and then to the masters of Sufi orders. Each step gradually increases in emotional intensity, towards the culmination. After all these stages comes the proper climax. Qadiriyya provides the sort of loud *Zikr* (*jahrî*), when each member should sing and shout the names of God (*Huw-Wa, Allâh, Hayy*) to achieve transcendence. So, forms of *Zikr* are still provided, taking place in deep secret in male society. Although this was not *Zikr* in its entirety, even the shortened form is proof that Sufi practice continues its difficult life in Central Asia.[107]

4

Female Sufism

13. HISTORICAL OVERVIEW

From the earliest days, women have played an important role in the development of Islam and Sufism. We have already mentioned above the name of one, who is considered to be one of the founders of Sufism – Rabi'ah al-Adaviyah. She was born between 95 and 99 Hijai (713–18) in Basra, Iraq. Much of her early life is recorded by Khawaja Farid ad-din Attar. She is reported to have been born free in a poor but respected family, and was the fourth daughter of the family and therefore named *Rabi'ah* (Arabic – fourth). When famine struck, she was kidnapped and sold as slave. However, when she grew up, her master discovered her piety and freed her out of fear for God. She was the one who first to set out the doctrine of mystical love and is widely considered to be the most important of the early Sufi poets.

> O, Lord, stars are shining, people close their eyes, kings close their gates...
> Everyone in love is alone with his beloved, and now I am with You.
> O, Lord, if I love You for the fear of Hell, rescue me there.
> If I love You for the hope of reaching Paradise, expel me from it.
> If I serve You for the sake of Yourself, don't hide Your perfection from me.

Much of the poetry attributed to her is, in fact, of unknown origin. She described her attitude towards God as divine love (*Mahabba*). 'The aim of her love is reunion with the Lord, association and unification with God.'[108]

> In love, nothing exists between breast and Breast.
> Speech is born out of longing,
> True description from the real taste.
> The one who tastes, knows;
> The one who explains, lies.
> How can you describe the true form of Something
> In whose presence you are blotted out?

And in whose being you still exist?
And who lives as a sign for your journey?[109]

Rabi'ah was the first person to speak of the realities of Sufism in a language that anyone could understand. Though she experienced many difficulties in her early years, her starting point was neither fear of hell nor a desire for paradise, but only love. 'God is God,' she said. 'For this I love God... not because of any gifts, but for Itself.' Her aim was to melt her being into God. According to her, one could find God by turning within oneself. As Muhammad said, 'He who knows himself knows his Lord.' Ultimately, it is through love that we are brought into the unity of Being.[110]

One of the many myths that surround around her life is that she was freed from slavery because her master, seeing her surrounded by light while praying, realised that she was a saint and he feared for his life if he continued to keep her as a slave. While she apparently received many marriage offers she remained celibate and died of old age, an ascetic, her only care from the disciples who followed her. She was the first in a long line of female Sufi mystics. One day, she was seen running through the streets of Basra carrying a torch in one hand and a bucket of water in the other. When asked what she was doing, she said, 'I want to put out the fires of Hell, and burn down the rewards of Paradise. They block the way to God. I do not want to worship from fear of punishment or for the promise of reward, but simply for the love of God.'

Ibn Arabi, the great 'Pole of Knowledge' (1165–1240 AD), tells of the time he spent with two elderly women mystics who had a profound influence on him: Shams of Marchena, one of the 'sighing ones', and Fatimah of Cordova. Of Fatimah, with whom he spent a great deal of time, he says, 'I served as a disciple of one of the lovers of God, a Gnostic, a lady of Seville called Fatimah bint Ibn al-Muthanna of Cordova. I served her for several years, she being over ninety-five years of age.... She used to play on the tambourine and show great pleasure in it. When I spoke to her about it she answered, "I take joy in Him Who has turned to me and made me one of His Friends (Saints), using me for His own purposes. Who am I that He should choose me among mankind? He is jealous of me for, whenever I turn to something other than Him in heedlessness, He sends me some affliction concerning that thing.".... With my own hands I built for her a hut of reeds as tall as she was, in which she lived until she died. She used to say to me, 'I am your spiritual mother and the light of your earthly mother.' When my mother came to visit her,

Fatimah said to her, "O light, this is my son and he is your father, so treat him filially and dislike him not."[111]

The wife of the ninth-century Sufi Al-Hakim at-Tirmidhi from Termez (now in Uzbekistan) was a mystic in her own right. She used to dream for her husband as well as for herself. Khidr, the mysterious one, would appear to her in her dreams. One night he told her to tell her husband to guard the purity of his house. Concerned that perhaps Khidr was referring to the occasional lack of cleanliness because of their young children, she questioned him in her dream. He responded by pointing to his tongue: she was to tell her husband to be mindful of the purity of his speech.[112]

Aisha of Damascus was one of the well-known mystics of the fifteenth century. She wrote a commentary of Khwaja 'Abdo'llah Ansari's *Stations on the Way (Manazel as-sa'erin)* entitled 'Veiled Hints within the Stations of the Saints' (*Al-esharat al-khafiys fi'l-manazel al-auliya*). Bibi Hayati Kermani belonged to a family immersed in the Sufi tradition. Her brother was a sheikh of the Nimatullahi order, and she became the wife of the master of the order. After her marriage, she composed a *divan* (collection of poems) that revealed her integration of both the outer and the inner knowledge of Sufism.[113]

A discussion of the female Sufism would not be complete without citing Professor Annemarie Schimmel, an expert in Muslim culture, in *Mystical Dimensions of Islam* she notes that 'Sufism, more than stern orthodoxy, offered women a certain amount of possibilities to participate actively in the religious and social life....A number of Sufi orders had women attached to them as lay members.'[114] Moreover she names women known historically to have been attached to Sufi orders. Among them are 'Shah Jihan's eldest daughter Jihanara who joined the Qadiriyya and was highly praised by her master Mulla Shah' and 'Bibi Jamal Khatun (d. 1639) who was one of the outstanding saints of the Qadiryya order during its formative period in the Punjab.'[115] As another scholar pointed out: 'One may assume that even in our day women are usually more concerned with ritual prayer and fasting than the average man in a Turkish or Pakistani household.'[116]

Among the Bektashis, an order in which women have always been integrated with men in ceremonies, many women have continued the tradition of composing sacred songs (*illahis*). In 1987, a songbook entitled *Gul Deste* (A Bouquet of Roses) was published in Turkey. It brings together sacred hymns written by women and men of the Bektashi tradition from the nineteenth century to the present.[117]

Mawlevi *sheikhs* have often guided both women and men. Rumi had many female disciples, and women were also encouraged to participate in *sama*, the musical whirling ceremony of the Mawlevis. (Women usually had their own *sama*s, though they sometimes performed together with men.) One of Rumi's chief disciples was Fakhr an-Nisa, known as 'the Rabi'a of her age'. One day, seven centuries after her death, it was decided to reconstruct her tomb. Shaikh Suleyman Hayati Dede, who was then the acting spiritual head of the Mawlevi Order, was asked to be present when she was exhumed. He later described that, when her body was uncovered, it was totally intact and the fragrance of roses filled the air.[118]

There is historical evidence of women participating in the development of Sufism in Central Asia too. Investigation of many ancient cemeteries and tomb complexes in Central Asia shows that women had a great influence. For instance, in the Sverdlov district of Bukhara is found the grave of Mastura Khanim, or Agha-yi Buzurg. She was a famous *murshid* or pupil of the *Naqshbandî* order who died on 30 July 1523. Agha-yi Buzurg had acquired her status as a *murshid* from Shaykh Shâd-i Giyati and his wife. She was brought up in the spirit of *murshid* by her grandfather and father. Among her disciples were both men and women.[119] Another leading female Sufi was a well-known head of the Kubraviyya called Bibi Khadicha, who lived near Khiva in the fourteenth century. Her grave is situated in Agahi village in the Khiva district. She had dealings only with women, whom she recruited into her order as teenagers, and with whom she shared her secrets. Another female Sufi, Bibi Zumrat, was known in the surroundings of Bukhara. Nowadays, the local old women come to her tomb to pay tribute and say their nightly prayers. It is also well known, for instance, that the Yassaviya Sufi order involved women participating in *Zikr*.[120]

Female rituals of the Qadiriyya Sufi order had a place in Tashkent at the beginning of the twentieth century. According to A.L. Troitskaya, Ishan-bu (the wife of the local Ishan, who is a descendant of the Prophet), together with her best female religious assistants, Halfa and Otin, wore the traditional white scarves and performed the *Jahryia* (open) version of Qadiriyya *Zikr*.[121] Each *Zikr* had a certain structure starting with Qur'an *Sura* number 1;[122] Salavat for the Ghavsuli Agzam.[123] The proper *Zikr* was based on Chor Zarb, which is 'La ilaha il Allah'.[124] The women danced in a circle, which preceded the third part of the *Zikr* with *Sura* 112. The poetry of Sufi poets Mashrab and Ahmad Yassavy would usually be recited.[125]

It was mentioned by Troitskaya that Ishan-bu, heading the *Zikr*, was of *Naqshbandi* Sufi origin though she performed the *Zikr* of the Qadiriyya Sufi order. According to Troitskaya, Halfa and Otin were highly privileged religious women who served the *Zikr* by helping Ishan-bu.

Among other forms of *Zikr* performed in that community Troitskaya mentioned Ashir-Oy, the celebration after the death of Hasan and Hussein, which has a special *Zikr*. *Zikr* also marked a celebration of the birthday of Muhammad, *Mavlyud*, usually performed four months after the Ashir-Oy. But *Zikr* could be performed just for its own sake, the author concluded.[126]

We conclude our historic overview of female Sufism with a quote from Shemeem Burney Abbas, the author of *The Female Voice in Sufi Ritual*, who defines the main areas of female participation in Sufism and its rituals on the basis of her research in the Indian subcontinent:

- Women as mystics in Sufi practices.
- Women as creators of Sufi poetry.
- Women who have influenced male Sufis in their roles as mothers, daughters, nurses, and mentors.
- Women as ethnographers and patrons of male Sufi mystics, such as the Mughal princess Jahan Ara, daughter of Shah Jehan.
- Women as singers/musicians/participants of Sufi songs, sometimes even called the *faqiriani* in the Sindhi shrines.
- Women as preservers and guardians of Sufi discourse or lore, such as Mai Naimat, a maidservant of Shah Abdul Latif, from whose memory his entire *Risalo* is said to have been reconstructed.
- Active female participants at the shrines (*hijras*). They have been identified as *khawajasara* in earlier shrine traditions during the rule of the Muslim kings in India.
- The aesthetics of the female voice, a poetic device in which the speaker is the female, even in the narratives of male musicians. The musicians play with the syntactic and semantic structures of the languages to speak as though they were females.
- Singing in falsetto, even by male musicians, to impersonate a female voice, as is done by the *faqirs* or musicians at Shah Abdul Latif's shrine in Bhit Shah. They mimic the heroines of Shah's poetry.
- The myths of female lovers, such as Sassi, Sohni, and Hir, used as aesthetic devices to speak of broader social, political, caste, and gender issues.[127]

How applicable this list is to female Sufism in Central Asia is discussed in chapters below.

14. SUFI POETRY IN CENTRAL ASIA: *GHAZAL* AND FEMALE POETS

Ghazal

Before we consider the issue of female Sufi poetry in Central Asia, it is necessary to define what Sufi poetry is.[128] The dominant form of Sufi poetry in Central Asia is *ghazal.*

So what is *ghazal* as a poetic form? There are many definitions, the first of which, by Shamsiddin Qays, dates from the beginning of the twelfth century: '*Ghazal* in its initial meaning is affection towards women, and also friendship with them...' The *Encyclopedia of Islam* defines *ghazal* as 'a song, the elegy of love, frequently also an erotic-elegiac genre, the song of man to woman'.[129] At the same time, the history of this poetic genre, beginning in the ninth century with Arabic poetry, developing and blooming on Persian soil (Attar, Saadi, Hafez)[130] and coming to marvellous fruition in the Turkic medieval literature (Nasimi, Navoiy, Fuzuli, Babur), testifies not only to the widest area of its propagation, but also the universal poetics of the genre, which in the process of this development outgrew the boundaries of its origin. If we summarise theoretical studies of *ghazal* as a poetic genre, its formal elements, standardised from the times of Saadi and Hafez, are namely: writing *ghazal* by *bayts* (two verses, meaning in Arabic 'a house'), rhyming *bayts* according to the formula A-A, B-A, C-A, and so on, the use of *Radif* (monorhyme), and also *Takhallus* (reference to the name of the author, usually in the last *bayt*).

Semantically, *ghazal* is a purely lyric, plotless form, which characterises, first of all, an internal state, but not external action; therefore, it is to a greater degree a statement about a state rather than a process. The semantics of *ghazal* are characterised by the presence of two semantic poles: the 'I' of the lyric hero and the 'you' or 'he/she' of his beloved, which are mutually impenetrable. Usually, between these two poles there is a space of separation, a break, unattainability, and so on. This separation creates the poetic, emotional stress of the *ghazal*. Furthermore, there are other relationships in the *ghazal*: 'I' – 'rival', 'I' – 'supporters' (e.g. sheikh, wine-waiter, doctor). To be more schematic, it is possible to reduce the functional structure of *ghazal* to the following universal structure: 'I' – the subject of a statement; 'you/he/she' – the object of the statement; the statement (a field between 'I' and 'you/he/she'); supportive forces (doctor, wine-waiter, wind); and obstructive forces (rival, enemy, etc.).[131]

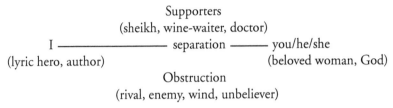

Of course, this universality was not assigned in advance, but rather revealed in the process of the development of the *ghazal*. Sufism played an enormous role in the universalisation of *ghazal*. The world of *ghazal*, in many respects, correlates with the world of ideas of the great Sufi theorists Ibn-Arabi and al-Ghazali,[132] and also of the most important representatives of Sufism in Central Asia: Nadjm ad-din Kubra, Ahmad Yassavi, and Baha ad-din Naqshbandi, all of whom wrote famous *ghazals* themselves.

For instance, the dichotomy is one of the basic principles of al-Ghazali's philosophy. In *Ihya ulum-ad-din* (Revival of Religious Sciences) it is manifested at several levels: linguistic (*zakhir-batin* (external-inner), *makhv-isbat* (hidden-proved), *sabr-shukur* (patience-gratitude), etc.), conceptual (action-state, reason-intuition, etc.), categorical, and so on. An important role in his philosophy is played by the three-part construction, which expresses, as a rule, the antinomy of two theses, which are resolved in the third. Accordingly, there is a triad of the functional parts of Sufi *Makam* (stations): knowledge – action – state. The same isomorphic structure pierces the entire world of al-Ghazali at the levels of text, consciousness, soul of man, structure of knowledge, man of universe.

In the Arabic language *ghazal* was perceived as just the amorous, erotic form of versification, but because there is grammatical gender in neither the Persian nor Turkic languages, there is in the *ghazal* poetry of both an ambivalence, with the possibility of turning your *ghazal* statement to refer both to the beloved and to God. Hence, there is a possibility of dual interpretation of the content of the *ghazal* and an interchangeability between *ishqi majoziy* (symbolical love) and *ishqi mutlaq* (absolute love).[133]

To see how *ishqi mutlaq* (absolute love of Sufism) is interchangeable with *ishqi majoziy* (symbolic love) of amorous poetry let us analyse the most famous *ghazal* of Uzbek classic poetry, which comes from Alisher Navoiy, and which is called *Munojat* (Appeal to God) by the people:

Kecha kelgumdur debon ul sarvi gulru' kelmadi,
Ko'zlarimga kecha tong otquncha uyqu kelmadi.
Lahza-lahza chiqtimu, chektim yo'lida intizor,
Keldi jon og'zimg'au ul sho'xi badxu kelmadi.
Orazidek oydin erkonda gar etti ehtiyot,
Ro'zgorimdek ham o'lgonda qorong'u kelmadi.
Ul parivash hajridinkim yig'ladim devonavor,
Kimsa bormukim anga ko'rganda kulgu kelmadi.
Ko'zlaringdin necha suv kelgay deb o'lturmang meni
Kim bori qon erdi kelgan bu kecha suv kelmadi.
Tolibi sodiq topilmas, yo'qsakim qo'ydi qadam
Yo'lgakim avval qadam ma'shuqqa o'tru kelmadi.
Ey, Navoiy, boda birla xurram et ko'nglung uyin
Ne uchunkim boda kelgan uyga qayg'u kelmadi.

My beloved was to come tonight
With his face like a rose and his figure like that of a cypress-tree
But he did not.
The whole night, sleep deserted my eyes
Full of hope, I would take a few steps on the road towards him
My soul was taking flight,
But this fickle betrayer didn't come.
Bereft of his angel-face, I wept and wept like a mad woman.
Whoever saw me must have thought that I was a fool
Is there is such a thing as a faithful suitor?
If there is one, why does not every step lead him to his beloved?
Navoiy, rejoice in the house of your heart
For sadness never floods a house where wine flows.

First of all, we can see that the model of *ghazal* is present here almost completely. Here is the semantic field of the lyric 'I', as well as the semantic field in which 'she' is located. There is an insurmountable field of separation, there are supporters like *kimsa* (someone) or *tolibi sodiq* (faithful pupil), to whom the lyric hero turns. The theme has two main components: the image of the amorous experiences of the lyric hero and the image of the beauties of the beloved, which are placed in contrast.

As far as a plot is concerned, the first *misra* (half-verse) of the first *bayt*: *Kecha kelgumdur debon ul sarvi gulru' kelmadi* (My beloved was to come tonight/But he did not), exhausting the story, displaces everything else into the sphere of imaginary nature, into conditionality, possibility. In other words, the *ghazal* begins, paradoxically, from the exhaustion of its own plot.

Let us examine how relations of time and space are constructed in this *ghazal*. As far as the position of the lyric hero is concerned, Navoiy does not place him firmly in any space, except suppositionally, transmitted through the time frame *tong otquncha* (till dawn). Navoiy constructs space subsequently in the following manner: *chiqdimu... yo'lida, oidin erkonda, kimsa bormukim anga ko'rganda*. In other words, everything occurs seemingly in free space. But then occurs the coagulation of space through *ko'zlaringdan necha suv kelgay*, a conditional step into the void, where there is no beloved: *yo'qsa kim qo'ydi qadam*, and finally, the last *bayt* locks and embraces all previous space coordinates by *ko'ngul uyi* – the 'house of the heart'. From this space began the initial motion. In other words, the space, assigned as external and expanding phenomenon: road – moonlight – separation, becomes the internal space of the soul, the space into which the beloved did not enter.

On the other hand, the space of thought, of imagination, in which the lyric hero and his beloved coexist divided, is gradually personified through the universal *kimsa* (someone), whose existence is hypothetical, conditional and abstract. Then, this 'someone' obtains the status of the collocutor, *tolibi sodiq*, who also does not exist. But there is a poet in his own alienation, whose alienation is formally described by the *takhallus*, when he turns to himself: 'Hey, Navoiy...'. In other words, in the negative space of separation the alienated name of the poet remains and by this token the poet leaves for himself the possibility of another, extra- or meta-textual space.[134]

A similar understanding of the role and value of *takhallus* in this *ghazal* makes it possible to assume that the intermediating forces (*kimsa, tolibi sodiq*) are the functions of the lyric 'I' of the poet in the sense 'I' – 'not I', 'I' – 'single', 'I' – 'special', 'I' – 'universal'. Thus, it is possible to reveal the duality of the space, which is illustrated through natural details (road, moonlight, etc.), but ends up in the absolute space of the spirit. So the time of the *ghazal* is dual. The temporary or pseudo-temporary coordinates of time in the *ghazal*, which are consecutively linear, again and again return to the very beginning of the promised meeting, to the beginning of this *kelmadi* (didn't come), which rushes about in time, first running forward, then returning to its beginning, which itself is an ending.[135]

Furthermore, one could say that the opposition 'I' and 'you', the lyric hero and the beloved in this *ghazal*, are reflected in all levels. Thus, together with those mentioned, at the meta-linguistic poetic level, for example, the opposition of logic and meta-logic, represented from the very first line *ul sarvi gulru' kelmadi* (that rose-faced cypress didn't come). If we read this statement from the point of view of formal logic, then *ul sarvi gulru'* cannot arrive anyway. A mechanical interpretation would explain thus: 'Trees do not walk.' And, from this point of view, the suggestion appears to be true. But with the meta-logic reading, when we deliberately allow the 'untruth' of this *ul sarvi gulru'*, we are shaken by its fraud with the same trustfulness: *Kecha kelgumdur debon ul sarvi gulru' kelmadi....*

If we take the metro-rhythmic level, then the combination of two *misra* (half *bayt*) in one *bayt* with their rhyming according to the pattern: A-A, B-A, C-A, and so forth are the combination of the variable and constant, of deviations and standards, absence of rhyme in the first of *misra* of a *bayt* and mono-rhyme in the second. The alliteration of *Radif kelmadi* (didn't come) is a combination of a constantly repetitive word with the variable environment. Each time this is the same *kelmadi* and each time it is different, revealing new facets. So whichever level or structural element of *ghazal* we take, all have this duality as a founding unifying principle, which creates a certain cognitive structure that is hierarchic and extremely flexible, correlating with the fundamental basis of human thinking and spiritual activity.[136]

No wonder that the main bulk of Sufi poetry, including the Sufi poetry of Central Asia, is written in the form of *ghazal*. Another factor which makes *ghazal* a universal form of Sufi art is the fact that it was, and is, sung. For instance, all the classic repertoire of traditional Uzbek and Tajik music is based on the *ghazal* form. *Ghazal* is also widely recited in Sufi communities, both male and female. Historic documents witness poetic gatherings like *Yassaviyhonlik* (readings of Yassaviy), *Bedilhoni* (*Bedilhonlik*) (readings of Bedil[137]), and *Mashrabhonlik* (readings of Mashrab).[138,139]

In the long history of Sufism, poetry, either recited or sung, was accepted as the best way to achieve spiritual ecstasy. The tenth-century scholar Al Farabi said that 'the most perfect is a melody united with verse. This is what can move a man and change his morals.'[140] From the beginning of the tenth century, the process of listening to poetry put to music, called *Sama'*, became a daily habit in the social life of the Sufi brotherhoods. Such innovation created discussion and critical protest among orthodox scholars, where music itself, as opposed to the reading of the Qur'an, was questioned. That discussion took widespread forms. The great Sufi and poet Al Ghazali (1059/1060–1111) in his principal work *Ihya ulum ad-din*, mentioned above, pointed out:

> Listening to the Qur'an occurs everywhere in our daily life. However, for social gatherings it is expected that singers are invited and music played, not the Qur'an.
> There are five reasons for this:
> 1 The Qur'an does not have associations with terrestrial love;
> 2 New songs and tunes could be sung and played but the Qur'an is always the same;
> 3 The voice and the rhythm of music make the heart beat faster;
> 4 The voice becomes stronger with the accompaniment of instruments;
> 5 Music can adjust to the mood, but not the Qur'an.[141]

So, the purpose of *Sama'*, which was based on the unity of poetry and music, was to create spiritual excitement, and this was supposed to come as a divine grace.

Music with poetry readings was performed at meetings of dervishes, Shaikhs' gatherings, Majlis in closed (*Khanaka*) and open places – each associated with a certain time and place. Love poetry with symbolic meaning was accepted for such purposes, often taking a simple form which originated from folk poetry, like Rubai. The demand for such poetry from the ninth century stimulated the flow of lyrics aiming to create particular emotional states: tolerance and obedience, terrestrial love, hope, and so on. Majlis, as the main form of social gathering, included conversation, discussion, collective prayers and listening to music. Originating from urban culture, this form maintained links with the vital force and beauty, initially of folk poetry and later of Sufi *ghazal*.

Central Asian Female poets: Zebunissa, Nodira-begim, Jahonotin Uvaysiy, and Anbar-otin

Women played a major role, not just in reciting and maintaining this poetry in Central Asia but also in creating it. Children of elite families were generally taught the basics of classic Central Asian poetry in Persian and Turkic languages by their grandmothers, reading their *Bayazs* (handwritten collection of favourite *ghazals* by different authors); and according to many memoirs, that way of transmitting initial knowledge of the poetry was quite common.

The first written collections of female Sufi poetry by Zebunissa came from the courts of great Mughals whose founder, Zaheriddin Muhammad Babur, was born in city of Andijan.

Zebunissa was the eldest daughter of the last of the major Mughal rulers of India, Aurangzeb. Her mother, Aurangzeb's first wife and a descendant of a Persian emperor, would have one other daughter and two sons before her own death in 1657. Zebunissa was born in the Deccan, where Aurangzeb acted as viceroy for his father, Shah Jahan. When she was in her early teens, her family returned to the north and lived first at Agra and then at the new capital in Delhi. As a member of the royal family, she studied not only Persian and Arabic, but also mathematics and astronomy, under the chief scholars of the realm.

In 1658, when Zebunissa was 21 years old, Aurangzeb seized the throne from Shah Jahan. For some years, his eldest daughter would have considerable influence over the new emperor. Contemporary chroniclers noted that Aurangzeb asked her opinion on palace appointments and that he sometimes accepted her decisions even when he did not agree with them.

Zebunissa never married, although some traditions give her an unwanted engagement and various love affairs. She had her own courts at Delhi and at Lahore to which scholars and poets came; at least some of her own poetry in Persian and in Arabic is from this period of her life. She established a library and had classical Arabic texts translated into Persian under her personal supervision.

Aurangzeb was a strict Muslim and, once in power, became increasingly strict in his requirements for the observance of Islamic law. However, his eldest sister was a Sufi. Perhaps through the influence of her aunt, Zebunissa eventually also chose that path of devotion. The Sufis held only a marginal place in Mughal society, but were tolerated unless they allied themselves with Aurangzeb's opponents.

In 1681, when Zebunissa was 44 years old, the younger of her two full-brothers, Akbar, rebelled against his father and proclaimed himself emperor. The rebellion lasted only a month; Akbar fled the country but continued to be troublesome. Zebunissa had some communication with her exiled brother and was accused by Aurangzeb of being the rebel's ally; for this she was imprisoned in a Delhi fortress and disappeared from the official record. We do not know how harsh her imprisonment was, nor if she remained in prison until her death in 1702.

Some of her poetry, written under the pen-name *Makhfi* (the hidden one) circulated among her contemporaries. Fifty years after her death, over 400 poems were collected and published in Persian as the *Diwan-i-Makhfi*. Most of the poems are *ghazals*. The most famous of her poems is the poem with the Radif *in jost* (is here), which is sung as a famous Uzbeko-Tajik song *Samarqand ushhog'i* (Lovers of Samarqand):

Come, a beauty with curly hairs and mascara eyes is here,
The beauty who kills with a warm look is here.

Her coquetry is a knife, her eyelashes are daggers, her sight is a diamond,
If you need a martyrdom, the steppe of Kerbala is here.

If paradise smiles to you, don't be deceived,
Don't go outside of the wine-house, because the place is here.

From feet to the head – wherever you look,
The coquetry breaks the heart, the place is here.

I searched the library of the world, turning page after page,
I saw your letter and said, my wish is here.

If you give a charity of beauty to God,
Come here, a begging Zebunissa is here.

Just as in the court of Delhi, Sufi poetry flourished at the court of Kokand in the Ferghana Valley, with the works of Nodira, Uvaysiy, and Anbarotin.

Nodira-begim (also known as Komila) was born in the family of Rahmonkulibiy, major of Andijan, in 1792. Her real name was Mohlaroyim. In 1808, she married Amir Umarkhan, who was then Mayor of Margilon; and went to Kokand together with Umarkhan, who had succeeded to the throne in place of his brother Olimkhan. After the tragic death of Umarkhan in 1822 she governed Kokand kingdom together with her son Madalihon. The madrasah, mosque and karavansarays were built at her instruction. She was a leader of the people of science and took care of poor people. She was killed by Amir Nasrulloh, khan of Bukhara in 1842.

Nodira wrote poems under the pen-names of Komila and Maknuna, writing in both Persian and Uzbek. Her work consisting of 10,000 bayts is widely known.

She used a wide range of genres such as a *muhammas, ruboi, fard*, but most of all *ghazals*. As a teacher she learnt Navoiy, Fuzuli, and Bedil. News of Nodira's life and poetry began to spread in her lifetime. Historical treatises such as *Muntahabut-tavorih* of Hakimhon Tora, *Tuhfatu-t-tavorih* of Avazmuhammad Attor, *Tarihi Fargona* of Isohon Tora, *Ansobu-s-salotin va tavorihi Havokin* of Mushrif and the stories *Voqeoti Muhammadlaihon* of Uvaysiy and *Haft Gulshan* of Nodir-Uzlat contain valuable information about her life and activity.[142]

Here are two *Ghazals* by Nodira (in my translation) reflecting the issue of Sufism:

Ah me, who am left on the ruins of separation with no direction,
because the beloved comes not as a guest to the ruins of my shelter
I could find no trace of you suffering in the desert
so I returned (sacrificing myself) once again,
wondering, to the house of sorrow.
I cried so much not partaking of the wine of your ruby lips,
so my life-force leaked as blood drop by drop from my eyes.
I was proud of her face as we met, but the dusk
finally burned my body with the flame of separation.
If I act in madness, do not blame me. That peri [sprite]
disappeared from my sight, and the light of her gaze became hidden.
Nodira, in wonder of that sun I became mad,
My love became apparent as the fame of time.

O straight cypress, what are your thoughts?
Your promise of rendezvous burnt my soul.
Bound, I pray for pardon,
My aim is your perfection.
You argue with the face of the moon,
O, sun, have you achieved eclipse?
For assets, water of paradise or water of Kaaba,
For me, the pure drops of your tears are enough.
You may not yet read them,
But your fortune-telling on holy sheets was blessed.
More precious than Jamshid's cup143
O Sufi-beggar, your broken ceramics.
Your lovers died in your sorrow,
But you have no particle of care.
O sick heart, in separation
You have not strength to beat.
O, Nodira, you speak about love,
And your condition becomes famous amongst the masses.

Jahonotin Uvaysiy, another famous female poet of that time, was born in Margilon in 1780. Her father Siddik bobo was an admirer of literature who wrote poems in two languages, Persian and Turkic. Her mother Chinbibi was an *otin*; and her brother Ohunjon was a singer.

Her parents married her to Hijohon, a craftsman, with whom she had two children. Unfortunately, she was widowed quite early and went to live with Nodira in Kokand in Khan's palace. She died in 1845 in Margilon, at the age of 65.

Uvaysiy's poems consist of 15,000 hemistiches. One of her *Divans* (collection of *ghazals*) is kept at the Institute of Academy of Science of the Republic of Uzbekistan. Her *ghazals, muhammas, musaddas, murabbas,*[144] and the poems *Shahzoda Hasan* and *Voqeoti Muhammadalihon* are included in that *Divan*. Her works and her *Divans* are very popular; and three copies of the her *Divan* were found in the 1960s.

Information about Uvaysiy's life and creative works can be found in her works and in some *tazkiras* and biographical books. Attention was given to the her creative work in *Majmuatush-shoiron* (1824), written by Fazli Namangoniy.

Here is an example of Uvaysiy's Sufi poetry:

Today, o friends, I miss my beloved child,
It's not my fault if I'm a beggar,
I miss my king of times.

I am a stranger, a foreigner, lonely and silent,
My body is full of suffering,
I miss my remedy.

Memory of my tongue, thought of my heart, my good child,
Sultan of my state,
I miss you, my dear, my only one.

Night and day I wait for him, staring at the road
Where he comes and asks how I am,
I miss my visitor.

God did not cast his lot if he finds no way out,
I miss my future, red blood of my liver,
Who says: My mother…

The world has darkened in my eyes through this separation,
I miss my shining moon,

The light of my eyes and of my heart.

I cry endlessly alone by day and night, Uvaysiy,
I miss the beauty of my home,
The light of my eyes, my khan...

Another famous Uzbek Sufi female poet is **Anbar-otin** (1870–1915).[145]
As her name reveals, she probably was an *Otin-Oy*, a woman who had
a religious upbringing. Anbar-otin was born in Kokand where she was
taught to write poetry by Dilshod Barno, the author of *Tarihi muhojiron*
(History of Muhajirun or Exiled). Anbar-otin was a lyric Sufi poet. In her
ghazals pure love is glorified. She was a poet who wrote lyric poems about
the soul and feelings of woman. She created a *Divan* with *ghazals* and other
poetic forms. However, it is necessary to point out that Anbar-otin developed social motives in her poetry and criticised very strongly the Sufis'
attitude to life and the Sufi orders Naqshbandiyya and Yassaviya.

During Soviet times, the female Sufi poetry of Central Asia went underground, though a certain ambiguity makes some of the *ghazals* of female
Uzbek and Tajik poets like Zulfia, Halima Hudoyberdieva, Gulchehra
Jo'raeva, Qutlibeka, Halima Ahmedova, Gulruhsor Safieva perfect examples of Sufi poetry. Here is an example by Halima Hudoiberdyeva:

Izlang meni
Agar to'lsam, bir jom yanglig' agar to'lsam,
Ko'ngillarni titrog'idan izlang meni,
Chechak yanglig' qovjirasa
Satrlarim kuzning kuyib o'tmog'idan Izlang meni.
O'ylasangiz bu dunyo tor, Bu dunyo keng.
Yaproqman, o'z daraxtimdan uzmang meni.

'Sen' tilingiz 'Siz'ga ketsa Bir murid deng.
Yassaviyning muridi deb 'Siz'lang meni.
Quiyosh bilan yursam, Yursam baland, bo'lib,
Xudo qo'lim tutmog'idan izlang meni.
Bir kun, bir kun topmasangiz, Bo'lsam g'oiyb,
Turkistonning tuprog'idan Izlang meni.

Look for me, seek from the shivers of heart's bottom
If my verses like a flower become faded
Look for me then from the sorrow of the autumn.

If you think that planet – narrow,
World is broad,
I am a leaf and kindly ask you
Not to pick off.
Reckon as a learner, esteem –
When you hold,
Respect as Yassaviy's pupil,
Whom I follow.
If I go with the Sun
In wealth, in eminence,
Look for me from
Mercy, blessings of Allah, and...
Once...you won't find me
When I once...evanesce
Look for me then
From the lasting Turkistan land.[146]

After the break-up of the Soviet Union, some of the female poets of Uzbekistan and Tajikistan returned to Islamic and Sufi poetry, using not just traditional *ghazal*, but also other modern forms. The poetry of Tajik poet Farzona or Uzbek poets Zebo Muminova and Khosiyat Rustamova show how female Sufi poetry is now developing in Central Asia.

This chapter has examined only the written, so-called 'professional' female Sufi poetry, but this does not in any way comprise the whole of female Sufi poetry. Chapters 9 and 10 feature little-known ritualistic and folkloristic forms of Sufi poetry, devoted to female Sufi rituals and its classification. We focus first on the phenomenon of knowledge transmission within Central Asian history.

5

Transmission of Sacred Knowledge in Its Connection to Sufi Tradition

15. USTAD–SHOGIRD TRAINING
IN MEDIEVAL SOURCES

Historically, Ustad–Shogird (master–apprentice) has been the only form of knowledge transmission for professional guilds. This chapter examines a medieval document which reflects on the Ustad–Shogird process of training and rite of initiation. *Ahloqul solihiyn* (On Ustad [Master] and his conditions) was written in fifteenth-century Herat by Husayn Voiz Koshifiy.[147] It explains many different issues related to Ustad–Shogird relationships, from its forms to its content. It is based on the Sufi way to perfection, of absorbing knowledge, and therefore includes certain ceremonial duties and obligations. The manuscript employs a particular terminology related to training systems within professional guilds: 'on the road' means during the process of training; 'fasten the belt' means initiating the relationship of Ustad–Shogird (master–apprentice); and 'stations' means stages in the process of professional and spiritual training related to Sufi tradition. In fact, this treatise is a manual on the master–apprentice (Ustad–Shogird) relationship and its connection with Sufi tradition.

The very first paragraphs of treatise emphasise the points that the Ustad–Shogid relationship lies in the very heart of any professional training.

> Know that no work is done without an Ustad, and every work done without an Ustad is in vain. There is a belief that even though a person might reach a certain degree and carry out a certain amount of work, if he had had no Ustad, or if his Ustad had not been a good one, his work would achieve nothing.

It is said that:

> Everyone without an Ustad works in vain, On the road to sense nobody is
> a better friend than an Ustad.

Therefore everyone who wants to achieve something with his work first of
all needs a perfect Ustad. It is obvious what an Ustad is for; without the
lead of an Ustad no work goes well:

> Everyone who starts his work without an Ustad is doomed in that his work
> never will gain attention. Keep close to the sleeve of the Ustad and be happy.
> Serve him for a certain time and become an Ustad yourself.

The person who fastens the belt of another person is called Ustad-the
tuner, and Shogird (Apprentice), whose belt suppose to be fastened called
Halaf.

The paragraph below shows what kind of character is needed for an
Ustad.

'If they ask what the preconditions of Ustad-the tuner are, say they are
six:

1) First, a perfect Ustad, who fastened his belt, should keep that belt beyond
   the hands of others (nobody should doubt his perfection) and he himself
   shouldn't touch the belt of his children/apprentices (not be rude to his
   children as well as to his apprentices).
2) Secondly, he must have all the features of a true man.
3) Thirdly, he must know small details of *Tariqat* (Sufi Way) and the sub-
   tleties of *Haqiqat* (Sufi Truth), to pass on to his 'child' (apprentice). If
   they ask who is the perfect Ustad, say one who follows the pure way of
   religion, who knows his own sins, who is a wise and tasteful person, who
   is not jealous and revengeful and mean.
4) Fourthly, Ustad, who fastens the belt, truly knows it, so the steps are
   taken in the right direction.
5) Fifthly, the belt on the child/apprentice should be fastened publicly, in
   the presence of Sheikh, Naqib and brothers in the Way, but not in a
   hidden place.
6) Sixthly, he must know the state of the child/apprentice, whether he is
   worthy of it.

If an Ustad sees that his Shogird is not worthy, he would not fasten his belt
on him, as it's evil.'

The paragraphs below are concerned with the process of fastening the belt from the way and conditions of doing it to its consequences.

'If they ask how many stations of fastening the belt, say they are six.

1) Firstly, the Ustad knows and describes parts of tuning and types of it.
2) Secondly, he orders his apprentice to serve forty days and the latter should bear it.
3) Thirdly, he prepares water and salt for the gathering.
4) Fourthly, he uses a five-wick lamp.
5) Fifthly, he fastens the belt conditionally.
6) Sixthly, for this ritual he must cook *khalva* (sweet).

If they ask how many conditions of fastening the belt there are, say – seven.

1) to spread out the rug for the prayer;
2) to put his left hand onto the head of Shogird;
3) to hold him with his right hand;
4) to prepare the belt;
5) to take the belt with his left hand;
6) to recite a relevant verse of the Qur'an;
7) to fasten the belt and take it off in seven days.

If they ask how many rituals there are in fastening the belt, say – ten.

1) to remember Pirs/Masters, who have passed away,
2) to introduce the Shogird to the community of Shogirds,
3) to recite a prayer, holding his hand,
4) to step away three steps from the prayer rug,
5) to take the belt in his left hand,
6) to recite a relevant verse of the Qur'an,
7) to turn the Shogird's face towards the way (i.e. tell him the truth),
8) take some khalva,
9) while taking Shogird's hand to touch by index finger to his same finger,
10) to explain the meaning of every step of the rituals.'

One can see from the paragraphs above that the meaning of every single step is explained in great detail. For instance, Ustad puts his left hand on Shogird's head because the left hand is closer to the heart. Or Ustad steps aside for three steps, because one step is meant to suppress the sinful soul, the second – Satan, and the third one – the desire for wealth. Unless he suppresses those, the Shogird cannot achieve his goal.

The next paragraph shows how the role of apprentice is related to religious and mystical study and based on an ascetic lifestyle.

On the conditions of being a Shogird
If they ask what is the basis of being a Shogird, say it is based on will.
If they ask what is the will, say sama'/mystical listening and piety.
If they ask what sama' and piety are, say to listen with the ears of the heart to whatever the Ustad is saying and accept it with sincere heart, and to fulfill it with the help of all his members.
If they ask what is good for a Shogird, say pure belief, because only faith brings people to their aim.
If they ask how a Shogird achieves his aim, say through his service.
If they ask what his service is based on, say on refusing pleasure and working hard.

The next two paragraphs describe the rules for the apprentice, including his attitude to the study and behaviour.
'If they ask how many stations of Shogirdness there are, say – four.

1) to start his venture bravely, because it is much worse to be scared of beginning, or to retreat;
2) to serve sincerely;
3) to coordinate his tongue with his heart, i.e. talk and act accordingly and truly;
4) to listen to advise and remember what his Ustad is saying, and follow it.

If they ask how many customs of Shogirdness there are, say – eight.

1) whenever he sees his Ustad, to greet him first;
2) not to talk much in front of his Ustad;
3) to bow his head;
4) not to look all around;
5) if he wants to ask something, first ask his Ustad's permission;
6) when his Ustad answers, not to talk back while he is explaining;
7) not to gossip in front of his Ustad;
8) to be polite in all his behaviour'.

The last paragraph describes how to tie the belt according to different orders:

'Alif' order is the order of 'maddahs' or 'eulogists' or musicians. 'Lam-alif' is the order of simple people. 'Mim' order is the order of philosophers,

'*Sayfiy* of military people, *Salmoniy* of cleaners, *Yusufiy* of craft workers and artisans, etc.

16. USTAD–SHOGIRD TRADITION TODAY

In discussions about the Ferghana Valley, its rural area and particularly the Andijan district, one should point out that a traditional lifestyle is observed in Uzbek households, within the family, and in the involvement of children in any family work (Photo 4).

According to Deniz Kandiyoti, 'Children, especially daughters from the age 10 and even younger, help mothers with domestic tasks, the care of younger siblings, the care of animals and at cotton harvest when agricultural season starts'.[148] Children do, indeed, help with the cotton harvest, as in Uzbekistan cotton remains a quasi-state monopoly. But it is worth mentioning that the agricultural season in rural areas of Uzbekistan and in

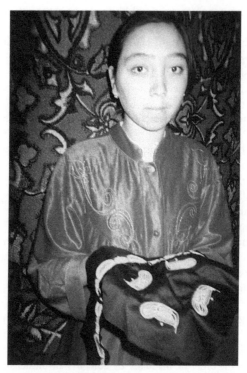

Photo 4: A girl-embroiderer from Ferghana Valley making traditional men's hat (*doppi*)

some parts of Tajikistan is a non-stop process taking place almost all year round, except for winter. Children help their parents with many difficult tasks like, for example, rice growing, which requires many long hours spent bending or standing in the water, or tending to silk worms, which are known for their 24-hour non-stop feeding on mulberry leaves, and so on.

So, children's involvement in agricultural work and domestic tasks leads to the development of strong family relationships supported by traditional social networks.

It is obvious that social structures and networks in Uzbekistan have been preserved from pre-Soviet times. Despite the Soviet regime, Uzbeks were allowed to carry on with previously established forms of social gathering, and therefore to maintain traditional social relationships (Photo 5). Notable among these relationships is *Gap-gashtak*, a social network where neighbourhood members – Mahallya – and friends assemble together. It can also be a gathering for special occasions such as a reunion for former classmates (*Sinfdashlar*), an assembly of teacher-colleagues (*Uqutuvchilar*), Ziyefat – friends' meeting, Maraka – a meeting on the occasions of mourning, or remembrance days. Women's *Gap-gashtaks*, based on economic, rather than spiritual, issues, sometimes take place on a regular basis among the female population. *Gap-gashtaks* in Uzbekistan are a

Photo 5: Female communities meeting *Gap-gashtak* in Keles

dense web of interconnecting networks. The origin of the female *Gap* is clearly related to male gatherings, as formerly *Gap* was a 'male activity consisting of a regular get-together, of about a dozen or so friends primarily for the purposes of entertainment and sociability', but later this began to become a female activity involving also some 'music and dancing'.[149]

The most interesting fact for this study is that '*Otin-Oys* gatherings are considered to be among the most prestigious and far away from pure social or entertaining purposes'.[150] These are the main focus of our attention, revealing how local society preserved centuries-old traditional links in networking and entertaining.

From our perspective, of great importance in such a process of preservation is the presence of traditional Mehterlik, professional guilds based on the Ustad–Shogird training system.

17. *MEHTERLIK* OR PROFESSIONAL GUILDS

Before providing examples of the forms of these activities, it would be helpful to offer some clarification on the concept of the Ustad–Shogird.

The oral knowledge transmission, from master to apprentice, from teacher to pupil, from professional specialist to beginner, originated in Central Asia in early medieval times. Historically, there were a great many professional guilds in every single part of this area with its strong focus on traditional culture, and also around the courts and palaces, where knowledge transmission by the Ustad–Shogird method was considered to be the only way of teaching and learning.

Musicians, artists, craft masters, or those who wished to be associated with correct, high-quality performance were all involved in guilds (*Mehterliks*). Those guilds consisted of 'clubs' of merchants or craftspeople formed to give help and advice to their members and to devise regulations and set standards for particular trades. All guilds were independent, and an exchange of knowledge between them was forbidden and prosecuted by law.

To belong to such a guild had deep spiritual meaning, and required total devotion, determination to follow the chosen life path and a lifetime devoted to improving skills. To be a professional musician meant to be a member of certain *Mehterlik* (guild), and to receive training in the Ustad–Shogird (master–apprentice) style.

In fact, the whole process and methods of *Mehterlik* training were related to the Sufi brotherhood system, where every step was related to religious training:

1) the way people worshipped Sheikh/Pir – they had to admire their teachers;
2) the whole process of knowledge transmission activity was surrounded by saints as protectors;
3) the respect given by the youngest to the oldest when advice was recommended.

Historically, each *Mehterlik* (guild) had a special *Risola* (book of guidance) for members to follow. This was document consisted of a programme of action adopted by a group of individuals, and at the same time, the set of principles on which it was based. One of these given below is '*Risola-I Mehterlik*'.[151] At the end of the Risola is a date, 1327 year of Hijra (i.e. 1909) and the name of the person the Risola paper belonged to: Ustad-Mehter-Kurchi Niyas-Mehter-ogly.

The *Risola-I Mehterlik* rules consist of:

1) a prayer;
2) a legend about the origin of professions and, related to them, Risola focused on the sacred roots of the named profession;
3) questions and answers on the religious significance of profession/skills mentioned (*farz, vadjib, sunnat, mystahab*) and an account of sacred representatives of that occupation;
4) questions and answers on spiritual mentors (Pir) from all stations of Sufism (*Shariat, Tariqat, Hakikat*), on the heads of four Muslim religious-law schools of Islam (Hanafiya, Hanbaliya, Maliliya, and Shafiiya), on 'Pirs of consolation/reassurance' (Mother, Father, Teacher, Master) and protectors of the present guild;
5) (The Most important paragraph of the Risola) questions and answers on prayers and sacred statements, which one should repeat during different stages of performance of named skills;
6) duties and restrictions for representatives of the above-named occupation;
7) policy of the named profession; attitude to the Risola; awards and punishments for breaking rules or guidelines/policy of the Risola.

The most interesting for us is the second paragraph, which relates the legend of the sacred origin of music and, particularly, of singing:

> One should know that the occupation *Mehterlik* comes from the holy man Gavryiil, Peace Be Upon Him. The great Allah said that the soul should enter the shape/body (*kylyb*) of Adam, PBUH, but the soul was scared to do so. Then the great Allah ordered *Mehter* Gavryiil to bring a Bird from Paradise to perform her song. From the pleasure and sweetness of singing the soul went into Adam-Safiulla shape/body. That is why *Mehterlik* comes from Gavryiil, Peace Will Be Upon His Soul. When a human hears music (Nagma) his soul is calmed and his love and joy increase.

So, here the divine origin of music is revealed as God's action. Also, it is closely associated with the fact of God's creation, mentioned in nearly every sacred book, and Adam became the first man to adopt music as a passion and a way of life. (Incidentally, Adam was also a Pir of butchers as well as musicians, because cow hide is used for making percussion instruments like Doira and Nagora.[152] So the material used by the guild for musical instruments united different guilds and their Pirs.)

Another strong guild association from those documents comes from Sufism and its relationship with Murid-Murshid or *silsilah* of oral knowledge transmission. The hierarchy of God–human, with the saints in between, was the framework for every *Mehterlik*, as confirmed by the example above.

We can observe, then, that every kind of professional training in music was deeply based on the Ustad–Shogird system of knowledge transmission and all authentic forms of Uzbek music are still taught this way even today.

18. *HOFIZLIK*: PROFESSIONAL TRAINING IN MUSIC

In discussing Sufi music and Sufi singing one should not forget that its history began with male performers who were at the centre of public attention. What is the Sufi traditional singing style? Who performed Uzbek Sufi songs in the twentieth century?

Sufi traditional music in Central Asia was based on a professional style of singing or the Hofiz training system, combining aesthetic perfection with technical excellence and accomplishment. The skill was acquired with Ustad–Shogird (master–apprentice) guidance, which had both practical and spiritual aspects.[153]

The term 'Hofiz' comes from Arabic, where *hifa* means a guard. Today, it has a wider meaning extending from the reader/narrator of *Sura* of Qur'an, documentary writer, writer or poet, epic singer baqshi/Hofiz, reader of classical poetry – *Ghazal* to simply a singer and musician.[154] In Hofizlik music training one can see traces of Sufi idea of perfection:

Shariat is a corpus of Muslim law, Tariqat is a mystical Way, Haqiqat is Truth. Ishq is passion and love, Shogirdlik is Apprenticeship, Hofizlik is Mastership.

The same resemblance comes from technical terms of performance where

Sozlanish is tuning, *Tayorlanish* is preparation, *Mukammallik* is Perfection. *Kirish* is entering, Anglash is comprehension, Yettite bosqich o'tish – ascending seven levels, Ijod faoliyat – creative action.

Here are main features of Hofiz's singing style: a) a beautiful, strong voice with a wide range; b) clear pronunciation; c) a capacity for structuring every single sentence of the songs, with the ability to extend them, adding well-developed decorations and ornamentations (*Hang*); d) the special long/chain-based breathing system illustrating the ability to perform not just one but two or even three melodic phrases on one breath; e) the ability to perform different instrumental passages, melodic forms that imitate percussion sounds, and so on; freedom in ornamenting rhythm and metre; f) skills in *Awj* (long, high culminations) performance; g) aptitude to build inner symmetrical structure with the use of *Hang* and *Shah'd* (the way of breaking the pulse or rhythm of the tune without affecting the whole song).[155]

Uzbek culture in the twentieth century was privileged to have three of the most outstanding Hofizes from Ferghana Valley: Sadyrkhon Hofiz (1847–1931); Djurakhon Sultanov (1893–1968); and Rasul Qori Mamadaliev (1928–76). Each of them deserves a special mention.

Sadyrkhon Hofiz's Ustadslar/teachers were Rummon Said Buzrukhon–hoja, and Qori Sangin-domla, from whom the singer learned the Qiroat (Qur'an's reciting style) with a focus on its poetry and content. Reciting the Qur'an requires the clear pronunciation of words and phrases, with melodically fixed and structurally well-developed delivery. He also played *Tanbur*. By attending *Honakoi* (mystical religious meetings) he learned religious genres such as Masnavyihonlik, Maroyahonlik, Na'thonlik. He was not allowed to attend any entertainment events.[156]

Hofiz Djurakhon Sultanov was more popular in performing both classical and folk *Katta ashula* genres related to outside (open air festivals) music celebrations. He was trained by Boltaboy Hofiz Rajabov (1867–1960) and Mamatbobo Sattarov (1885–1967). He was named a Pir of *Katta ashula's* singers (*katta a ashullachilarning piri*). His interest in folk genres (Kushik, Yalla) has enhanced and enriched his style in Maqam performance (Evvoi Chorgoh, Dugoh Husainyi, Savti Suvora, Sadyrkhon Usshogi).[157]

The blind musician Hofiz Rasul-Qori's childhood training mostly concentrated on recitation of the Qur'an. Because of his amazing voice, he was named the Daud's voice representative (*Daudi ovoz sohibi*), the nightingale. His achievements in singing included: a) ornamented decorations; Hudo (poetry Salohyi), Ghazalhonlik, (poetry Chishtyi), Mehmonsan (poetry Huvaido); b) scale and mode arrangement within the ascending ladder of structure; c) instrumental improvisation, including imitation of percussion sounds; d) incorporation of the new style 'Ist': – when, within the same melodic structure, the tempo slows down to reflect dramatic/dynamic/emotional expressiveness...as in *Katta ashula* or Suvora.[158]

It is clear that Hofizlik methods required a serious training, which covered style of performance, musical structure, frame, and ornamentations including a fine ability for improvisation. Very often, Hofiz performed his own compositions, and developed a distinctive and personal interpretation of the song.

In the next chapter we shall look at the case of female performers.

6

Music and Female Sufis

19. SUFI MASTERS IN MUSIC

'Music is called *Ghiza-i-ruh* (the food of the soul) by Sufis. Music, being the most divine art, elevates the soul to the higher spirit; music itself being unseen soon reaches the unseen; just as only the diamond can break the diamond, so musical vibrations are used to make the physical and mental vibrations inactive, in order that the Sufi may be elevated to the spiritual spheres,' wrote Sufi Pir-o-Murshid Inayat Khan in his book *A Sufi Message of Spiritual Liberty*.[159]

Chapter 4 quoted the views of Al-Ghazali, as to why music affects Sufis more strongly than reciting the Qur'an, and how it is used for their *zikrs*. But not all theologians in Islam hold the same views. The practice of music and dance in Sufism is, in fact, rather contentious. It is by no means universally accepted by all Sufis, and some orders frown upon it. Others may rejoice in the recitation of mystical poetry, accompanied by musical instruments and performed as part of their prayers and devotions. Some Sufis consider such music conducive to 'mystical ecstasy'. These Sufis maintain that music can arouse passion, either sensual or spiritual. It is spiritual passion (longing for God) that is the Sufi's goal. Hence, musical concerts are a regular feature of some Sufi orders, like *Mawlaviyya*, *Chishtiyya*, or *Kubraviyya*.

Music has always been the favourite Sufi means of spiritual development for those orders. Rumi, the author of the *Masnavi*, introduced music into his *Mawlaviyya* order, and enjoyed the memory of his blessed *murshid's* association while listening to it. Since that time, music has become the second subject of Sufi practices. They declare that it creates harmony in both worlds and brings eternal peace.

The great mystic of India, Khwaja Moin-ad-Din Chishti, introduced music into his *Chishtiyya* order. Even today, musical entertainments for the elevation of the soul, called *Sama'*, are held among Sufis.[160]

Sufi music is about union with the Beloved, with God. Music is the vehicle to reach the heart and attain a state of grace or enlightenment, a 'stateless state' or *Ma'rifat* – inner knowledge. Music is an essential part of spiritual life and practice for many Sufis. In that sense, Sufism is not simply about theories or the intellect; the goal is the experience of union with the One. So, Sufi teachers lead their *murids* towards the One through practical experience in ritual, movement, voice, and music.

Sama' (which means listening in Arabic) is the key concept, which defines usage of both poetry and music among Sufis. The greatest Islamic theologian and Sufi Master Imam Al-Ghazali, in his fundamental work *Ihya ulum ad-din* (Revival of religious sciences) – considered to be the encyclopaedia of Islam and Sufism – devotes two separate chapters to the nature of *Sama'* and practice of poetry and music in it. In his conclusion he says: '*Sama'* could be sometimes *haram* (disallowed by religion), sometimes *mubah* (admissible), sometimes *makruh* (undesirable), sometimes *mustahab* (beneficial). For those who are enslaved by their worldly lust, and for most youngsters, it is disallowed, because *Sama'* confuses their souls full of beastly lust. *Sama'* is undesirable for those who are routinely using it just for the sake of fun but not turning themselves into beasts. It is admissible for those who are enjoying just the beauty of the sound. *Sama'* is beneficial for those who are woken up to the love to Allah and to good deeds because of it.'[161]

Imam Al-Ghazali sets out five principles of *Sama'* reflecting on issues of Time, Place and People, *Zikr*, concentration on *Sama'*, participants' behaviour and involvement. He points out that *Sama'* has three relevant prerequisites: Time, Place and People. As to Time, *Sama'* is useless while eating, fighting, praying or when the heart is not quiet and calm. As to Place, *Sama'* is not arranged in the random street, or in a disgusting environment, where the heart is distracted. As to People, they should not be hypocrites – those for whom *Sama'* is disallowed or undesirable. Also, Imam Al-Ghazali argues, the mental state of people at the gathering should be considered. Some people could be happier with *Zikr*, or helping poor people, but having no union with God in *Sama'*. As Imam Al-Ghazali suggested, participants should not be distracted by what is happening in the gathering, but should concentrate fully on *Sama'* and should not simply pretend to achieve ecstasy. They should not jump, dance or cry unless they cannot control the impulse, indicated Imam Al-Ghazali. But at the same time, 'if someone naturally comes to ecstasy and starts to dance, others should follow him.'[162]

Imam Al-Ghazali quotes the views of many famous Sufis regarding *Sama*'. Zunnun al-Misri said: '*Sama*' comes from God and turns the heart straight to Him.' Abu-l-Huseyn ad-Dirac said: '*Sama*' made me dance, gave me the knowledge of Allah as a gift, made me drink from the purest cups and I was elevated to the Gardens of the Heaven.' Shibli said: 'The external side of *Sama*' is a rebellion, but the inner side is an example. Those who are aware of meaning are allowed to follow the example. Those who are unaware of them might drown in rebellion and end up in confusion.' He also said: 'Those who are listening to music in a natural way share the tenderness of music and nature, connect the purity of the mystery in the heart with the purity of music and *Sama*'.'[163]

Talking about listening and the comprehension of music, Imam Al-Ghazali defines four states (*hal*), which end with a wonderful symbol of Sufism:

1) the state when one enjoys music just as a matter of nature: he/she is not different in that sense to any living organism;

2) the state when one enjoys music in a comprehensive manner: this is the state of youngsters and lustful people;

3) the state when one separates what he listens from his relation with Allah: this is the state of inexperienced *murids* (Sufi apprentices);

4) the state of those who are absorbed by Allah: these people are like those Egyptian women, who cut their fingers and didn't feel the pain, while looking at the beauty of Joseph. 'They are true Sufis,' states Imam Al-Ghazali, crediting those women in his main religious and Sufi work.[164]

Hazrat Inoyat-khan mentions five aspects of music in the Sufi perspective. He says: 'Music consists of vibrations which have evolved from the top to the bottom, and if they would only be systematically used, they could be evolved from the bottom to the top. Real music is known only to the most gifted ones. Music has five aspects:

1) *Tarab* – music which induces motion of the body (artistic);

2) *Raga* – music which appeals to the intellect (gnostic);

3) *Qul* – music which creates feelings (emotional);

4) *Nida* – music heard in vision (inspirational);

5) *Sawt* – music in the abstract (celestial).'[165]

Keeping these views of the Sufi masters in mind, we now look at the Sufi music of Central Asia.

20. SUFI MUSIC IN CENTRAL ASIA: FROM COURT TO FOLK TRADITIONS

The existence of a cultural division between the nomads and the settled people of Central Asia is reflected in the kind of music they each perform. Historically, the urban population of the cities is made up of Tajiks and Uzbeks and their music is based on the urban classical, or professional, music tradition called *Maqam*. The very word *Maqam*, which means in Arabic 'a station, a degree', is the key word for Sufism, defining the stage of proximity of a Sufi to God. Therefore, the whole *Maqam* music is directly rooted in the Sufi tradition of *Sama'*. This music is discussed in greater detail in this chapter.

As for the Kazakhs, Kyrgyzs, and Turkmens, who are of a nomadic origin, their music follows the rural, or folk, traditions of bards such as the Kazakh *zhiraus* and the Kyrgyz *manaschies*. This distinction, however, is flexible. Indeed, during the twentieth century many nomadic people took to the settled way of life, and it is also worth noting that the Tajiks and Uzbeks have their own rural communities and musicians, the Baqshies and the *Otin-Oys*. Nonetheless, the deep-rooted traditions of these two kinds of people have survived the progress of time and changes in lifestyle, and the distinction between their music is still discernible as part of their ancestral identity.

The Sufi influence is the common thread which, nevertheless, ties these different types of music together and it is rooted most significantly in the poems by, for instance, Saadi (1184–1292), Rumi (1207–73), Hafez (1318/25-unknown), and Navoiy (1441–1501), which form the basis of song. The singing style of these countries is very distinctive, reflecting the singer's meditation and concentration. The Sufi content is also evident in the structure of classical song, which is analysed later in this chapter, but which represents that of a whole *Zikr* ceremony with the same sort of introductory, developmental, and climactic sections that, in turn, reflect the broader spiritual stages of the Sufi 'way' to divinity.

Uzbek and Tajik religious and Sufi music has not yet been classified among the acknowledged musical categories studied by musicologists. The reasons for this are not purely political – when all religious confessions, including Islam, were banned – but are also of a musical nature. Religious and Sufi music was, and still is, performed mainly without instruments.

This fact led to the genre not being taken seriously enough. However, it is said that: 'The conceptualization of religious music as a chant or recitation, rather than music or song, reflects a fundamental Muslim belief in the supremacy of the word as the basis of all religious communication, starting from the revealed word of the Qur'an itself, which constitutes the very foundation of Islam.'[166]

This statement is also true for Central Asian, and particularly Uzbek, religious music. According to one of the existing classifications, Islamic religious music could be roughly divided into:

- Mosque music (reciting the Qur'an)
- Sufi order music
- hymns and songs for festivals.[167]

Another classification of Islamic music is given in reference to Indo-Muslim religious music considering: a) liturgical music; and b) non-liturgical music, including Sufi music.[168]

Uzbek and Tajik non-liturgical music is distinguished by its particular variety and richness and it differs from one local area to another. For example, the full range of hymns expressing devotion to God (*Hamd*) or the Prophet (*Na't*) combining the celebration of *Mavlud* (Prophet Muhammad's birthday) along with the Sufi rituals are still found in the Ferghana Valley.

This kind of music is still popular in Uzbekistan and Tajikistan (also southern parts of Kyrgyzstan and Kazakhstan) and has various distinguishing features. One should point out that only a few genres of the Islamic musical tradition (e.g. *Azan* – the call to prayer) are still performed in male society. But all other genres are seen only in female performances. So far, this issue has not been discussed in the context of Uzbek and Tajik religious music.

21. CENTRAL ASIAN SUFI MUSIC AND FEMALE SINGERS

Maqam and Sufism
In Central Asia, Maqam music has a particular role in religious, cultural, and social life.

The very word Maqam reveals its Sufi origin. Sufi teachings became extremely widespread as Islam was adopted and reconciled with local traditions and culture. That is one of the explanations why so many Sufi orders were born in Central Asia. These teachings were very often supported by the Central Asian khans and emirs, almost all of whom had their spiritual masters or *Pirs*, who were true Sufis. We can therefore, thank the rich and robust medieval court culture, strengthened by major developments since the fourteenth century (as four different kingdoms grew up in Samarkand, Bukhara, Khorezm, and Kokand), for maintaining the Sufi tradition, including its music.

Originating in the courts of these *emirs* (emperors) and *khans* (kings), the music of *Maqam* tradition developed over a long period, and in different ways, in various regions of the country. Today, the music of Uzbekistan encompasses different forms of *Maqam* – the classical musical form with a Sufi flavour, including the *Maqam* from Bukhara – '*Shashmaqam*', the *Maqam* from Khorezm, and the *Maqam* from Ferghana-Tashkent.

The *Maqam* system of Sufi court music was founded on a particular aesthetic and ethical code. Each *Maqam* had to be played in a hall decorated with an appropriate and specific colour, and everyone present at that reception had to wear clothes of the same colour, which reminds us of Najm ad-din Kubra's Sufi theory of colours and states of the Sufi. In addition, each *Maqam* had to be performed at a fixed time of day, so, for example, the *Maqam* '*Iraq*' should be performed in the early morning during sunrise. The terrace, hall and musicians' gowns where that particular *Maqam* was played should be white. *Buzruk* (great) was performed accompanied by red colours, *Ushshoq* (lovers) and *Rost* (straight) in dark yellow, and *Navo* (melody) would have been performed after midnight in black or grey costumes. The evidence is clearly depicted in the miniatures of Kamal ad-Din Behzad, the founder of the Herat school of miniature painting in the fifteenth and sixteenth centuries.

In paintings such as *Sa'bai Sayar* (Seven Planets) by Alisher Navoiy, and particularly 'Bahram in the Gold Pavilion' or 'Bahram in the Green Pavilion', the scene is laid out in beautifully decorated pavilions. The emperor is pictured sitting comfortably within the arcades of the palace. Beneath the vaults, the female musicians sit on the floor, and among the warmly glowing candles soft music is performed, played by delicate instruments such as the *ghidjak*, the harp (the predecessor of the *chang*, or box zither) and the *doira*, or frame drum.

Shashmaqam is a cycle of six *maqams*, which was formed towards the eighteenth century. Information about initial *maqams* is mentioned in treatises of the tenth and eleventh centuries (*Farabi, Ibn-Sina*); and in treatises about music of the fifteenth to seventeenth centuries (*Abd al-Qadir Maragi, Abd al-Rakhman Djami, Darvish Ali Changi*, and others) they figure as the compilation of twelve *maqams*.[169] The term 'maqam' was first used in a musical sense, as the system of modes, by the Persian scholar Qutb ad-din al-Shirazi (d. 1311).[170] In the process of development, six *maqams* remained out of twelve: *Buzruk* (great), *Rost* (straight), *Navo* (melody), *Dugoh* (two moments), *Segoh* (three moments), and *Iroq* (Iraq, far away). Named in accordance with the varieties of similar harmonies, they seemingly assimilated the remaining *maqams*.

In one of our articles, written on the similarities between Sufi literature and Sufi music, my husband and I argued that, just as Sufi poets created a cycle of *Hamsa* (five poems) from the open literary form of *Shahnameh*, where each of those five poems was devoted to one of the Sufi degrees – Benefit, Grace, Good, Beauty, and Truth[171] – the same process has happened in the development of *Shashmaqam*. Moreover, *maqam Iraq* is the shortest in the cycle. It is half the length of the other five *maqams*, which makes it possible to assume its residual value. Possibly for this very reason, in contrast to the first five *maqams*, which have independent cycles, *Iraq* is performed extremely rarely as a separate work.

So here we can, once again, refer to five Sufi aspects of music as stated by Inayat-khan: artistic, gnostic, emotional, inspirational, and celestial. Indeed, researchers of *Shashmaqam* assert that each separate *Maqam* initially corresponded with five characteristics, which are applicable to *Hamsa* poems. Thus, *maqam Buzruk* is characterised by majestic, heroic, courageous, open, glad music. *Rost* is described as bright, but very restrained like the shining of truth. *Maqam Navo* characterises the state of bright melancholy, languor, hope, and love. *Dugoh* is joyfully glad, winged. *Maqam Segoh* is amorous and tragic, extremely dramatic, which resembles by its endlessness Mejnun's love for Leyla. *Iraq* has a profound philosophical meaning – the meaning of sorrowful meditation.

Thus *Shashmaqam* in its composition follows the stages of the Sufi Way: from the courageous, majestic elevated heroics of *Buzruk* (great) through the bright but restrained *Rost* (straight, truth), then the wearisome hope and the grief of *Navo* (melody), winged *Dugoh* (two moments), and tragically amorous *Segoh* (three moments) to the deeply philosophical finale of *Maqam Iraq* (far away).[172]

Each of these six *Maqams* has an instrumental section *Mushkilot* (complication) and a vocal section *Nasr* (victory, prose). Each suite contains a series of pieces related by melodic resemblance, but set in different metric-rhythmic genres. In general, every single suite relies on an older distinction between a fixed, canonical sequence of pieces and an open-ended sequence that followed it.

At the centre of the *Maqam* tradition is vocal music. Singers have the greatest cachet among performers, and the ability to reach a high tessitura pitch in the *Awj*, or culmination, of a song and sustain it over an entire long breath is much admired by connoisseurs of classical music. Singing *Maqam*, however, is far more than a display of virtuosity. 'The lyrical expressiveness of the *Maqam* is also a means of conveying the beauty and symbolic power of the poetic texts....The text composed in classical forms as *Ghazal*...are redolent with symbols drawn from Sufism, the mystical trend in Islam. The most salient of these symbols is love, which while describing human feelings and activities alludes metaphorically to the love of the divine.'[173]

The similarity to the path of spiritual wisdom in the Sufi Way – *Tariqat* is quite obvious in the melodic development of each *Maqam*. Its vocal piece *Shu'be* (part), which is based on *Ghazal* poetry, progresses through a series of structural divisions distinguished by tessitura: an introductory section, *Daramad* (entrance), set in a low tessitura leads to a section called *Miyankhona* (mid-room), typically set at an interval of a fifth above the introduction. *Miyankhona* leads to *Dunasr* (double victory), set an octave above the *Daramad*. *Awj* (zenith), the culmination, follows *Dunasr*, after which the piece gradually descends to the original tessitura in a concluding section called *Furaward* (exit). The high tessitura *Awj* is both the musical and the dramatic climax (Figure 2).

On the other hand, every single *Maqam* is identified with development from the wisdom of the first part of the *Maqam*, *Sarahbor* (main message) to a quiet *Interpretation* or the second stage – *Talkin*; observation of *Nasr* (third stage), and then the optimistic finale, conclusion, to the fourth stage – *Ufar* (fragrant).[174]

Most of the historical chronicles give the names of famous male performers of *Maqam* – some, among them, sang in a high-pitched feminine voice. Thus in Ferghana Valley some historic documents name a famous *Maqam* singer, Hudoyberdi, whose performing nickname was *Zebo-pari* (Beautiful fairy).[175] The Sound Archive of the British Library keeps early recordings of Central Asian traditional Sufi music, made by the company

SHU'BE

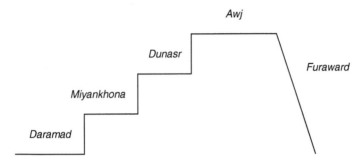

Figure 2: Melodic development in Shu'be

'Gramophone' in 1906. One of them is a Sufi song, sung by three male singers in a falsetto voice. The first female performers of *Maqams* were also recorded at that time. They were the famous women singers Netayhon and Tojinissa.

22. FEMALE MAQAM SINGERS

Berta Davydova and Kommuna Ismailova

Female *Maqam* performers became more common during Soviet times. The names of Tamara Hanum, Halima Nasyrova, Nazira Akhmedova, Hadia Yusupova, Fotima Borukhova, Barno Is'hakova, Shohista Mullajonova, Zainab Palvanova, Rakhima Mazokhidova, Mavlyuda Agzamova, Saodat Kabulova, Berta Davydova, Kommuna Ismailova, and many others make up the pride of Uzbek and Tajik *Maqam* musical and performance arts, and embellish the history of the Uzbeko-Tajik Sufi musical tradition.

Berta Davydova (b. 1927 in Margelan, Ferghana Valley, d. 2008 in Tashkent), was one of the leading performers of *Maqams*. She was born to a rich Bukharian Jewish family, and loved to sing from her early childhood. In 1938 her family moved to Tashkent. After finishing school she graduated from medical college and worked as a nurse in a health centre. Berta liked to sing, and sometimes performed at evening concerts for the local hospital. Once, on a big occasion, famous Uzbek artists came to perform in front of all the wounded soldiers, and one of the young soldiers on crutches suddenly shouted in the middle of the concert, 'We also have a singer here!' People called her and she had to go onto the stage and, feeling embarrassed as she was in her nurse's white medical gown, she sang a few songs.

'After the concert the Uzbek People's artist Imamjon Ikramov came to the Hospital's director and said that I had a special voice and he would like to invite me to work for the Radio. The head of the health centre said that very soon, on reaching eighteen years of age, I would have to go to the front line to fight the Germans in World War 2. To avoid that, it would be better if they took me to sing.

My mother didn't want me to become a singer. So, I asked my colleagues to help me and Imamjon Ikramov went to talk to my mother to explain to her that it was the only way to avoid me being sent to war. After that my mother didn't mind me singing for live broadcasts. I remember I sang at that time *Munojat*, which was the first classical song I learned with Imamjon Ikramov. With this song I became Berta Davydova. Halima Nasyrova was a famous female singer at that time. She was lady in her prime but I was just 17 when I started.

After Imamjon Ikramov retired Yunus Rajabi became the head of our ensemble. I learned all the Uzbek *Maqams* with him during the five years I was working for his Maqam ensemble. In the past only men sang Maqam. I was the first woman who sang Maqam, and I learned it from Imamjon Ikramov who said my voice was appropriate for Maqam-style singing and taught me how to do it. I sang "Bayet 2", "Bayet 5", "Talkini Bayet", "Taronai Bayet". Then I went to Tajikistan to their Maqam ensemble there and learned "Nasry Bayet", "Taronai Bayet", "Talkinnin Baayet", "Ufori Bayot", "Ufar oromijon", "Orazi Navo", "Sarahbori Oromijon", "Kashkarchi Savty", "Usshok", altogether about ten *Maqams* from Shahnozar Sohibov (People's Artist of Uzbekistan) and Zirkiev, who was a Maqam singer himself from the Bukharo school. I sang Navoiy, Zebunissa, Uvaysiy poetry in Maqam.

As head of a Shashmaqam ensemble Yunus Rajabi had set Uzbek poetry to the Shashmaqam and published six volumes of Shashmaqam with only Uzbek poetry in it, leaving the Tajik poetry behind. Six *maqams* were transcribed as six wonders! God bless his soul!'

> If you sing Maqam in the right way you never get tired! In the 1960s, I often went on holiday to Anjijon, I was sometimes singing up to twelve Maqams at once during the same public concert. On one occasion I was taken by helicopter to Jalalabad (a city 100 km away in Tajikistan) where an instant public concert was arranged for me to perform. After the concert,

returning to Andijan, I was told that again another concert was to follow on that very evening as the *Kolhozchilar* (farmers) had asked for another performance. And I was the only singer in those long non-stop concerts!

I have had many students who I taught *Maqam* performance: Nasiba Sattarova (People's artist of Uzbekistan), Maryam Sattarova (People's artist of Uzbekistan) are the most famous among them, then Mahbuaba Sarymsakova, and many others.[176]

Another outstanding Maqam performer in Uzbekistan was **Kommuna Ismailova.**

During her interview, she told me her story – how she became a singer, and particularly a Maqam singer.

'I was born in Khiva city in Khoresm district on the 15 December 1927. I was singing from early childhood. In 1934 Tamara Hanum and Karimzor Kariev came to Khorezm, and all the time I sang songs from their repertoire. Finally my parents took me to Tamara Hanum, saying, 'She likes singing so much!' She blessed me in a way, advising me to carry on, to participate in amateur school groups and performances. At the time when World War 2 began the Soviet army music group came to Urgench under the guidance of Gavhar Rahimova. Once, when I sang for a school performance, artists heard me from outside the window. Artists came to our place and their director asked, 'Who sang a song just now? Can we see that girl, please?' After listening to me they asked if I would like to be taken to Tashkent. Later, in the spring of 1943 I was taken as a 16-year-old to perform in Tashkent for the Uzbek front line group.

'My parents didn't understand I was going to perform for the WW2 front line Ensemble. They thought it was just the Uzbek state ensemble. My Usto at that time was Fahritdin Sadykov. I remember once, for the 1st May celebration, I performed *Yakkahon Ashula*. I sang two songs very well, receiving long applause. But for the third song I had forgotten the lyrics for the Awj (culmination). I started introducing the Awj ornamentation with…a-a-a-a-a-a---' but the words would not come. I tried again and again but with no success…. Finally, after a long, loud 'a-a-a—a' I had no words to sing and I made up the end with the words 'Borey!' (Get lost!)

I ran from the stage and there the Uzbek People's Artist, the Director of Philharmonic Boborahim Mirzaev, came backstage and pulled my ear. I started to cry but he said, 'You made a new folk song! Do you hear the applause? Now they want you to come to the stage again!'

We sang many folk and classical songs like Karokolpokcha, Azerbaijoncha, Gruzincha, Belorassia, Ukrainian, Russian and many others.

On 15 August 1943 we were taken to the Front line, the 1st and 2nd Ukrainian front line in 1944, also the Baltian front line. The most memorable was our performance for the second Belorussian front, when on 23 February 1945 we performed for Sabir Rahimov's (the Uzbek General's) 37th Uzbek division. In July 1946 I came back to Khorezm to be given the honourable title People's Artist of Uzbekistan. After that I performed in the Philharmonic ensemble as a soloist, performing in festivals in every decade.

In 1959 I was invited to Uzbek Radio where I worked for 30 years. I was involved in 468 recordings, performing songs in Uzbek, Russian, Kyrgyz, Tajik and other languages. I sang forty-three songs by Fahritdin Umarov, eleven by Kamiljon Jabbarov, thirteen by Ganijon Toshmatov, seven by Kamiljon Otaniyasov, five by Muhammajon Mirzaev, songs by Sabir Baboev, Nabi Hassanov, Sultan Haiyt, and other composers.'

'I sang Shashmaqam with Berta Davydova and that was great opportunity for us. Look, now there are no such singers as we were at that time! Together with Berta, I sang all six maqams! And we did it!

From 1960 I sang Maqams together with Berta Davydova and with the other most outstanding male singers like Arif Alimaksumov, Karim Mumin, Ortykhoja Imamhojaev, Shokirjon Ergashev, Siroj Aminov. Six of us sang Shashmaqam and also the legendary Jurahon Sultanov from Ferghana and Tolmasov from Samarkand were invited to perform several Awjes (culminations) for our recordings. We learned Maqam ways and performance style from Yunus Rajabi. By 1965 the Shashmaqam recordings were finished. For recordings we used to stay in the studio till midnight and even till 6 o'clock in the morning, before the trams started to run. Then we would go home. We used to 'cook' the part of Shashmaqam for ten to fifteen days and then we would record them. Yunus Rajabiy used to listen to our singing and change the notes for the next session, constantly improving it. When we started Buzruk, he fell ill and then Arif Alimaksumov took over. Professor Rajabi wanted to get stereo recordings but it didn't happen, so we have a mono recording of the whole Shashmaqam, but not in stereo. Our singing was transcribed into notes and put in six volumes books and LP recordings. Yunus Rajabi used to say, 'I will leave this world but my Shashmaqam transcriptions and LP recordings will remain.'"

'I have a number of bright and talented students I am very proud of. I teach in the Theatre Institute, in the Pedagogical Musical College. My students were Munojat Tajibaeva, Shahzoda Ismailova, Mavluda Asalhojaeva, Karima Ismailova and other talented girls. I am very proud of them. There are 468 songs in my repertoire from teachers who have now passed away. Now on TV, singers do not say their teachers' names but one needs to remember their names! It's so important! The poet or musician should be named and the Teacher/Usto appreciated. The souls and spirits of our teachers will be happy! We have so many outstanding poets and musicians to be remembered.'[177]

Maqam, which used to be performed in long elaborate cycles, is today very often performed as a short extract from the cycle in only one piece of music. However, the significance of its relation to the Sufi dimension is still very high, according to statements by local musicians – that the mystical dimension of Islam can be expressed in musical terms. The subject of such music is remembrance of God. One of the most popular examples of this kind is the song related to the Ferghana Maqam style, called *Munojat* (prayer). This song has become famous, and has been performed by famous female Uzbek and Tajik singers such as Barno Is'hakova, Berta Davydova, or Munojat Yulchieva. Every performance of this song awakens an image of *Zikr* based on a long developed flow of tension in the form of dynamic waves to culmination and back to the foundation. It is a classical song about spiritual assimilation with God and symbolises the Sufi way to perfection.

Female performance of Maqams flourished in the twentieth century. After the break-up of the Soviet Union, the art of Maqam became one of the key elements in nation building, both in Uzbekistan and Tajikistan. Young Maqam singers like Munojat Yulchieva, Maryam Sattarova, Matluba Dadabaeva, Nasiba Sattarova, Khurriyat Israilova, and Zamira Suyunova have largely determined the way that modern Maqam art is developing.

23. MUNOJAT YULCHIEVA

There is not a single fan of Uzbek music abroad who does not know the name of Munojat Yulchieva. In fact, she has outshone the fame of all the Uzbek artists, even those who have ventured abroad. She is unsurpassed in her skill and perfection of vocal technique, and in the beauty of the songs she performs. Nowadays, her name abroad has become a synonym for Uzbek classical music.

Munojat Yulchieva is indeed the brightest star among performers of the classical Uzbek music in recent decades. Even her name, *Munojat*, means 'ascent to God', which represents the true meaning of Sufism. One of the common traditions of Sufism is the continuity of a spiritual chain or *silsilah*. In those terms, Munojat has inherited her musical knowledge from her spiritual and musical *murshid* (teacher, master) Shavkat Mirzaev, who in his turn inherited this knowledge from his father Muhammajan Mirzaev, to whom the knowledge was passed by the famous musicians Fahriddin Sadykov and Djurahan Sultanov. So the beginning of this chain melts away in the mists of past centuries. Despite Soviet political and cultural pressure on the texts that have been transformed over last century, the music continues in the same traditional way.

Munojat is not just a singer who follows on the traditions taught by Shavkat Mirzaev, she is a great singer, the only one who managed to absorb the essence of Sufi singing style. Born on 26 November 1960, in Andijan village of Sherman Bulak (Ferghana Valley), Munojat studied music at Tashkent State Conservatoire from 1978 to 1985 under the guidance of Shavkat Mirzaev. She studied hard, and was well trained by her famous teacher, concentrating on the proper repertoire of Uzbek classical music. Following her diligence and devotion to Uzbek music, she has never performed at weddings, which is a well-known and well-paid custom for that kind of musician in Uzbekistan. She performs only at concerts and

Photo 6: The Uzbek Sufi singer Munojat Yulchieva

different sorts of festivals. After one of these, a remarkable concert on TV (1978), she became an overnight success (Photo 6).

She worked at Ensemble '*Maqam*' at Uzbek State Radio from 1980 until 1982. Since 1982 she has worked with the Uzbek State Philharmonic Ensemble. She received the awards for 'Honoured Artist of Uzbekistan' (1991), and 'People's Artist of Uzbekistan' (1994) and was decorated with the order 'Respect and Order of the People' (1998).

Munojat took part in many regional and International Festivals and Competitions, gaining first prizes (including, in 1997, the 'Golden Nightingale' at the Samarkand International Festival *Sharq Taronalari*). Since 1989, she has toured many countries, including the United States, and European, Asian, and Latin American countries.

Her repertoire consists of the best examples of Uzbek Maqam music and music of *Bastakors*-composers in traditional Uzbek style. Thanks to her unique voice (mezzo-soprano, extending to 2.5 octaves), owing to Shavkat Mirzaev's training, Munojat not only revived female songs well-known from the history of Uzbek music, but performed for the first time many male songs with really difficult composition and dynamic development. Her repertoire includes Uzbek Sufi music and the poetry of Alisher Navoiy, Fisuli, Mashrab and Huvaido among others.

The most remarkable fact is that Munojat Yulchieva received the same Usto-Shogrid training from her teacher, Professor Shavkat Mirzaev, as other Sufi singers in pre-Soviet times. In spite of the Soviet cultural policy to sideline classical heritage, she was brought up in the traditional way. The basics of that oral tradition was built on long hours of individual sessions and a careful selection of Sufi poetry for her singing repertoire, rather than the popular modern Uzbek poetry that flattered Soviet ideology. This method restored the style of the old singing school.

Professor Mirzaev took a risk in training the traditional singer Munojat during her long association (nearly 30 years) with her Usto. Building such master–apprentice relations during the Soviet times, when conservatory classes were full of students practising in groups, on a five-year course, was both a challenge and an outstanding achievement.

I remember that, as a student, Munojat was a shy young girl who followed every word of her teacher's advice. In 1990, at the Barbat Symposium and congress in Dushanbe, Munojat was staying at the same hotel as me, and I often met her at breakfast. One day, I met her in the corridor and noticed that she needed some help. She was looking for somebody to go to local market. But why, I asked her, pointing out that the market was just around the corner, two minutes away from the hotel. It turned out her Usto Shavkat Mirzaev had prohibited her from leaving the hotel so as to avoid the crowds of her fans and admirers.

Shavkat Mirzaev, coming from musical family, understood very well the advantages and disadvantages of fame, particularly for a female singer. It is so important for a popular artist not to be exposed to the public, or to become a toy in the hands of communist authorities. As a wise teacher and an outstanding Usto Shavkat Mirzaev tried to protect her from every single danger.

As a result of his devotion, Munojat and Shavkat have become famous all over the world. Together, they have toured many countries in Europe, America and Asia during the last 20 years, conquering the public and winning music lovers' hearts. In Munojat's repertoire today there are songs of Sufi poetry and Maqam pieces. This is the most outstanding achievement in Uzbek music, when most of the Maqam pieces have been forgotten. In fact, Munojat has become a symbol of yesterday's culture, singing classical poetry, using classical idioms and performing the classical music of vanished palaces. The beauty of court music is revealed today when Munojat performs her songs. Her stunning strong voice and wide range tessitura enable her to include even male songs in her repertoire.

When in 1978 Professor Shavkat Mirzaev found a peasant girl from Ferghana Valley crying in the corridor after failing to gain a place in the Uzbek State conservatory, he was attracted by her extremely strong and powerful voice. The timbre of her voice reminded him of the best voices of the Sufi singing tradition. So he decided to help Munojat to become professional singer – but only a Sufi singer. Certainly, Munojat must take the credit for her success as it only came about because of her sincere devotion to that kind of singing. How special was his training style? First of all it affected the voice range. To be able to produce a strong Sufi style sound the voice has to be trained in the way of the old Sufi professionals. What was the Sufi style of singing?

In order that Munojat's voice could be trained in the Sufi style Professor Mirzaev invented new techniques, which included both local voice techniques called *guligi* and *biligi* and the technique from Italian *belcanto* singing style based on chest breathing. His training was, therefore, based on the symbiosis of not only local styles combining throat and cupol/head/nose singing, but also on the best singing style of European opera. To learn the latter, Professor Mirzaev went to Moscow State Conservatory to consult with the best representatives of vocal skills training, returning to

Tashkent with a clear view of how to develop vocal techniques and integrate their basics within the classical Uzbek singing style.

In fact, Shavkat Mirzaev's training system for the voice and breath development was based on Sufi tradition but enriched with the best innovations of contemporary European style. As a result, he has created a completely new technique of singing rooted on the use of the nose, head, and throat but with the creation of deep chest sound.

Being both an instrumentalist (playing Rubab) and a composer, and a musician with a deep knowledge of Sufi poetry and music, Professor Mirzaev established a completely new vocal technique within Uzbek classical music that was adjusted to the female voice.

That is why Munojat's singing is so moving: because she combines the old-fashioned system with the up-to-date methods of European opera and pop music styles. In her voice, one can find all the elaborate nuances of a highly professional singer from the twentieth and twenty-first centuries: from a deep low voice at the beginning through whispering sounds for the most intimate declarations to the thrilling voice-blow at high dynamic conclusions. Professor Mirzaev has offered Munojat the whole system of training for a professional singer, which includes not only the voice but also certain body movements (hands and head), posture, alternate use of the chest-nose-throat in singing, and distinctive breathing system.

From numerous interviews with Shavkat Mirzaev I learned that, as a very responsible teacher carefully extending Munojat's repertoire, he introduced songs from the simple to the ever more difficult, developing her voice from the central to the peripheral, most powerful and strong areas of tessitura. Finally, all famous Sufi songs were included in her collection! Freed from the traditional Sufi training (living in the family, cleaning shoes, doing housekeeping duties, and so on), Munojat's dream of becoming a star came true, thanks to her extreme good fortune in meeting Professor Shavkat Mirzaev, her own 'Professor Higgins'.

24. SUFI ORIGIN GENRE *KATTA ASHULA*

Katta ashula (big song) is a vocal genre of Sufi origin, which is quite similar to Spanish *cante hondo*. It could be regarded as remnants of separately performed Maqam, but at the same time it is a distinct genre of Uzbek and Tajik vocal music, which is deeply rooted in Sufi *Zikrs* and *Sama'*. *Katta ashula* is usually performed by two or more unaccompanied singers. Other elements of it are: a) reciting parts, b) improvisation, and c) exclamations in the high pitches – all of which are similar to the structure of the Sufi *Zikr*. The Russian scholar Alexander Semyonov studied that genre of Uzbek music in the mid-1930s, when he was invited to collaborate with the Scientific Institute of Arts Researches. He mentioned two other genres of Sufi music of the ninth to twelfth centuries like *Sama'i* and *Khanaqa'i* (*Khanaqa* is a place of Sufi gatherings) as the origin of *Katta ashula*.[178]

Another name for *Katta ashula* is *Yovvoyi Maqom* or *Wild Maqam*. Therefore, the main structure of Maqam's vocal parts or *Shu'be*, which corresponds to the Sufi Way *Tariqat*, is followed here too: an introductory section, *Daramad* (entrance), set in a low tessitura leads to a section called *Miyankhona* (mid-room), typically set at the interval of a fifth above the introduction. *Miyankhona* leads to *Dunasr* (double victory), set an octave above the Daramad. *Awj* (zenith), the culmination follows *Dunasr*, after which the piece gradually descends to the original tessitura in a concluding section called *Furaward* (exit).[179]

According to Orifhon Hatamov, one of the greatest performers of *Katta ashula* in Uzbekistan, the Ferghana-Tashkent school of singing is distinguishable in two ways: a) *Maqam* ways of singing, and b) *Zikr Maqams*. In the *Yassaviya* Sufi order *Zikr* is performed in a loud (*Jahriya*) way in which music, and particularly *Katta ashula*, played an important role. In that order *Zikr* has the same structure as *Katta ashula* and follows three stages: a) *Hal* or entering the relevant state; b) *Vajd* or giving up yourself and obtaining a state of ecstasy; c) *Mukashafot* or discovering Allah and finding union with Him.

The high-pitched exclamations correspond with the part of the *Zikr* when the gathering starts to exclaim short names of God: *Haqq, Hu, Huw-wa* (True, He, and Himself). From the musical perspective, this part is based on *Chorzarb* (four beats) *usul*. The rhythm could be changed to *Yakzarb* (one beat), *Duzarb* (two beats), *Sezarb* (three beats), or *Chorzarb* (four beats), depending how many times the names of Allah are repeated.[180]

Here is one of the most famous examples of *Katta ashula*, performed by Munojat Yulchieva, a leading Sufi singer of Uzbekistan.

> *Ey dilbari jononim, hay sen tarki javob etma,*
> *Yuz jabru jafo birla holimni harob etma.*
> *Mastona ko'zingdan dod, qoshing qilichin tortib,s*
> *Qo'lingga hino bog'lab bag'rimni kabob etma.*

> Hey, my Beauty, don't leave me without your answer,
> Don't ruin me with hundreds of tortures and suffering.

I cry because of your intoxicating eyes, don't use the sabre of your eyebrows
And don't cut my body into blood, painting your hands with henna.

Munojat said about this song: 'When I sing it, I use what I call a Sufi voice.
It's like a prayer. Singing quietly can be much more powerful than singing
loudly. When you are praying, you do not bother with other things. When
I sing in this way, I concentrate on my inner state. I experience a kind of
ecstasy and the music helps me in this. When I sing, I think of God.'[181]

As a matter of curiosity one must mention that during the Soviet time
the same *Katta ashula* was sung with completely different words:

The working people made the desert of Farkhad to blossom.
Steppes are now turned into gardens; crows are not flying above them.
The enemy can't bear it, he cries, his body covered with ulcers,
Enjoy your labour, tireless friends and comrades!

7

Interaction of Shamanism and Sufism in Central Asian Female Performance

25. FROM HEALING RITUALS TO PROTECTIVE SONGS

Shamanic practices extend, today, all over Central Asia. From my experience of witnessing Shamanic practices in Uzbekistan I remember that they offer different forms of healing.

On one visit to Eski Noukat village (Osh district, Kyrgyzstan) in 2002, I saw two women whispering and talking rapidly, using sayings and tongue twisters, pretending they spoke in other people's voices, bending over a girl who had fallen ill. The two Azaimhans (Shamans) continued in this way until the girl started vomiting and fell asleep. They said the girl had fallen ill because ghosts disturbed her as she went to see ruins of a centuries-old house. They said that they had exorcised the bad spirits and now the girl would recover.

On another occasion, in Boisun village, an old lady cured her granddaughter by chopping off a hen's head. She then soaked her fingers in the hen's fresh blood and spread it inside her granddaughter's throat. 'It's the best treatment against sore throat', she said. In Boisun village the most famous Shaman/*Baqshi* was a man called Turi Shaman. He practised in a smoky room (the central room in his house) heating a knife over the fire preparing for the culmination of his healing ritual. Shaking his head, vibrating his lips, emitting louder and more forceful eerie sounds, he twirled the knife around the head of his patient who was sitting on the floor. The visibility was obscured by the increasing smoke when finally his patient started to move and, crawling slowly, left the room.

Later, Turi Shaman would continue his performance of healing rituals, joining a Boisun group programme and becoming a kind of 'stage performer' showing off his Shamanic skills to an amazed audience.

But the most interesting healing rituals in Central Asia of the twenty-first century are certainly those that contain musical elements. Mostly performed by women, they reflect numerous features of religions from Shamanism to Islam. Various examples of female music-making forms are examined below.

26. FEMALE SHAMANISM IN TURKMENISTAN

Shamanism has always been part of Turkmen culture. The Shamanic idea of the upper, the middle, and the lower worlds (i.e. the main concept of Shamanism) is present in Turkmen arts, primarily in the decorations of rugs, carpets, and kilims. Two main elements of Tengrianism – earth and sky – are depicted by skilful Turkmen female weavers in ornaments that symbolise the Turkmen view of life, as well as their philosophy.

A linguistic approach, according to Dr. Yusuf Azemoun, shows that the archaic word for the carpet in old Turkmen and Turkic languages is *kowuz* or *kowur* (this word has become kovyor in Russian), derived from the word *kopuz*. *Kopuz* is the oldest Turkic musical instrument.[182] In the remote past, the *kopuz* was a long-necked bowed lute, which was widely used in Shamanic practice. It is believed that the sound of *kopuz* helps to attract good spirits and to repulse demons.

The principal design of Turkmen rugs and carpets, which has been used for centuries, is called *göl*. Literally, this means a lake, symbolising the cult of water, over which birds are flying. But it is also believed that it was originally a reflection of sky on earth, or stars on water on the earth beneath.

In Turkmen carpets the world is divided into three: the Upper World (heaven), the Middle World (our world), and the Lower World. Soren Neergard argues that the *göl* design on Turkmen carpets might represent the Turkmen image of heaven.[183] In the old Turkic language, a star (in heaven) has always been used as an important ornamental element of the world. A line in *Kutadgu Bilik*, a Turkic book of poetry written in the twelfth century, says: '*Bu kökteki yulduz bir ança bezek*' (the stars in heaven are such beautiful ornaments).[184]

The springs are perceived as the eyes of Mother Earth where, in connection with the cult of water, people make sacrifices.[185] As we notice here, the Shamanistic *yir/sub* or the cult of water and earth play an important role in the art of carpet-making.

Among the people of Central Asia and the Altay mountains, the ram has long been regarded as sacred. Archaeological studies in Central Asia and the Altay mountains have confirmed this fact. In Shamanic traditions the ram is a divine animal, which protects the heavenly spirits from evil spirits. For this reason it is sacrificed. The influence of Shamanism continued among the people of Central Asia, namely the Turkmens, even after they became Muslims. The ram's horn, which is a Shamanic element in Turkmen art, was, and still is, a popular design used both in carpets and felts. It is even used in the decoration of mosques. We also find Orkhun Runic letters as carpet patterns, each with a Shamanistic and mystic connotation. The letter *r*, in particular – beside being a beautiful design, represents the flow of water which symbolises the flow of life.

In twelfth-century Central Asia, as Sufism began to develop, based on the poetry and teaching of Khodja Ahmad Yassavi, his followers established the Yassaviya brotherhood. When the area was invaded by Mongols, those Sufi followers fled to Anatolia, where started the new Sufi order, the Mawlaviyya. The poems of Yassavi, widely used in *zikr*, contain many Shamanistic motifs and elements. *Zikr*, among the Turkmens, is a recital of Sufi poetry with dance rituals, performed by men as well by women, until they reach a state of ecstasy. The Turkmens were prohibited from carrying out the *Zikr* by the Soviet Union. However, it was carried out to treat sick or depressed people, or to exorcise an evil spirit from their souls and bodies.

Curiously, while Sufism was prohibited in the former Soviet Union for being religious, it was prohibited by the Turkmen mullahs in northern Iran for being anti-Islamic.

While singing and dancing, Shamans and the crowd very often produce guttural sounds which correspond to *Hu*, meaning 'God' among the Sufis, with an Islamic connotation. However, it is believed that the ritual and the repetition of a guttural sound similar to the Sufi *Hu* is related to the legend of a spiritual leader who, while preaching vegetarianism, was caught eating meat. As a punishment, he was wrapped in tree bark and cut with a saw. Therefore, the guttural sound in the Sufi ritual is said to be the sound of the saw cutting the bark, which, in time, has turned into the sound of *Hu* – the repetition of the name of God. The guttural sound is present in Turkmen music even today, bringing a mystical property to the song. It is interesting that it is used in both male and female performance.

The four elements of earth, air, fire, and water play an important part in Sufi mysticism. Makhtumkuli, a Turkmen classical poet of the eighteenth century, says in his poem entitled 'The Pains of Love':

Ishq o'tina tushtim, parvona bo'ldum emdi,
Shavqing ko'zina kuydim, biryona bo'ldim emdi,
Jismim kaboba do'ndi, giryona bo'ldim emdi,
Ganch isteyinlar gelsin, vayrona bo'ldim emdi,
Ayri bo'ldim ag'yorlardin, begona bo'ldim emdi.

Love caught fire within my heart, and burned and blazed.
Smoke whirling in the wind whipped me like something crazed.
Fate caught me, spinning me upon its Wheel.
Who came to see me through the eyes of real desire?
Separation was a storm and – both flood and fire.[186]

In Sufi doctrine the meaning of separation is very important. A Sufi needs separation to reach spiritual perfection. Separation makes a man burn and turn to ash; in other words, it helps a man to be 'annihilated' in God. In the same poem Makhtumkuli says:

Mahdumquli, har zamon naylayin o'lmay giryon,
Fakrliyna botdim, chiqa bilmasman bir yon,
Ko'r, mehrobtin tarab, ko'nglimning uyi vayron,
Jon jismdek aqldin ayrilib qoldim hayron,
ish geldi bosha dushdi, vayrona bo'ldim emdi.

O hopeful slave to the beloved's charm, whereby
I lost my heart! A songbird of sweet tongues was I –
Encaged! But separation scorched my soul.
Then yearning burned me up, to ash was turned my mind.
And Makhtumkuli's life was tossed upon the wind.[187]

In Turkmen classical poetry as well as folk literature, the words 'pain' and 'burning' proliferate, because some Sufis summarise the stages of their lives in three phrases – being raw, becoming mature (by the fire of tribulations) and being burnt (and turning to ashes).

In Turkic-speaking world culture, before Islam came to Central Asia, women were highly respected. They were called *khan emme* or *beg emme* literally meaning 'the mother lord' which, with time, turned into the words *khanum* and *begum* that in modern Turkish mean 'my Lady'.[188]

Turkmens had lived in a matriarchal society before they became Muslims, where women sang and even played musical instruments. One can find Shamanistic elements in Turkmen folk songs, which usually are pre-Islamic songs. Women improvise the lyrics for the euloegies in which praise the deceased and define his or her virtues. In the villages and in the countryside, young girls in groups under the moonlight sing 'Laleh' in the form of quatrains to express their feelings towards their beloved or to complain about social obstacles which obstruct their meeting with their loved ones.

No wonder that in matriarchal society there were female musicians and even female *Baqshi*. One of them – Heley-Baqshi from the tribe of Yomuts or Chaudyrs which originated from Khiva – was Turkmen Baqshi, the winner of many male musical competitions.

Her brothers shunned her because of her habit of constantly singing, which they deemed inappropriate. To find an accompanist for her songs she followed the Amu Darya upstream to the Kerkenskyi district, where she found a man, the *Dutar* player, who later became her husband. Her name became well known and many famous Baqshi sought the chance to meet her in competition. When she was in final months of her pregnancy the legendary Kyer-Kodjali wanted to compete with her. The competition began in the evening and audience was divided, one side supporting Heley-Baqshi and the other Kyer-Kodjali. 'Let's see if the mare will win in the horse-race!' said Kyer-Kodjali, and Heley-Baqshi answered, 'Let's see!'

Around midnight Heley-Baqshi felt that she was going into labour. She asked her husband whether he would like her to win or to give birth. 'Win!' was his answer. She went out, gave birth to her baby, and returning, continued playing until she won the competition. Kyer-Kodjali admitted his failure and fled from that place forever.[189]

Today, in Turkmenistan, a broad range of folk songs are performed, which are related to family, and daily life. If we look at their titles we find a connection with Shamanic or Sufi nature.

For example, the popular Syut-Gazan – a song calling for rain; Like many other Central Asian people, Turkmens still practise Islam together with pre-Islamic religious beliefs. The call for rain, for instance, is addressed to Syut-Gazan, protector of animals, who was able to bring rain using magic rain stones *Yada*. That genre reflects both the ancient agricultural, Shamanic cults of Turks-Oghuz and Islamic influences. Nowadays children sing this song as a game.[190]

Other songs known in the area include Yaremezan – festive songs, and Monjukatdy – fortune-telling songs.

Zikr (*Zyakir*, *Zykyr* in Turkmen) are commonplace at Turkmen weddings. Originating from Sufi tradition, mixed up with Shamanic derivation in a form of *Jahr* (or *Jahriya* – a loud form of Sufi *Zikr*) which has developed in two directions: as a healing ritual, and as an entertaining genre for wedding and house-warming ceremonies. Together with wedding songs, with the exclamations *Alla*, *Huv-hu*, 'Eh-ha', it is based on dancing forms.

Zikr for weddings plays an important role as a form of protection for the new family. Its form is based on alternating parts contrasting in rhythm and content: the impulsive Divana and Bir-depim change to quiet Sedratom, the fast *Uch-depim* contrasts with the peaceful *Oturma-Ghazal*, while the final Zem-Zemom concludes on the highest range of emotions. The link between the forms of *Zikr* is based on construction, architectonics, rhythm, and common melodic patterns.[191] Some songs reveal the influence of Sufi *Zikr*, and include repetitive body movements like, for example, *Ayak-lale* (jumping on one leg combined with intense body movement).

The female group of songs is quiet wide-ranging, including wedding songs such as Yar-Yar, the lullaby Hundi, and other songs-laments (*Agy*). Other groups of female songs consist of game songs: Lale – girls' songs; and the same genre in the form of a game; *Daman-lale* (accompanied by clapping on the throat producing harsh and grating sounds made in the throat or towards the back of the mouth); *Dodek-lale* (in which the lower lip is nipped with the fingers); *Egin-lale or hymmyl-lale* (tong-twisters or brain-teasers songs).

27. GALEKE: THE KAZAKH SHAMAN

It is well known that music has the power to affect our mood and our health. We listen to music to raise our spirits or, on sad occasions, to give relief from deep sorrow or grief. Music can be used specifically for its healing effects, as in the case of Galeke, an exceptional personality who is famous in Kazakhstan for her unique ability to heal people using song. I had a chance to witness her performance. When her divine, tender, and pure voice starts flowing over the audience, people forget all their troubles. Her voice brings such a memorable joy that people ask her to sing again and again.

The image of Galeke is a very special one.

At the age of five, Galeke acquired the power of prophetic prediction. She has never received any training in the healing rituals, acting only through intuition. She sings and her voice – unpolished, and untrained – purifies your soul like a stream of water. She senses immediately what problems are affecting your body from the first time she sees you, and during her singing sessions helps people to balance their health. The basis of her repertoire comprises such genres of Kazakh traditional musical culture as *kara olen*. But she also sings Tatar, Russian, and Kyrgyz folk songs with or without accompaniment. 'Galiya's birth was preceded by amazing and memorable events. The wolf is a common ancient totem of the Kazakhs and, more widely, of the Turks. The she-wolf, who legendarily reared the Turkic Prince Ashin, is the heroine of many ancient Turkic myths. Well, a large pack of dark blue wolves had overwhelmed the small settlement in the north of Kazakhstan at the time when Galiya Kasymova was born. For days people could not venture out for fear of the wolf pack. The nurse who had to help deliver the child was strong and determined. She took an axe for self-defence and went to Galeke's parents' house ignoring the danger of wolves around the village.' No doubt that was the moment to mark the arrival of, in Basilov's term, 'the chosen one of the spirits'.

The sound of music in Galeke's performance impacts on the listeners in a manner similar to a Baqshi's healing seance. Through the sound of her voice, especially notable for its high vibrations, pure energy enters the mind to purify and cure those who hear it.[192]

In daily life, Galeke is an outstanding personality who combines two different images; she is a Shaman, and at the same time, she is a scholar who tries to understand her own power in her reflections and observations. According to Galeke,

Sound is a channel of energy. The effect on your body depends on what the song sounds like. Music reflects the harmony of universe, bringing a stream of information which affects our mind and body. Humans live without identifying the stream of time, like floating in water. When we are listening to music our mind is resting though our body does not rest at all: the heart still pulsing, the breath is inhaled and exhaled, the blood is moving in our vessels etc. so, music is curing our body. I feel immediately the physical problems of every human around. When I perform a healing ritual, when people are sitting around in the hall and listening to my singing for two or three hours, they feel better after just one performance.

'All folk songs have extreme magic power. Not pop or jazz music but old folk songs. It doesn't matter what language they are sung in or what ethnicity they represent: Kazakh, Tatar, Kyrgyz, Russian. These folk songs are energetically active and are supposed to have healing effects on ill people. The same happens with traditional instruments. Music played on those instruments possesses healing power. Abu Ali ibn Sina recommended listening to the music of traditional instruments to take preventative measures to protect your body. I know from my experience that traditional instruments can heal even drug addicts. Classical music is also available for healing. It could be Mozart, Beethoven, Bach, Tchaikovsky, Rachmaninov. Some carefully-chosen pieces of music from other composers' music have a special effect as a means of healing.'

'Prayers, casting spells and chanting are also effective means for the healing process. Not only should my medicine/melody therapy work here but also it requires a personal involvement. The ill person should read prayers himself to clean the body.'

'Not only Sound but also Water is a substance with strong healing power. A molecule of water has the power to heal as was proved by scholars in 1995. Seventy per cent of the human body consists of water. No wonder that water also has a powerful impact on the human body due to mechanical vibrations which form a bio-magnetic field. Music can change the code of water, as water remembers the information and can acquire sacred or healing features. No wonder that there is sacred water, Holy water. If prayers and sayings are said to the water, imbuing it with the spells' effect, it can be used afterwards for the healing process.'

'I never had teachers for my healing ability. I have healed intuitively from the very beginning using non-contact therapy. In my childhood I could call for rain. I don't know how it happened, how it occurred to me, the knowledge or the way how to do it. I can foresee people's destinies. They come to me as a picture of colours or a code of digits.'

(from my original interviews: February 2006, July 2007, July 2008)

28. FEMALE SHAMANISM IN TAJIKISTAN

Hojent is a city in the Ferghana Valley where the Uzbek and Tajik populations are mixed together. In the Soviet past, Hojent, which used to be called Leninabad, was the most Russianised, industrialised, and densely populated city, counting the regional Communist elite among its 175,000 inhabitants. At the same time, common Tajik-Uzbek traditions maintained close links between these ethnicities for centuries. Many rituals are carried out here in both the Tajik and Uzbek languages. In 1997, when I visited

Hojent, the city was in deep economic crisis with crowds of jobless people all over the places. Depression was in the air.

In such an atmosphere, I recorded a healing ritual which involved a huge crowd of people. People gathered in the Central Square around a small house (the former Club of Culture), forming a long queue. Waiting patiently in line to experience the cures of well-known Sitorabanu-Otin, were people who had travelled long distances from different parts of Tajikistan. She turned out to be a magician who helped everyone absolutely free of charge. People said she was able to cure not only different kind of illnesses and disease but even some neglected conditions such as alcoholism or the behaviour of bad-tempered husbands.

The story of her healing power was moving. Six years ago, one day both of her children disappeared. She desperately looked for them everywhere and then, people said, she had a dream where the Hazrat Ali advised her to start helping people, to heal them for twelve years and then her children would safely return. When I met her she looked depressed, but was performing her duty with a devotion to the process of healing that was astonishing. She spent long hours trying to cure people, gaining enormous respect. People consider that Sitorabanu-Otin is an angel who has come to the troubled city to rescue them.

Those who joined her sessions were asked to attend ten sessions of twenty minutes each. Every person had to be covered by white headscarf. Nearly everyone had a jar of water front of them. Usually a session started with a prayer followed by a collective prayer, her speech (very much of religious content) and a long musical meditation during which people sat on the floor, sinking into a deep trance, after which the session was over. People said that her cure came from her image, her appearance and her way of praying over their heads. Her style of healing was simple: prayers were recited in her very genuine beautiful voice with dynamically wavy structure, tapes were played in musical sessions, during which she continued slowly walking around. She was just strolling between seated patients, touching each head during the session and making gentle gestures with her arms. Not only the patients themselves but even those people who could not make a journey to see the Sitorabanu-Otin but whose photographs were displayed, got restored to health.

Other wonders surrounded the Otin's presence in the city include the following. A girl who sat next to me later on that evening at the local wedding told me that after attending Sitorabanu-Otin's session returning home she found a couple of pearls in her tea cup! Many people told me that they were saved by this inexplicable experience. A teenage boy who was previously unable to walk, but later was miraculously cured by her, was assisting his mentor.

All kinds of music were used for these sessions, including local pop music, and local stars' hits with a traditional flavour. But all the music was heard in the background. *Otin-Oy* herself said that she had a well-known spiritual teacher in Kokand (a neighbouring city in the Ferghana Valley) from whom she acquired her spiritual power. Her teacher also practised with prayers, and by reciting classical poetry by Navoiy, Fuzuli, Nodira, Uvaysiy, and other Uzbek Sufi poets.

29. ELEMENTS OF SHAMANISM AND SUFISM IN UZBEK FOLK MUSIC

Our journey of examination continues with Uzbek music. Although we have numerous examples of the relationship between religion and music in Uzbek culture, we focus here on the most common form: music of celebration, and in particular, a wedding song performed by local women (Photo 7). This song is heard at every single wedding throughout the nation. How have pre-Islamic beliefs and practices developed in folk music? Have they mixed with Islamic features? To answer these questions, to get an idea of religious symbiosis, let us analyse just one example: the Uzbek wedding song *Yor-Yor* (beloved, beloved).

Hoy-hoy o'lan, jon o'lano, o'lanchi qiz,
Yor-yorey o'lanchi qiz,
Va'dasida turmagan–o, yolg'onchi qiz,
Yor-yorey, yolg'onchi qiz.
Tog'da toycha kishnaydiyo ot bo'ldim deb
Yor-yorey bo'ldim deb.
Uyda kelin yig'laydiyo yot bo'ldim deb,
Yor-yorey yot bo'ldim deb.
Yig'lama qiz, yig'lama yo, toy saniki,
Yor-yorey, toy saniki
Ostonasi tillodano uy saniki,
Yor-yorey uy saniki.
Osmondagi yulduzniyo sakkiz denglar
Yor-yorey sakkiz denglar,
Sakkiz qizning sardoriyo keldi denglar
Yor-yorey, keldi denglar.

Photo 7: Uzbek wedding *Toy*

Sakkiz qizning sardoriyo biz bo'lamiz,
Yor-yorey biz bo'lamiz,
Sakkiz bog'da ochilgano gul bo'lamiz,
Yor-yorey gul bo'lamiz.
Hovlimizning o'rtasida bir tup anjir,
Yor-yorey bir tup anjir,
Bir tup anjir tagidayo tillo sandiq,
Yor-yorey tillo sandiq.
Tillo sandiq simlariyo uzilmasin,
Yor-yorey uzilmasin.
Kelin-kuyov taqdiriyo buzilmasin,
Yor-yorey buzilmasin.

Hello riding woman, horse woman,
You didn't keep your promises you deceiver-woman.

A foal is in the meadow and thinks he is already a horse
At home the new bride is crying saying she is a stranger here.

Don't cry girl, don't cry girl, it's your wedding
The golden threshold of the house is yours.

In the sky there are stars, they say you are the eight stars
The eight star girls have come.

We will be the head of the eight girls
As sight in the garden we will be like open flowers.

In the middle of the garden there is a fig tree
Under the tree there is a golden chest.

Let the hinges of the chest not be broken
Let the bond of the bride and the groom not be broken.

At first glance we find no obvious religious references, in the song's lyrics, either to Islam or Sufism. This song, which has been handed down from ancient times, is sung all over Uzbekistan. The tune and rhythm are simple, easy to remember and to repeat, and is said to have protective meaning. No wonder every family encourages performers to sing and play it again and again! However, in analysing the song's poetry in the more detailed way one can find that the meaningful symbols of local religions and beliefs are present here in the most dynamic way. What first draws our attention is a record of hidden symbols in lyrics of the song. Why are the words and phrases, 'threshold', 'house', 'eight flowers', 'eight stars' so widely used here? What is their origin? What do they mean?

To answer those questions we should turn our attention to another phenomenon of Uzbek traditional culture, to the local decorative art and particularly to its special example – Suzane.

These large decorative wall-hanging silk embroideries – Suzanis – originated in the nineteenth century and were made exclusively by women. These embroideries were popular only in the Central Asian region, where different Suzane designs developed in different areas. By the mid-nineteenth century the art of Suzane was formed as a standard system of patterns and developed its traditional styles. The composition, colour, and ornamentation based on floral motives and vegetative-style images were the supreme manifestation of the harmony of universe. The semantics of their appearance testify to a long evolution of this art.

The tradition is characterized by picturesque and complex coloured patterns, placed against a background. Each Suzane was designed by a professional craftswoman, known as a *Kalamkash*. These skills were passed down from mother to daughter, or between other female members of the family. The genesis of Suzane embroidery was closely connected to family life. Though these were primarily designed as domestic articles, the ornamentation was intended to give protection from the evil eye. The language of ornamentation was a language of metaphor whose usage and interpretation were determined by tradition. Behind every conventional sign there was a meaning. It employed a space-related symbolism where each element of ornament goes back to astral motives, whose source was probably in religious belief. Embroideries played the part of protective objects, but in the patterns the women saw a way to express certain ideas and content connected with real life.

Some decorative motives of the Suzane, expressed in ornamental details and floral roundels symbolise a house and a threshold, pointing to the hidden meaning of a protected space where no evil eye could reach and affect you. According to Ashirov, 'a door as a threshold possesses a deep symbolic meaning, bringing the image of the frontier between good and evil, light and dark, new and old, associated with sunrise and sunset. As archaeologists found out in the seventh–eighth centuries in Afrosiabe and Pandjikent areas, sacred rituals occurred on the thresholds of Sogdian shrines' (Ashirov, p. 30).

However, one of the most popular motifs in Uzbek Suzane is certainly the floral roundel in the shape of an eight-cornered star, emerging very often as an eight-petalled flower.

Originating in the Shamanic past, the symbol of the eight-cornered star symbolises the cosmos, the power of universe. Eight items is so significant for that culture that you can often meet the symbol in old folk songs like the one above. However, here in the Suzane those Shamanic symbols are combined with later Islamic decorations: the eight-cornered star, the astral Shamanic symbol, sign of the universe has become the symbol of Sufism.[193]

Today, in the most popular songs like the Uzbek wedding folk song *Yor-Yor* one can find a close connection between Shamanism and Sufism which is expressed in different signs and symbols of decoration and in ornamental arts.

8

Musical Instruments and Dance in Female Communities

30. MUSICAL INSTRUMENTS: FROM SHAMANISM TO SUFISM

Central Asian musical instruments are historically associated with extreme power related to Shamanic spirits, for example, the Kazakh instrument, *Kobuz*, or from Sufi concept of divine power. Some of these are discussed here.

In the Kazakh myths and legends the creator of the first musical instrument, *Kobuz*,[194] was Korkut, the first musician and the patron of the *Baqshi* – Shaman. The first musical instrument of the *Baqshi, Kobuz,* preserved its archaic features up to the middle of the twentieth century. The form of this musical instrument and the way it is held during the performance represents for Kazakhs the trinomial structure of the Universe: the High World, inhabited by gods, divine spirits, and birds, the Middle World, which is the abode of human beings and warm-blooded animals, and the Lower World, where evil spirits live, as well as those that creep and float, such as fishes, snakes, and lizards. The shovel-like head (*bas*) of the *Kobuz* is decorated with metal pendants in the form of rams' horns (the creatures of the High World) and birds' feathers (inhabitants of the High World). The case of the instrument, in the form of an open ladle from which, it is believed, the spirits rush out after the *Baqshi*'s appeal, symbolises the Middle World. The Lower World is embodied by a mirror placed inside the case. It represents the World Ocean, or as the Kazakhs say, 'the lower sights'. The sound of *Kobuz* – dense, rich and with pre-sounds, or harmonics, or overtones,[195] – is the signal for the appearance of spirits.

Legends, widespread among the Kazakhs, testify to the belief that *Kobuz* is an animated creature. It participates and wins in *baiga* – a horse-race,[196] and is capable of producing sounds without human input.[197] It also has deep symbolic protective meaning: Russian philologist V. Zhirmunsky wrote that the Kazakhs hang the *Kobuz* in the yurt (Kazakh nomad's tent) to provide relief for a woman during childbirth.[198]

Women in Central Asia have always been involved in music making. Many manuscripts, classic literature and art provide evidence about the place and role of women in Central Asian traditional culture, both in settled and nomadic communities. In Navoiy's epic poem, 'Seven strangers' (planets), seven different princesses in their beautiful palaces tell seven stories to the King, like Sheherezade of the *Arabian Nights*. This is an example of women protecting and preserving the sacred culture. Navoiy's poems, beautifully illustrated with miniatures and vignettes by Kamaleddin Behzad (1450–1535) documented for later generations a number of female musicians, playing spike fiddle and frame drum (*Bahram Yashil Kasrda –* Bahram in the Green Palace) or harp and frame drum (*Bahram Oltin Kasrda –* Bahram in the Golden Palace). We do not know the names of those musicians but their very presence in the medieval book miniature reveals much.

Certain musical instruments were widely used in connection to Shamanic or Sufi practice. However, the main Sufi instruments in Central Asia, for example, *Nay* (flute) and *Chang* (dulcimer) were played by men. *Masnaviy* – the greatest Sufi work by Mevlyana Rumi, for instance, starts with the famous words, which became a motto of Sufism:

Bishnav as Nay, ki hikoyat mekunad,
Az judoiho shikoyat mekunad.

Listen to *Nay*, who has story to tell,
Who complains about its separation.

Before proceeding with description and classification of musical instruments in Sufi tradition, we direct to the readers' attention an example of relationship between Sufi musical instruments and Uzbek classical poetry.

Muhammadniyaz Nishoti (eighteenth century), who was born in Khiva (nowadays Khorezm, Uzbekistan) wrote a famous Sufi poem called *Husnu Dil* (The Beauty and The Heart), about a King, Mind (Reason) in the kingdom of Body, who has a son, Heart. When the son reaches adulthood the father presents him with a kingdom and his mother gives him a book. In this book the Heart reads about *Obi Hayot*, the Water or Source of Life, and then falls ill. His father talks to him and, realising what the problem is, he calls his servant Nazar (the name means Sight) and sends him to find the source of life. In the 15,000 lines of the poem narrating his search, Nazar encounters Pride, Honesty, Shame – in fact, every human attribute, or failing – but nowhere does he find the source of life. Some kind people, like Intuition, tell Nazar that the source he is looking for lies between the lips of Beauty, who is the daughter of another king called Love (Passion). Before the Heart can find Beauty there are battles between the two kings, Mind (Reason) and Love (Passion). Love is victorious. Finally, all the poem's heroes are united in the Garden of Perfection, and there is a Feast where everyone sings and dances. Heart wins Beauty, and at the same time finds the Source of Life.

Part of this Sufi poem tells the story of *Daf* (a round Drum), *Nay* (flute), and *Chang* (Dulcimer), the main musical instruments used in Sufi rituals.

Mehr dafin kafga sipehri barin
Oldi oningdekki guli otashin.
Charx ko'rub oni bulub charxzan
Raqs ila o'z jismiga berdi shikan.
Raqsu samo' ila bo'lub ko'hsor
Gulshani davr ichra edi zaravor.

Like a flaming flower
Drum of the Sun was taken by Sky.
Heavens noticing it started to whirl,
Breaking itself into dance.
Dance and *Sama'* have overtaken mountains,
Which were closing their circle.

This is an introductory paragraph about *Daf*, which describes the functions of that musical instrument in Sufi music and rituals. Many existing Sufi rituals are still performed with accompaniment of *Daf/Doira*, and are discussed in greater detail in Chapter 9 devoted to female Sufi rituals, especially those based on dance. Here it is enough to say that, for instance, Barno Is'hakova, one of the leading performers of Maqams, often sang to the accompaniment of *Doira*.

There is a well-researched theory into *Doira's* rhythms or *Usul* (Method) theory, which goes back to the Treatises on Music by Al-Farabi and Ibn-Sina. In my book on the correlation between *Usul* and the rhythm of melody in Maqams,[199] I tried to summarise these theories and to show that, on one hand, *Usul* sets up a rhythm of the piece, which is a crucial element of Sufi *Maqams*. Thus *Usul,* which is called *zarb-ul-qadim* (ancient beat) is in fact related to the heartbeat, while other *Usuls* are related to different modes of breathing, etc. On the other hand, *Usuls* support the rhythmical structure of *Maqams' Ghazal* Sufi poetry, making bigger its affective, suggestive power.

31. *DUTAR*

Among the large group of Central Asian musical instruments is one that is famous for its 'feminine' image, and widely used in female performance. That is the long-necked plucked, fretted lute, *Dutar.*

Apart from *Daf/Doira,* the *Dutar* plays an extremely important role in Central Asian female Sufism. In Uzbekistan, the Uzbek *Dutar* has interesting historical connections with women's domestic music, women performers, female poets, and poetic images of femininity, including the Sufi one. In many contexts, it is the only acceptable melodic instrument for use in female performance. Uzbek musicians consider the shape of *Dutar,* with its light elegant body, long slim, long neck, and round belly, to be similar to a stork's image. Its tender sounds are associated with sounds of a cooing flying flock.

The *Dutar* is an ancient instrument. Some scholars link it to the *Tanbur* that existed in Khorasan, a historical cultural area covering Turkmenistan, western Afghanistan, and eastern Iran.[200] The name *Dutar* means 'two strings'. There are several distinct regional types of *Dutar.* Of these the Uzbek *Dutar* is comparatively large, being about 125 cm in length. The Uzbek *Dutar* has retained its two silk strings, whereas other types of *Dutar* may have more strings, and use materials such as wire, gut, or nylon.[201]

The *Dutar* seems to have been one of the main instruments for all entertainment events in the cities and villages of Uzbekistan. It was used by both male and female professional and amateur musicians as a general instrument in all kinds of settings. Because it has silk strings and a soft sound, it was played indoors, and its muted sound made it suitable for the quiet home atmosphere. Its role has been to accompany the voice or other instruments. In the classical Maqam tradition, which has been dominated by male professional specialists, the *Dutar* has an accompanying role providing background support to other instruments.[202]

It is important to remember that, for centuries, women in Muslim Central Asia, and particularly in Uzbekistan and Tajikistan, were largely segregated from men, keeping within secluded parts of the home. Islamic law and local interpretations of Islam meant that many classes of women were traditionally subordinated to male power and authority, although female members of royal and aristocratic families were actively involved in literature and the arts. The chronicles of Uzbek history were written by men, and in musical treatises many men have been identified as great masters of *Dutar*, but the role of women with regard to *Dutar*, as well as other music has been largely unrecorded. Nevertheless, drawing on a variety of sources, including literature, painting, and the oral tradition, we can trace evidence of women's historical involvement with this instrument.

Other types of long-necked lute, similar to the *Dutar* are depicted in fifteenth- and sixteenth-century miniature paintings, which portray musical entertainments inside palaces. The evidence suggests that during that period, women played various instruments, including long-necked lutes, in indoor court music. It is likely that they were both aristocratic women and professional entertainers.

Central Asian poets have traditionally recited their poetry aloud, and in Ferghana the *Dutar* may well have had a role in performances by female poets. In past and present Uzbekistan, it has been quite common to see romantic miniature-style images of beautiful women playing the *Dutar*, and a recent edition of Nodira's work contains an illustration of her composing poetry with a female companion playing the *Dutar*.[203] Given that so many outstanding women poets lived in Ferghana, it is not surprising that female *Dutar* traditions in Sufi music have been particularly strong in that region.

Girls and women created music at their own private gatherings (*gap*). A *gap* is any convivial gathering for men or women, either with or without music, very often bearing the traces of Sufi gatherings. The *Dutar's* softness made it suitable for female gatherings at any time of the day or night, while its percussive quality (from the fingers plucking the strings) gives sufficient rhythmic support for dancing and singing in small indoor spaces.

Late nineteenth-century photographers have captured images of young women holding *Dutars*. One such photograph was taken, not later than 1896, by the Russian traveller, Voljinski, in Khiva, the capital city of Khorezm.[204] Sitting in an opulent setting, a group of five elaborately dressed young girls pose holding a *Dutar*, a frame drum (*Doira*), a book for singing poetry, and flowers. From their clothing and demeanour I conclude that these were professional entertainers. It is very likely that they played the *Dutar* in connection with marriage ceremonies or female Sufi events.

We find descriptions of amateur female *Dutar* playing in early twentieth-century novels. The novel *O'tkan kunlar* (Days Gone By) by the eminent author Abdulla Qadiry (1893–1938) has a scene set in nineteenth-century Margilan, a town in the Ferghana Valley. This depicts the beginning of a wedding ceremony with a female party in the women's area of the house known as *ichkari*. In an amateur capacity, and in the context of celebration, Qadiry's female characters – Zebi, Qumri, and others – play songs and dances accompanying themselves on the *Dutar*.[205] Another description occurs in a novel by the eminent Uzbek writer Abdulhamid Cholpon (1895–1938), *Kecha va Kunduz* (Night and day). His heroine Zebihon and her female companions play music to make the journey to another village exciting and lively; they play the *Dutar* and sing songs as they travel in a private enclosed ox-drawn carriage.[206]

The *Dutar* remained especially prominent in Ferghana's female professional traditions. The British National Sound Archive houses recordings by *Tajiniso*, a famous female Sufi performer, whose semi-classical and folk pieces on the *Dutar* were recorded in 1906 by the British company, Gramophone.

For some time, female actresses played the *Dutar* on stage in the Theatre of Musical Drama in Andijan (Ferghana Valley's largest city), which was established in 1920. By 1997, the theatre had become moribund, but one old retired actress, Sharopat Ahmedova (b. 1907) still maintains her skill as a *Dutar* player. During my research on female *Dutar* players in 1996, she told me that all actresses were required to be *Dutar* players. The dramas were heavily interspersed with musical interludes, and some sections were purely musical, so the actresses sang and played the *Dutar* on stage.

Various female professional performers from Ferghana became prominent. Muhtaram Azizova (1930–95) and Kimsanhan Ahmedova (b. 1942–2004) sang in the demanding improvisational style of *Katta ashula* or *Jo'ranavoz*, a classical genre from the Ferghana-Kokand court tradition (Photo 8). *Jo'ranovoz*, which is also a remnant of Sufi *Zikr*, is usually performed by two highly-skilled musicians singing alternate verses.

The world of Uzbek music rests on many multifaceted ideas, myths, and legends, some of which hint at interesting connections between the *Dutar* and women or the female role. Uzbek musicians admit that the two long-necked-fretted lutes form the main basis of traditional music: the *Tanbur*,[207] which has three strings and is played with a brass plectrum, and the *Dutar*. Their musical relationship is unequal, with the *Tanbur* as a dominant and leading instrument and the *Dutar* in an accompanying

Photo 8: Famous *Dutar* performer Kimsanhan Ahmedova

role. In the Uzbek system, the *Dutar* is the shadow of the *Tanbur*, and its follower and accompanist. It is equated with the female role, which entails being secluded and occupying a position in the background. The *Dutar*'s silk strings and soft whispering tone give it a gentle sound corresponding with idealised expectations of female behaviour, whereas the *Tanbur* has a lower, louder, and brighter sound which equates with male dominance and authority.

To a certain extent, the *Tanbur* and *Dutar* represent two prototypes of the same instrument. According to an Uzbek legend, the inventor of the *Dutar* was the Greek philosopher Aristotle, whose name, as Arastu, is well known in Uzbekistan. (He was the tutor of Alexander the Great, who conquered the lands of Central Asia in 330–27 BCE.) Ryhzhon Hojahanov, a well-known Tashkent *Dutar*-maker, recounted the legend to me.[208]

The story says that Aristotle's teacher Plato invented the *Tanbur*, which he often played for his own pleasure. He kept his invention secret, jealously hiding it from the world, and he would play it for hours in the privacy of his terrace. However, the *Tanbur*'s wondrous sounds attracted the attention and curiosity of his pupil Aristotle, who approached the house in search of a clue about the instrument's identity. There he saw a vivid shadow of the performer and instrument. With the imprint of this image in his mind, Aristotle attempted to reproduce the instrument – with a pear-shaped body and long neck along, on which were stretched the strings. However, this resulted in a totally new instrument: the *Dutar*, with its slightly larger body and softer voice.

This myth of origin alludes to the master–pupil role[209] and the idealised submissiveness and respect of the pupil for his master. We may detect an implied equation between the *Dutar* and the female role, which respects male authority. The relationship between the *Tanbur* and *Dutar* corresponds with idealised notions about masculinity and femininity, according to which men lead and women follow.

The evidence for the mystical origin of the *Dutar* is reflected in other local myths and legends, such as the following.[210] Once upon a time, Hazrat-Ali (a cousin and son-in-law of the Prophet Muhammad) noticed that his favourite horse Dyul-Dyul was gradually getting sicker and sicker, and he became increasingly worried. One day, entering the stables he noticed that his groom Baba Kambar was playing a strange instrument – a long-necked lute. Seeing that he had been caught in action, Baba-Kambar was so frightened that he wanted to break the instrument into pieces, but Hazrat-Ali stopped him and asked what kind of instrument it was. Baba-Kambar told him that he had made the *Dutar* out of the mulberry tree but that the instrument was voiceless. Then Baba-Kambar called for devil's help who given the *Dutar* this beautiful voice. After that, the *Dutar* acquired the intriguing/evoking/haunting voice that had made the horse sick.[211] In different sources, Baba-Kambar appears also as the inventor of *Dutar* or even as a female saint (Kambar-Ana).[212]

According to another legend, Plato wanted to invent the instrument with sounds like a peacock wings. He investigated the nature of that sacred bird's wings and then made the *Dutar*, which sounded amazingly mysterious, similar to the sounds of her wings.[213]

An example from female repertoire of the Ferghana Valley area is the tune called *Chertmak*, played in 2/4 rhythm. *Chertmak* is a general name for plucked lutes in Central Asia. In southern regions of Kyrgyzstan, the lute, Komuz, is also called *Chertmak*. In translation, *chert* means to flick or to snap, producing a sharp cracking sound. *Chertmak* is a piece where the main beat (*Usul*) provides the colour, tempo, and energy of that particular character of music. The melody gives you a sense of direction, the flow of energy distributed through each stage: beginning, development, culmination, and recapitulation. *Usul's* energetic beats echo the energy of a dance, which could be associated with Shamanic performance.

The repetitive melody ascending in fourths, with short phrases leading with dynamic development towards the culmination. Suddenly, in the middle of the flow of music, the soloist strikes the wood of the *Dutar*'s belly with a lightning effect. It sounds as if drums are interrupting the lute's performance. Such alternation of string sounds and percussion sounds, performed on the same instrument, brings extreme power to this piece of music. So, as we see from this analysis, even the *Dutar*, with its gentle and tender sound, can at times become emotionally dynamic and expressive.

We also find associations between the *Dutar* and the female role in poetry. The early nineteenth-century Sufi woman poet, Uvaysiy, evokes this relationship in a *ghazal* about the sorrow of separation. In the first and principal line of the poem (which is constantly repeated in performance), she refers to the traditional pairing of the *Dutar* with the *Tanbur*:

Manga chertgan dutor chogi
Chalib tanbur qachon kelgai

To me, who plays the *Dutar*,
when will he who plays the *tanbur* come? [214]

The passivity of the female role is expressed in the idea of the woman waiting for her loved one. The romantic notion of the appropriate pairing of musical instruments (that will play together) is also implied.

The early twentieth-century author Abdulhamid Cholpon (whose novel is mentioned above) was also a poet. He makes an analogy between the fate of an Uzbek woman, imprisoned within the four walls of her house, and the sorrowful sounds of the *Dutar*, whose music itself is limited within the range of two strings.

Men dutor gberlan tug'ungan, kuhna bir devonaman
Ul tug'ushgonim bilan utda doim yenaman
Dallarida g'am tula bechoralarga yerman
Vaqti hush g'amkurmaganlardan tamon bezorman

I [a woman] was born to be like a *Dutar*, with restlessness inside me
We burn with the same flickering flame
I try to find a place to hide my sorrow
But my pain is endless: every note I play reflects it. [215]

The *Dutar* underwent significant changes in image and musical role during the early Soviet period of the 1930s. Instead of playing traditional Sufi music, musicians were expected to adopt an optimistic style, playing new pieces that expressed Soviet values, which ran counter to the melancholic and spiritual ethos of Uzbek classical music.

Sovietisation brought revolutionary changes to Uzbek musical and social life, and the authority in Central Asia has always emphasised the emancipation of women as an extension of the aspirations of the October Revolution. In Uzbekistan, there was a dramatic rise in female education and women were incorporated into the paid workforce. A positive outcome for women was the fact that female professional musicians felt encouraged to become poets. In Ferghana, several women musicians – Lutfihonim Sarymsakova, Mehro Abdullaeva, and Bashorat Hojaeva – sang the poetry of Mukimy, accompanying themselves on their *Dutars*. Another musician, Mavluda Agzamova, sang pieces by the female poets Toshmapulat and Furkat.[216] But at the same time Mavluda Agzamova was a singer who maintained the Sufi tradition of playing *Dutar* and singing Sufi songs throughout the whole Soviet period. Archives of the Uzbek State Radio house her recordings of Sufi songs such as *Topmadim* (Couldn't find), *Munojot* (Ascend to God), among many others.

The new Soviet cultural policy favoured popular art on a large scale. According to the Communist slogan, art should be 'taken out of narrow national confines and opened to boundless internationalism'. The government encouraged female music-making, and female *Dutar* ensembles were created. However, these new ensembles were quite out of character with *Dutar* traditions. The *Dutar*'s silk strings were replaced by nylon ones, which were stronger and gave a louder, brighter sound, but the silk-stringed *Dutar*'s spirit and distinctive sound was lost.

Male musicians appointed by Communist authorities implemented the new Soviet policy. They recruited inexperienced girls to project an image of female emancipation, regardless of their musical talent. These girls were taught to play the *Dutar* in a class, playing in unison and reading from sheet music. This had never been done before, and these innovations eliminated the traditional improvisational style. Sometimes, when official performances were prepared at short notice, the musical director might give the girls a simple Russian melody such as an easy *Svetit Mesyats* for balalaika to play within these ensembles, sightreading from the sheet music.[217]

For local audiences, the results were musically unsatisfactory. As mentioned in Chapter 1, commenting on the first Uzbek women's *Dutar* ensemble, formed in 1939, the leading Uzbek musicologist Ilyas Akbarov remarked: 'Most of the girls had [only] a very vague idea of their instrumental technique.'[218] In fact, the technique was that of the balalaika, not the *Dutar*. Suddenly, the *Dutar* was expected to be loud and artificially lively, and its soft and lyrical nature was completely destroyed.

Across the Soviet Union, similar innovations were taking place, with the development of massed instrumental ensembles and the recruitment of female performers to create an image of emancipation. Later, in the 1950s, the *Dutar* underwent further reconstruction and innovation. In line with the expectations of his Soviet masters, the professor of Tashkent State Conservatory of Music, Ashot Petrosyants, tried to adapt Uzbek traditional musical instruments for use in Western-style symphony orchestras. A family of four different-sized *Dutar*s was created, paralleling the orchestral string family of violin, viola, cello, and double bass, but this experiment did not gain popularity.

The situation changed for the better in 1972, when the Tashkent State Conservatory established its department of Oriental Music, whose aim was to revive Uzbek traditional styles, free from outside influences. The eminent Uzbek musician, performer, composer, and teacher, Fahriddin Sadykov, who was brought up in a Sufi musical tradition (his name means Pride of Faith), was appointed to teach the *Maqam* repertoire on the *Dutar*. For the first time, girls were accepted as students of the *Maqam*, learning classical Uzbek Sufi music and performing on authentic instruments (rather than the new ones with their different sizes and nylon strings).

One of these students from the Ferghana area, Malika Ziyeyeva (b. 1955), became a celebrated performer, teacher, and innovator of *Dutar* traditions in her own right.[219] Malika Ziyeyeva has made many recordings as a soloist, both with the State Radio of Uzbekistan and with the Moscow Recording Company, *Melodia*, who awarded her a Golden Recording Disk (Photo 9). Her recordings include pieces from the Sufi *Maqam* repertoire, which she learnt from Professor Sadykov, and many of her own arrangements of folk tunes.

In 1991, she began teaching at the Tashkent State Conservatory, and there she founded the only existing female *Dutar* ensemble not only in Uzbekistan but in the whole of Central Asia. This ensemble has much more in common with the traditional image and repertoire of the *Dutar*. Ziyeyeva has revived the old traditional repertoire enriched with soft and delicate ornamentations and decorations of the Ferghana performance style. Her ensemble is not commercial and it does not really perform in public.

Photo 9: Shavkat Mirzaev's ensemble with Malika Ziyeyeva (*Dutar*)

Its members generally play together for their own enjoyment, like female Sufi gatherings, to experience a genuine interaction between the *Dutar* and the female spirit, and to create a setting for the Uzbek female *Dutar*-playing Sufi tradition (Photo 10).

An interesting observation on *Dutar's* association with Sufi tradition was made by great Uzbek musician Turghun Alimatov, who confirmed: 'There is something spiritual/divine in Dutar! Sometimes you can hear the music of the universe throughout its tender harmonics. Also as your colleagues-musicians claim you can keep it playing while you sleep! They swear they heard me snoring and playing at the same time! The most spiritual piece of Dutar music related to the old Sufi tradition is certainly Tanovar where the weeping sound set on regular rhythm is reminiscent of the inhale/outhale breathing nature of Sufi *Zikr*.'[220]

The image of the *Dutar* is very important not only because it signifies a female presence in local music culture but also because the instrument is of the highest importance in the local cultural identity. As the most popu-lar Uzbek musician in Afghanistan, Usto Gafar Qamolitdin (1908–2008), had claimed 'Nothing in Uzbek culture could be done without a Teacher! My Usto [teacher] was Sadreddin, Shogird [pupil] of legendary musician Sadyrhon from the court of the Emir of Bukhara. I received my Nohun [a Tanbur plectrum made of silver and iron] from my Usto, who in turn

Photo 10: Group of female *Dutar* performers led by Malika Ziyeyeva

received his Nohun from Usto Sadyrhon. I was so happy to get it! Today I have none to pass it on.' During my interview with him in October 2006, he said: 'What kind of Uzbek are you if you don't play *Dutar*?'

It has become apparent that the very image of the Uzbek was always associated with music-making skills and the ability to play the classical traditional instruments like *Dutar*. The *Dutar* performance was considered the genuine proof of 'Uzbekness'. Certainly, music for Afghani Uzbeks was, and is, much more important than for Uzbeks from the motherland, when, owing to political changes, music was an oasis, or an intangible cultural heritage that kept the national identity alive. However, one should not underestimate the fact that even in mainland Uzbekistan, the *Dutar*'s presence helps to maintain that culture, and continues to be played by both men and women. Women in particular helped to preserve the national identity!

32. DANCES IN CENTRAL ASIAN CULTURE

Another important function of *Daf* and *Doira* instruments playing *Usul* comes out in Sufi *Zikrs* and dances based on Sufi *Zikr*.

Historically, dance was always a part of any religious worship, being a part of mystical Sufi rituals. Sufi rituals had compulsory closing dancing sessions, with the length of the dancing session being dependent on the brotherhood. But many Central Asian Sufi rituals have been built up on extensive ecstatic dances to close the ceremony (Qadiriyya, Yassaviya, Naqshbandiyya).[221] Although there were no sophisticated elements of dancing involved, massive crowds of whirling people (up to 10,000 in Turkestan, even at the beginning of the twentieth century) arranged in circles, became a prominent feature of religious dancing.

One should say that alongside the Sufi or religious dances there also existed other forms, like dances in the women's gatherings, as well as the so-called *bacha* (boy) dances. Descriptions of these are recorded in the works by *Jadid* writers at the beginning of twentieth century. In his novel *Kecha va Kunduz* (Day and Night) Abdulhamid Cholpon describes a young ladies' gathering where the heroine Zebi plays the *Dutar* while other girls are dancing. Another famous Uzbek writer and philosopher Fitrat in his novel *The Indian Traveller* depicts a dancing performance of a *bacha*, who was a subject of paedophilia – a phenomenon which still exists in Northern Afghanistan. The dance of the *bacha* is also mentioned much earlier in *Ba'daul Voqea'* by Zayniddin Vasifi (sixteenth century).

When the Soviets invaded Central Asia, dance as a meaningful form of music was used to express the joy of new social system. New groups were quickly built up, even where there was no precedent in the previous history of these republics. One should point out that the majority of dances in modern-day Uzbekistan and Tajikistan are performed by women. 'Today national dances of Uzbekistan are almost always female' noticed Mary Masayo Doi, emphasising that for traditional Muslim society it is not at all common. In that case, 'why and how did unveiled female dancers become a beloved national icon during the Soviet period?.'[222] Well-known and later world-famous, *Bahor*, a female dance group from Uzbekistan, became an icon of the new happy life, though, historically, public female dancing was not established in this culture.

Female ensemble *Bahor* (spring season) was the most famous dancing institution in the history of Uzbekistan and Central Asia. Created in 1957 by choreographer Mukaram Turgunbaeva in response to a request from Moscow, *Bahor* became the first female dance group in the history of the area. This art was characterised by an emotional sense of *joie de vivre*, reflecting the main spirit of the socialist age: the inspiration of collectivisation, the admiration of mass art, the beauty of the youth, and dynamic energy. Its repertoire was created by highly professional choreographers and *bastaqor* (composer), Muhammedjan Mirzaev using styles and tunes deeply rooted in local ancient traditions. As a result, an outstanding success followed the group from its very inception. Later, despite the 'iron curtain', *Bahor* became the only musical group from that area to tour abroad.

In the style of *Bahor's* dances one can, today, detect the connection with traditional Sufi dances and whirling experience.

Since Central Asian republics gained Independence the Sufi tradition of dances has been reborn both in Uzbekistan and Tajikistan. Folk dance ensembles, like *Boysun* or *Falak* are now performing *Zikrs* on the stage. Some Sufi female dances like *Larzon* (trembling), *Ufori Qalabandi* (fragrance imprisoned in the castle), *Orom* (meditation), *Ufori chillyaki* (fragrance of ascetic 40 days), and *Ey dilbari jononim* (O, my beauty) have been restored, all of them accompanied by *Daf/Doira.* Only the names of some movements reveal the link with previous Sufi dancing traditions. So, for example, tiny decorative movements from Ferghana dances called *Mukomlar,* consist of: *Qarsaklar* (clapping), *Barmoq qirsillatish* (finger snapping), *Quldasta Titrama* (hands trembling), *Quldasta ailanish* (wrists turning), *Qyig'ir bo'yin* (neck movements), *Iyak h'arakati* (chin movements), *Elka qoqish* (shoulder movements), *Elka titrama* (shoulder shaking), *Gavda tibranishi* (body movements), and so on. So, the shadow of Sufism has affected present culture in its rich use of dancing forms in daily life and celebrations.

9

Female Folk Sufism

33. FEMALE RELIGIOUS PRACTICES

There is a well-known metaphor to the effect that, in all things, a woman is the keeper of the home fire. One can assume that the roots of this saying lie in the far distant past, when men would leave the camp to hunt and women stayed behind to keep the precious embers of the hearth alive. But, of course, the metaphor is meant to indicate the role played by women in many aspects of society – family tradition, rituals, and ceremonies connected with the major rites of passage. The question is: to what extent has this behavioural archetype changed in today's world, with respect to culture and ritual?

Human history gives us many examples of 'staying behind', that is, of those occasions at different times and in different places when women have provided help and support for the community while remaining excluding from the historical records. Women's names are rarely mentioned in the great historical enterprises, ranging from the discovery of America to the conquest of the Poles, or outer space, and precious few women's names are represented in the annals of any sensational scientific revelation. No wonder that the role of women in maintaining cultural tradition is still so poorly documented in relation to the history of art and music.

Our research until now has shown the same trends in the Sufi history of Central Asia and particularly in its most Muslim areas – Uzbekistan and Tajikistan. With regard to female Sufi rituals, I shall concentrate initially on Uzbekistan, and then show similarities in other Muslim areas of Central Asia separately.

We begin by looking at the lives of women in the most traditional and densely-populated part of Uzbekistan, the Ferghana Valley, which is situated south-east of Tashkent, the capital city. It covers some 80,000 square kilometres where the three newly independent states of Uzbekistan, Kyrgyzstan, and Tajikistan meet. Between 9 and 10 million people live there, and families are extremely large, as a rule. The Ferghana Valley has always had the highest birthrate, not just in Uzbekistan, but of the former Soviet Union. (The increase in population in rural areas there in 1991, for example, was about 34 people for every 1,000.) Almost the entire population is Muslim.

Figure 3 gives some information about the daily life in rural areas and particularly in the Ferghana Valley. It compares the positions of men and women in different aspects of human activity.

As one can see, the position of women in Uzbekistan as a whole is much more restricted and dependent than that of men. It is a tradition, in rural areas, that when a girl graduates from her school she is expected to get married almost immediately. The wave of weddings in the villages starts mainly in summer – straight after the end of spring term. In the widespread but

	MEN	**WOMEN**
Education	A larger proportion of individuals receive higher education	Rarely educated
Job	Mostly employed, or go to Russia as *Gastarbeiters*	Almost no employment but handicrafts and tailoring at home, seasonal work in the fields, moving now towards commercial travelling abroad, in groups comprised of female relatives or friends (*chelnochnichestvo*)
Family Life	Dominant position in the family, the dictator Has the right to express opinions publicly	Always dependent on husband's opinion No right to express opinions publicly
Religious Life	Worship at mosque Many other forms of religious activity	Prohibited from attending the mosque, worship at home. Restricted forms of religious activity
Celebrations and Entertainment	*Toy* (weddings) *Gap* (gatherings)	*Toy* (separate participation) *Gap* (separate meetings)

Figure 3: Life of men and women in Ferghana Valley

narrow Uzbek view there is no need for women to be educated: a woman's duty is to stay at home, be a housewife, give birth to children, and so on. In these circumstances, when the educational level of the rural population is rather low (only 80 out of every 1,000 village residents are known to have received higher education), these views are quite common.

The same attitude is shown with regard to paid employment. What is the point in having a job if you are going to be the slave of your husband?[223] This view is widely held among the women in the Ferghana Valley as well as in other places in Uzbekistan. So women are deprived of the opportunity (or even lack the will) to work and to be independent.

This sense of dependence becomes stronger when we turn to the domain of religion. The mosques of Central Asia have no place for women – the presence of women in the mosques is still prohibited. Female worship can only take place at home. So, men and women are segregated even at the time of religious rites. One might say that Uzbek men and women follow different paths in both daily and spiritual life.

The general attitude to women in Uzbekistan differs strongly from that in the West. In pre-Revolution society it was prescribed that outside the home a woman should keep her face and figure hidden under some sort of cover. Through the whole of Central Asia women wore a kind of cloak called *parandja*, covering their faces with netting.[224] Nowadays the situation has changed a little. But, generally, women play a subordinate role and are still viewed as less important, and less respected than men.[225]

Although the policy of the Uzbek government involves placing women as deputies to the governors at each level, the position of women in ordinary Uzbek families, particularly in rural areas, is unenviable. On the surface everything is calm but underneath discrimination is rife. Medieval attitudes within society stimulate patriarchal relationships within the family. There are some regions where, when a woman gets married and starts living with her husband's family, she is not even permitted to speak aloud to any of her in-laws. She is doomed to be like a dumb person, merely indicating by signs or nods of the head if she agrees or disagrees. So, even though she lives with her husband's family, and may meet members of a usually numerous community every day, she should give no sign of having a voice! Obviously, she is not allowed to express her opinion or her wishes at any important decision-making gathering in the family.[226]

The only place where Uzbek women have a right of presence or can join men is at a wedding party or feast, called *Toy*. Here they all participate, but, nonetheless, they have to sit in separate places. Sometimes *Toy* takes place at two different houses: the bride's house and the house of her neighbours. Then women fill one house and men another. They seem to be together, but in reality they are separate.

Another occasion where women are able to go and to be on their own is *gap* (talking) – gatherings for close friends and members of community. Usually these take place on special occasion, like returning from *Hajj* (religious pilgrimage) and so on. In that case, women meet together in the house of the hostess of the festivities and celebrate the occasion by sitting around the *dastarkhan* (a tablecloth on the floor), having a meal and chatting. But, of course, women here are usually separated from men, who have their own *gap*.

These detailed explanations about different social positions are necessary in order for Western readers to appreciate the essence of being an Uzbek woman. This division is the basis of many special religious rites and part of the conditions of being a woman in the Ferghana Valley. One should point out that the Ferghana Valley is not an exclusive place, where women are treated as second-class creatures. Women's lifestyle in many parts of the world involves absolute isolation from the outside world and complete focus on husband, children, and family duties. This, according to psychologists, results in a need to find an emotional release, and consequently engagement in escapist activities. Common forms of so-called escape include the assumption of roles in domestic amateur drama, and listening to tales about those who have passed away, thus transferring the listener into the world of myths and fairytales, legends and miracles. The escape to another, fictional dimension is vital for mental relaxation, allowing women to avoid the stresses of daily life. But can this reason be the only one for the continuing involvement of women in ritual; mythical, imaginative worlds conjured up by performance?

Another, according to scientific opinion, is that women's emotional domain is greater than that of men, and, being more developed and sensitive, it requires constant maintenance, which involves a considerable effort of regeneration. Performance is one of the ways to act out accumulated concerns and problems – to act out another life for a short while. Thus, it represents one of the ways of replenishing one's emotional resources and achieving psychological balance.

This explains the psychological inclination of women to perform in artistic genres – singing, drama, and mystical forms of reading and spells, various kinds of stage display – thus strengthening the connection between their daily life and the spiritual world. One could say that, indeed, women have carried on playing the role of guardians of cultural heritage owing to their biologically-predetermined capacity as child-bearers and nest-defenders, and their historical experience. It is well known from history that women always followed their men. In exploring the world and in the conquest of new geographical spaces men were the pioneers, and the first to arrive, with the women following on bringing the children and domestic possessions. Thus did the 'tradition' itself trail behind the conquerors, carried by those cultural pack-horses, the women of the society, who had in the storage bags of their imaginations the necessary lifestyles, customs, habits, and rituals of daily life.

The traditional Muslim household in Uzbekistan is divided into two separate parts: *tashqari*, the outer, male part and *ichkari*, the inner, female one. Historically, a woman's life in a Muslim family was spent in this separate part of the house. *Ichkari* is off-limits to strangers, with entry strictly limited to family members, relatives, and children. Males from outside the family are never allowed to enter the *ichkari*. It is a separate world with its own rules, traditions, and life. This isolation of the female part of the household has played a crucial role in preserving and maintaining religious traditions, which have been mostly lost in the more exposed male part of the society. During my fieldwork I have met women who have never ventured beyond their *ichkari*, who have spent all their lives behind the high clay walls, bringing up their children. Usually, the *ichkaris* of one household are interconnected with those of the neighbours, and so the female part of the society lives a hidden life, moving from one house to the whole village.

This spatial phenomenon reflects an ancient order of gender segregation. Scholars have associated it with the old arrangement in palaces, where the *harems* were always situated at the back of the buildings, hidden from strangers and guests. The *harems* of the Akhemenid rulers' palaces (seventh to thirteenth centuries) provided the template for the later establishment of separate male and female quarters within Islamic palaces. The female area was where many women developed their performance and poetic skills.[227]

This same structural division survives today in Uzbek and Tajik households, even through the times of different rulers and ideologies. Every household in Uzbekistan, particularly in rural areas, still follows the *Tashkari/Ichkari* division, with the *Ichkari* remaining as an inner sanctum that is at the very heart of the house (Figure 4).

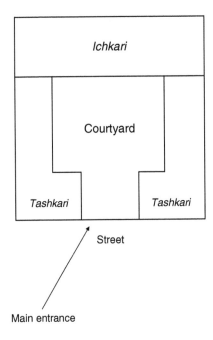

Figure 4: *Ichkari*

Ichkari was off-limits to strangers. Entry was strictly confined to the family members only, as well as relatives and children. In this fashion, women lived in an enclosed environment, subject to few outside influences.

So, under Soviet influence, the numerous prohibitions resulted in the creation of a very refined and highly hierarchical cultural environment, where the present and the past were tightly interwoven, by providing points of contact for the levers of protest. And maybe for this reason, the flow of modern life still continues in the manner of past times. Every step taken today is taken cautiously, with a backward look, as if today's world were only an approximation of the truths and lessons learnt yesterday.

Alongside the metaphorical substitution of religion for everyday culture, reflecting also on the female environment, the culture of Islam was, nevertheless, being not only preserved and maintained, but also passed down to the children, in the relatively undisturbed environment behind the walls of *Ichkari*.

The life of women developed in this enclosed environment, subject to few outside influences. So, deprived of contact with the outer world, women concentrated their efforts on their inner lives, like nuns for whom religion played the most important role in life. If we remind ourselves that even nowadays, in regions such as Khorezm in the South–West of Uzbekistan, in a perfectly urban environment, a daughter-in-law has no right to voice her concerns and even if asked something is only allowed to indicate her consent by nodding, little remains to be said about the place of women in the past.

One can only appreciate the scope of the culture of the women's world in the traditional society of Central Asia by looking at it from the outside. They possess their own school of life, passed down from grandmothers to children and grandchildren; their own school of religion, practised purely in the confines of their homes, similarly passed down from old to young; their own perceptions of the history and development of the world; and their own specific music and song. So, on one hand, there is the influence exerted on these rites by the Muslim tradition (some containing reflected Sufi forms), while on the other, their integration into domestic life provides convincing historical proof that they have emerged as examples of practices related to the rites of passage (Gennep 1960), which have incorporated the old, traditional rites as their major components.

Women played a crucial role in maintaining the Sufi tradition throughout the Soviet period. The Bolsheviks were determined to create an atheistic world; therefore, Islam was seen by them as the most reactionary ideology and Muslims were persecuted, under various slogans such as fighting *Basmachis* and later as Enemies of the People. As a result, almost all Mullahs, Ishans, Sufis, and any clerics or religiously-learned people were either killed or sent to the camps of the Gulag. Some managed to flee the country. Women were less exposed and vulnerable towards this Bolshevisation, so they kept the religious traditions of their families, passing the sacred knowledge to their children. It was a kind of 'reflected' Islam, 'reflected' Sufism; and music played a very important role in maintaining the religious rituals and traditions.

The most interesting fact is that, even today, the whole of traditional culture finds itself largely in the hands of women. The reason for this is not only because of Islam, with its division of the world into the categories of all things male and female, but also to some extent the original turn of history involving numerous prohibitionist regulations and persecutions enforced by the politics of the Soviet regime. So, for instance, it was one was simply not allowed to speak one's native language in public places, to believe in God or even in spirits generally, to carry out prayers, or in any way to identify your world outlook as different from the one prescribed by the Soviet regime.

However, since the Bolshevist politics of the Soviet Union could only offer brash slogans of the kind 'All the Power to Soviets!', 'Communism is Our Bright Future', or 'Let Us Proudly Fulfil the Five-Year Plan!', as a substitute, and since these slogans were unrepresentative of reality and far removed from the essence of people's everyday lives, they actually assisted in pushing the boundaries of common reality towards a surreal existence. As a result, it seemed as if the world was turned into a realm of subtext and underlying meanings. Under Soviet influence, the common pronunciation of Allah's name was replaced with a mental remembrance of His name.

Thus, in spite of the changes in social structure and disruption of social life on a vast scale in Central Asia, it is apparent that the foundations and influence of the old culture and the traditions were stronger and more solid than those innovations of new socialist growth.

History has recorded numerous occasions when secluded societies of any kind – religious, economically undeveloped as well as those in need of political intervention, or experiencing crisis situations – became hosts to spontaneously formed groups of psychological supporters among their members. As a rule, a hierarchical network arises within these groups, with the power ending up in the hands of the strongest. In female societies a similar trend can be observed in many different parts of the world, where an aged woman is usually chosen as head of the group on account of her experience and knowledge of all things mystical and religious – knowledge which, in conditions of a state ban on religion, is equivalent to mysticism. The dissemination of this knowledge takes place, as a rule, on domestic occasions, in the semi-public sphere, in the form of collective singing, representation of scenes from religious and historical heritage and appeals to the spirits of ancestors. Where bans exist on religious and spiritual rites, in some secluded societies, these are often transformed into artistic phenomena, marking the birth of rituals. In Uzbekistan, these women who lead the Way (even in Sufi terms), are called *Otin-Oys*.

34. *OTIN-OY* AS FEMALE SUFI *PIR*[228]

The etymology of the word *Otin-Oy* is unclear. The term may have originated from the Chagatay word *Hotin* (*khâtin*) meaning 'schoolteacher' but a more descriptive explanation would be desirable, as Chagatay and

Uzbek languages are almost identical. However, in Uzbek, *Hotin* means only 'woman' or 'wife'. Hence, one can assume that this term represents an amalgamation of two different words, for example, *Ohun(c) Hotin* or *Ota-Ona-Hotin*. Here *Ohun* means 'the educated', whereas *Ota* means 'father' or, at the same time, 'holy person'. The second part of term, *Hotin* stands for 'woman' or 'wife'. So, presumably, *Otin-Oy* could signify the particular woman who is spiritual leader of community, sometimes, *Otin-buwy* (*Otin* – 'granny' in Uzbek) or *Otincha* (pet-name). In modern translation this means 'religiously educated woman', a kind of female Mullah.

Normally they are descendants of *mullâ* and *qârî*, people who were trained in religious schools and who have studied the Qur'an in a thorough manner. These women are held in great esteem in times of both trouble and peace. On weekdays or on holidays, the *Otin-Oys* are welcomed in each family and in every house. They give help, support, or advice to anyone who needs it. They perform ancient rituals in a music and poetic form, which 'comment' on the occasion that is to take place. Generally, *Otin-Oys* are invited at each important stage in life (birth, marriage, and death) or to numerous dates celebrated in the Muslim calendar. They sanctify each event by performing spiritual songs and incantations.

Who, then, are the *Otin-Oys* in Uzbekistan? Very often they are secularly uneducated women. Nevertheless, from the point of view of social life, they are the upholders of a spiritual and religious knowledge, which is accessible only to chosen people, the descendants of a spiritual social stratum. Though suppressed by the Communists, they remained underground for almost 70 years, but continued to be held in great esteem by the local population.[229]

Where do they come from? As mentioned above, female activity in Central Asia and Uzbekistan, particularly, was rigidly separated from that of the male. However, there is historical evidence of women participating in the development of Sufism in these lands. Many female Sufis are named in written sources of the Middle Ages. For instance, some were mentioned by Abd al-Rahman Djami (fifteenth century) in his book of biographies of famous Sufis.[230]

According to some historical sources, the tradition of storytelling, and educational narrative, were widely performed during the time of Tamerlane the Great. For example, *kissakhons* (narrators) were highly ranked in his Palaces with *sayids* (scholars), historians, astronomers, and doctors. Also favourably estimated were readers of Qur'an (*Khofizs*), preachers (*Voiz*) and interpreters of the Prophet's sayings (*Muhaddis*). He also respected poetry (*Sherkhonlik*). The best of them he maintained in his Palaces.[231] One might conclude that, today, many genres in *Otin-Oy's* repertoire are related to the former court tradition of storytelling, educational narratives, and entertainment.

As a rule, *Otin-Oys* are middle-aged or older women of unstained reputation, who are valiant mothers and wives. In country life, *Otin-Oys* are without exception participants at all major events and happenings in family life and in village life as a whole. However, their activity is strictly restricted to the women's sphere. As a rule, they are invited only into *Ichkari* – the women's half of the house.

The appearance and lifestyle of *Otin-Oy* is, in other respects, the same as that of everyone else. It is not easy to distinguish an *Otin-Oy* in a crowd. The only distinguishing feature is the traditional item of clothing called *Oq Rumol*, a large white head scarf which is to be worn during ritual performance. Obviously, the question arises – is any Uzbek girl or young woman able to become an *Otin-Oy*, and what are the requirements? Also, how do they earn the right to become an *Otin-Oy*?

In order to become an *Otin-Oy* one must fulfil the following conditions:

1) to have come from a religious family of a Mullah, or to have experienced a difficult destiny, for example, being widowed early in life, or having a handicapped child;

2) to possess the required religious knowledge, such as knowledge of the Qur'an, and to be religiously observant – keeping all Muslim holidays and following laws and prohibitions dictated by Islam;

3) to have musical and performing/acting talents such as the ability to express emotions well, a good voice and a good ear for music, including good communication skills and cheerfulness, which are also important qualities;

4) to possess poetic skills – sometimes this allows for creative work, such as composing poems for particular occasions;

5) to have a pleasant appearance or good looks, and woman's natural charm – often *Otin-Oys* are physically strong and naturally healthy;

6) to have received a specified level of training from an older *Otin-Oy.*
   This is considered to be the main requirement which must be fulfilled
   in order to gain the right to become an independent *Otin-Oy*. Here
   we can see the traces of Sufi concept of *silsilah* or spiritual chain.

A further stage of mastering the requirements of the *Otin-Oy* involves
learning in the 'school of life', from one's own married life and mother-
hood, which is so necessary to gain the prestige and status of a respected
woman in Uzbek society.

Lastly, the final stage in obtaining the status of *Otin-Oy* is actually the
start of this new independence – 'going out into the world', the beginning of practice. Often this happens after the *Otin-Oy's* own children have
grown up, thus releasing her from her parental duties and allowing some
free time for her activity. At this point, there is at last, the opportunity to
put knowledge into practice and improve her skill on a regular basis. As a
rule, at this stage the newcomer *Otin-Oy* receives a blessing, *Fatiha*, from
her spiritual teacher.

Nowadays, along with other changing circumstances in Uzbekistan, the
status of *Otin-Oy* has become somewhat fashionable. Many young women
and girls in various parts of the country gained the right to receive religious
education and become *Otin-Oy*. However, to become true *Otin-Oy* they
will need to gain experience in the tough school of life, which will certainly
take time.

Otin-Oys, being the organisers and conductors of ritual ceremonies, are
represented by members of the most aristocratic social circles in the perception of the villagers, namely individuals held in high esteem by the rest,
holders of important posts and significant roles in the community. Their
leadership and orchestration of the process thus projects the hierarchical
composition of the ritual's content onto the mass of participants in these
gatherings, mirroring the structure of the ritual.

The participants are divided into active members, with *Otin-Oy* as the
focus of attention (where there is more than one present, the oldest and
most respected occupies the central place), and passive observers, with
the size of the audience depending on the time and nature of the event.
How do they perform these rites? They sit down on the floor around the
dastarkhan (a tablecloth on the floor set with traditional food and drinks).
At first glance they appear to sit at random, but in fact they sit according

to a strictly observed order: the eldest woman sits opposite the door, in the centre of the circle. The women seated nearest to her are of similar age. After them come the younger women, with the last one – usually a young girl – sitting near the door. She brings the tea and some food for the *Otin-Oy* during the gathering. Naturally, that last place is the lowliest. One can see that this order illustrates the entire hierarchy of Uzbek women's society. The same order exists for singing. The right to begin the singing belongs to the most respected woman, the main *Otin-Oy*. She starts and others follow.

The chain of regularity of rituals characteristic of Sufi assemblies, taking place for instance every Thursday, was broken by *Otin-Oy* practices. This can be easily attributed to the restrictions experienced during Soviet times. On the other hand, the involvement of the *Otin-Oy* became an indispensable accompaniment to every single significant occasion, no matter how big or small (the prom night, enrolment into the army); that is, it moved away from religion and drew closer to everyday life.

The question which now arises is: what occasions do *Otin-Oys* mark with their chanting?[232] In fact, every stage in life is supposed to be signified by the *Otin-Oy*'s performance, from the birth of a child, the beginning or end of every stage of child-rearing (teeth or hair growing/cutting, first sitting/walking, beginning of nursery or school attendance); the ritual of initiation for boys (*Sunnat-Toy*); meeting classmates after graduating; applying for, obtaining or leaving a job; betrothal, wedding, divorce; hospitalisation/discharge from hospital; death and mourning rituals; days of remembrance or commemoration. So, one can see that *Otin-Oy* appears at nearly every single situation in life.

The role of the *Otin-Oy* in a female community consists of:

1) priestly function, when she performs all religious activity among women: however, in Central Asia in the absence of female mosques or opportunity for women to join communal prayers, the *Otin-Oy*'s responsibilities are not a complete substitute for the Imam in male congregation;

2) master of ceremonies, whatever its nature (religious, rites of passage, calendar);

3) teacher and role-model for young generations;

4) the social authority, the leader in female community.

One can compare *Otin-Oys* in contemporary village life with psychoanalysts. When someone is in trouble they are responsible for problem-solving, 'negotiating' with the Almighty, trying to support and to comfort their people. At the same time, *Otin-Oys* are remarkable public figures heading the social hierarchy, representing the upper level of society.

35. HOW TO BECOME AN *OTIN-OY*: MALIKA ASQAROVA'S CASE

During Soviet times the activity of *Otin-Oys* was considered illegal. For example, *Otin-Oy* Malika Asqarova (b. 1955) from Dudur village tells how, as a schoolgirl, she went to see an old Ruzi-Otincha, at night-time in order to learn the skills of *O'qish* (reading, i.e. performance). Nobody knew about these lessons except her parents. The lessons consisted of a set programme of learning, progressing from simple to more difficult repertoire. The piece first learned was *Salavat Assalomu*, the prayer glorifying of the Prophet, and after that *Haftiyak*, 1/7 part of the text of Qur'an.

Malika tells the story of her studies: 'There were 32 of us pupils and we always sat in two lines. Ruzi-Otincha was more than eighty years old. We did not understand how old she was. We were very demanding pupils... She completely devoted herself to teaching. She gave us all her knowledge, certainly, free of charge. Sometimes we would sit at her home till 2 or 3 o'clock in the morning and would finish our lessons only when our angry parents came to pick us up. Every day we spent our free time at her home. She never told that she was sick and tired of us, she was a real saint. We continued to learn reading of Arabic texts, little by little we shifted to *Haftiyak* [see above], then we started to read Qur'an and then we went on to the *Chahor kitob* [Fourth book] and *Ishan Bobo* [Comprehensive religious books by Sufi Allahyar] (Photo 11). We learned pieces mostly by heart. Then I finished my studies, because I had to get married. In a few years' time my mother-in-law asked me to continue my regular studies... I came back to Ruzi-Otincha, but she was very old at that time and having listened to my reading she said that I can practise now on my own. She told me: 'Read regularly and when you are ready come here to see me to bless you and for initiation. And then you will become an independent *Otin-Oy*.' Eventually I was blessed by Ruzi-Otincha. And now I read. Sky is the limit as they say.'[233]

Later, Malika Asqarova herself started to teach others. Initially her neighbours asked her to teach their daughter, and then others brought their

Photo 11: Classical poetry in Arabic script from *Otin-Oys* notebooks

children. So she put together a group of ten pupils. Some of them were from the families of *Otin-Oys*, others were just very eager to learn. Now she has plenty of religiously-educated pupils in the area. Malika's grandmother could read as well and Malika remembers many pieces like *Dediyo* and others from her childhood. Nevertheless, the ultimate polishing of her knowledge she definitely received from Ruzi-Otincha. So we can see that among the *Otin-Oys* there are two types: those who have great knowledge of religion and rich practice in rituals, and who perform on a regular basis, and those who practise but who also pass this knowledge to their pupils. Their role has its equivalent in the *Murshids* in Sufi orders. Apart from for their knowledge, they are respected for their pure and almost holy way of life (Photo 12).

Otin-Oys occasionally include reading and practising outside the sphere of 'sacred' knowledge. That is why, for example, Malika Asqarova went to Ruzi-Otincha to study, rather than to her own grandmother, who was also able to read the Qur'an. One important aspect should be pointed out: apparently there is a kind of *silsilah* between teacher and pupil in the *Otin-Oy's* practice similar to the chain between *Murshid* and *Murid* in the Sufi order, which is said to pass mystical knowledge from person to person. Despite the political and ideological changes during successive periods, in

Photo 12: *Otin-Oy* Malika Asqarova

modern Uzbekistan the *Otin-Oy*'s chain has maintained sacred religious knowledge among the women of Uzbekistan. As we showed above, sometimes this knowledge has been received from Sufi persons, either women or men.

Once in Dudur village, it was suggested that I should meet the young girl Nodira who was learning how to become an *Otin-Oy*. She had a really beautiful voice. She recited a few examples which she had learned from her teacher. I noted their musical simplicity. They sounded like the skeleton of future incantations with a simple tune developed on the basis of three or four notes. In fact, her example seemed more of a recitation than a musical piece from the professional *Otin-Oy* repertoire with their long- and well-developed patterns.

However, training in the professional skills of the *Otin-Oy* depends not only on purely musical or vocal gifts but also on devotion to the chosen professional path. Not everyone could devote oneself to an *Otin-Oy*'s life. Recently, I was invited to meet a young *Otin*, Halida, living in Tashkent. I had heard she was about 17 years old and had a strong and beautiful voice. Under the pressure of her parents in early life she had been trained as an *Otin-Oy*. Her teacher was a famous *Qory* (Qur'an expert) from Ferghana, to whom she went regularly for lessons. The teacher and his student were of different ages and social positions. Moreover, they were not relatives. By Uzbek tradition they were not allowed to see each other's faces, so they conducted the lessons separated by a curtain, with the teacher on one side and the student on the other.

When I visited her, she started to sing assiduously, performing the stanzas one after another. Her voice was really impressive. But gradually I began to feel that she did not seem to be a really convincing *Otin-Oy*. Why? I tried to understand what was happening. I noticed that she became irritable and tense. She often looked at her watch. I understood she was in a hurry. 'What is happening?' I asked her mother, who sat next to me. 'Sorry, she is in a hurry, because she is going to the swimming pool!' Can you imagine an *Otin-Oy*, an eternally mysterious religious female image, with the modern look of a half-dressed woman's body in a glamorous swimming pool? Later, I heard that she did not become an *Otin-Oy*. It turned out her destiny took another path.

Recently, visiting the tiny city of Denau (South Eastern part of Uzbekistan), I found that the area's lifestyle, city architecture, local traditions, social network, all reminded me of the Ferghana Valley (Photo 13). Carefully painted houses with tidy gardens were a distinctive feature, proving the presence of a settled population. In fact the difference between the close neighbouring townships of Boisun and Denau is quite remarkable: Boisun is an area of nomads whereas Denau is an agricultural area with a settled population. The *Otin-Oy* I was shortly introduced to, Mukkaram Halilova, was stunningly beautiful and looked so young that at first I doubted whether she ever had any appropriate training at all (Photo 14). However, it turned out she had. Her pure voice, emotional performance and her ability to perform rituals in a highly professional manner were very impressive. When I asked how old she was she explained that her training had been traditional and intensive. Mukkaram Halilova learned her professional skills from local *Otin-Oy*. Having four children, a husband and a number of family duties kept her very busy. The only excuse for her to go out was the obligations of the *Otin-Oy*. She helps people and people love her in return.

Photo 13: Female community – mixed generations in Denau

Photo 14: *Otin-Oy* Mukkaram Halilova is performing ritual *O'qish*

The house where I was invited to observe her rituals was one of the richest in Denau: with spacious rooms, traditionally decorated with local ornaments, massive lavish furniture, exclusive carpets on the floor, a refined set of cups and dishes, delicious food – all the necessary attributes of wealthy people. The purpose of that particular family ritual, with the popular *Otin-Oy* in attendance, was to mark the husband's recent promotion (he had become the head of the local railway station). *Otin-Oy* Mukkaram was surrounded by a circle of friends and neighbours. She practised for a couple of hours, performing a large range of *Suras* and *Ghazals*, with rare taste and confidence, accordingly to her own preference and choice. Repetitions of rhythmical patterns, dynamic waves, and clear tone development were typical features of her style. After the session finished, I was invited to her place to continue my interview. Her unique voice, entire devotion and bright personality made this meeting with *Otin-Oy* Mukkaram Halilova unforgettable. So indeed there are no limits to the appearance of new, distinguished *Otin-Oys* in Uzbekistan.

36. SUFI RITUALS LED BY *OTIN-OY*

The Ferghana Valley is today the most strictly Muslim area of Uzbekistan. Some of the rituals women perform there are songs and incantations praising different historical figures. The very broad repertoire of the *Otin-Oy* includes some incantations devoted to the founders of different Sufi orders such as Qadiriyya, Naqshbandiyya, Yassaviya.[234]

When you ask *Otin-Oys* about *Tasavvuf* (Sufism), some are very articulate and can elaborate on it at length, others can barely understand this word. On examining their rituals, in some places, the essential elements of loud *Zikr* can definitely be found, and further investigation almost always reveals that one of their predecessors was from a family of *Ishân* (Sufi *Sheikh*), who followed and performed loud *Zikr*, reading the *Hikmat* of Ahmad Yassavî. However, modern *Otin-Oys*, particularly the most prominent stream from the Ferghana Valley, do not belong to any particular *Tariqat*, but hail from a mixture of various Sufi branches. There is probably a simple explanation for this: as the wives of *Ishâns* from different *Tariqats* no particular one became dominant, but they just retained the principal manner of devotion to God, by gathering together to recite the Holy Qur'an.

It is worth mentioning that today this huge number of incantations is performed as the proper stuff of performance without following the rules of a particular Sufi order. One can assume that there are several reasons for this. It is likely that modern female rites are mostly viewed as a broad collection of items for rituals consisting of different incantations and poetical works, in the style of Qur'anic *qira'at* (singing/reading) or *tilâwat* (singing/declamation). They were probably collected for different reasons, for example, their poetical and melodic beauty. In those lands where many Sufi orders have been found, from medieval times, female rites nowadays include a mixture of different parts of Sufi *Zikrs*, quite unlike the *Zikr* from centuries ago. One can say that *Zikr* might be a part of each special female meeting for certain religious or family events.

Zikr was set as a part of devotional gathering. It could be a part of a funeral event, as I saw in Boisun – a series of prayers of increasing emotional intensity, culminating with weeping, alternating with the performance of ancient poetry. *Otin-Oy* Mutaborak-hola from the village of Butaqora (Andijan district) had performed the song, which is actually properly applied to the history of the *Qadiriyya, Tawba tazarru* (repentance). This was a glorification of the founder of the Hanafi Sunni *mazhab* – Ghavsul Aghzam (Ghawth al-A'zam or Imâm 'Abd al Hanîfa).

Tawba tazarru (repentance)

Sharmandalya rasvolighim haddin oshdi
Ghavsul Aghzam podshohim madad qiling.
Osyi jonu gunohkorman ilohimga,
Ghavsul Aghzam podshohim, madad qiling.
Jaborrimga hech kim mandek sharmandamas,
odam hulki manga u'hshab yomon emas.
Tawba qilsam, gunohlarim tamom bu'lmas,
Ghavsul Aghzam, gunohlarim tamom bu'lmas,
Ghavsul Aghzam, podshohim, madad qiling...

My disgrace became unlimited,
Ghavsul Aghzam, my sovereign, my king, help me.
I am very guilty, God,
Ghavsul Aghzam, my sovereign, my king, help me.
No one so disgraced himself before God as I,
There is no one in the world so bad as I,
Even if I confess, my sins do not disappear
Ghavsul Aghzam, my sovereign, my king, help me.
Ghavsul Aghzam, my sovereign, help me.[235]

It is interesting that the line *Ghavsul Aghzam podshohim, madad qiling* has 11 syllables. Bearing in mind that the number 11 was a holy number for certain Sufi orders, the use of 11 syllables was probably intentional.[236] Even considering 11 as the common number of emphasised or accent syllables in *Barmak* – the folk system of poetry based on particular number of syllables – the question as to why that number of syllables was used could not be answered easily. All other songs from the *Otin-Oy* repertoire are addressed to other Sufi principals like Hasan, Hussein, Naqshband, and others have a totally different number of syllables.

37. *ZIKR*

Nowadays, *Zikr* in Central Asia are a mere residue of the old style of worship, and the passing of time has led to the transformation of rituals. They change not just in their inner development but also through external pressures, as in Uzbekistan. Today, they are only a shadow of the past, an enigmatic but a very essential shadow, melting in the vacillating image of time. They are a shadow not just in terms of their lost intensity, but also in the way they have been reflected by women who, during the Soviet suppression, were the only stratum of society that could maintain the Sufi tradition in the forms of rituals. Therefore, I call this form of female Sufism 'reflective Sufism'.[237] Innovations in the policy of modern independent Uzbekistan could lead to the revival and revision of Sufi tradition or, on the contrary, to its disappearance. But as we have seen, that tradition has the inner resources to survive, despite external pressures.

Zikr is originally a Qur'anic word, commanding 'remembrance of God', and an act of devotion during and after a prayer. As Nikolay Lykoshin witnessed, in Tashkent in the beginning of the twentieth century, male Sufi *Zikrs* were carried out in two ways: *Dashgariya Jahriya* (aloud), and *Hufiya* (in silence).[238] This act can be observed during the sessions of *Otin-Oy*. In 1992, I was an eyewitness at a gathering of several *Otin-Oys* in the very heart of the Ferghana Valley in Uzbekistan, in the village of Dudur in Andijan province. The reason for that gathering was very solemn – namely, the end of *Ramadan*. The very process of this gathering was full of ritual: the *Otin-Oys* arrived slowly and ceremoniously at the house of *Otin-Oy* Mutabarak-hola, a respected woman, the widow of the former chairman of the local *kolkhoz* (collective farm). All of them wore white shawls, which covered them fully, and were slow and graceful in their movements and in their speech as they sat around the *dastarkhan*.

A short introductory conversation while drinking tea helped them to get into the mood of the *O'qish*, or 'reading'. *Otin-Oys* chanted from the small

Figure 5: Music Line Antalho

books called *Bayaz* or *Kulliyat* (collection of religious or semi-religious texts with some *Suras* of the Qur'an, Islamic myths, and Sufi poems). A wide range of very different poetry was performed on that day: from Ahmad Yassavi (twelfth century), Mashrab (seventeenth century), Sufi Allahyar (seventeenth century), and some female poets, such as Nodira and Uvaysiy (both from the nineteenth century). Sometimes, *Otin-Oys* read their own poetry. The general name for these gatherings is *O'qish* (readings), although the texts are sung. The musical features of this rite are obvious. Developing slowly and monotonously it starts as a recitation but gradually develops into song. One song after another is performed until the climax, which is actually the pure *Zikr*, is reached. The performance of *Zikr* was set on the well-known *Shahada* of *Ahmad Yassavi*. This tune is better known by its ubiquitous first line *La ilaha il Allah* (There Is no Other God but Allah!), widespread through the whole Islamic world (Figure 5).

Antalho

> *Bismillahi-r-rahmoni-r-rahim!*
> *Antalho dey antalhaqq, laysallahu illahu,*
> *Asli rabbim Jallolloh, mohi qalbim xayrulloh,*
> *Nuri Muhammad salllaloh, La ilaha il Allah (6 marta)*
> *Har kim maysa o'rguncha, La ilaha il Allah,*
> *Go'ri bo'lar dunyocha, La ilaha il Allah,*
> *Ochar bihishtdin darcha, La ilaha il Allah,*
> *O'lib o'g'lon kelodir, La ilaha il Allah,*
> *Doim xizmat qilodir, La ilaha il Allah,*
> *Go'ri bo'lar qon asta, La ilaha il Allah,*
> *Yotar qushdek qafasda, La ilaha il Allah,*
> *Mehnat qilar payvasta, La ilaha il Allah,*
> *Tahlil degan ushbu nom, La ilaha il Allah,*

Tinmay ayting subhu shom, La ilaha il Allah,
Hamroh bo'lgay imoning, La ilaha il Allah,
Qorong'u go'r charog'ing, La ilaha il Allah,
Imon islom a'losi, La ilaha il Allah...

I celebrate you, God
I celebrate you, Almighty,
There is no God but the Deity
Indeed You are my Lord
My Lord who created the universe.
I sacrifice my heart to you, God.
Resplendent Muhammad is the messenger of God.
There is no God but Allah
There is no God but Allah
There is no God but Allah
While everyone is cutting grass
There is no God but Allah
His grave will be the whole world
There is no God but Allah
He will open the window of paradise
There is no God but Allah
A dead son is coming
There is no God but Allah
He will constantly serve God
There is no God but Allah
His grave will slowly be filled with blood
There is no God but Allah
He will lie like a bird in a cage
There is no God but Allah
Suffering will come and will bind him
There is no God but Allah
This is cleansing
There is no God but Allah
You talk continuously from morning to night
There is no God but Allah
Your faith will be your companion
There is no God but Allah
In the dark grave there will be light
There is no God but Allah!

This *Zikr* is performed as a chorus, when the right mood is achieved at the very culmination of the gathering. The leader of the session gives a sign and then everyone joins in. Musically, it seems quite ominous. They start off in a very slow rhythm and with quiet voices. Then the tempo accelerates and voices rise, finally reaching the pure repetition of the unique phrase *La ilaha il Allah.*

One of the most remarkable events I witnessed was the *Zikr* in the village of Gushtyemas in the Andijan district, in October 1999. The women were gathering together for a special purpose. A well-respected, elderly lady called Chinny-hola – a friend to many of them – had not been feeling well for the past month after recovering from pneumonia. As women came to visit her, sitting, and drinking tea, later having dinner, they called for the closest neighbours. Gathering together a dozen of them, sharing the latest worries and news, they finally became more and more excited about the state of Chinny-hola's health. Finally, trying to comfort and support her, they fell into the ritual with prayers, *Fatiha* (*Sura* n1 of Qur'an), Sufi poetry of Mashrab, Uvaysiy, turning later into the dance form. One of the *Otin-Oy*, Sabokat-hola, took the *Doira* (frame drum) and started playing. The evening became joyful and dynamic, lifting the spirits of all those present. Next morning, all the neighbours who could not come expressed real regret that they had been unable to participate in such a remarkable event.

There is a tendency towards special features in *Zikr* performance within women's circles. Here I am talking of the recreation of 'quiet' *Zikr*, when tears come to the eyes of the participants and hearts fill with sadness. In this sense, *Sama'* of such kind suggests a particular form of transcendence, reflecting the qualities of women's nature, the tendency to gentleness and emotional sensitivity. In contrast to the harsher forms of men's *Zikr*, where the ecstatic state is displayed as a total loss of perception of reality, the culmination of women's *Zikr* can be discerned as a tradition of immersion into quiet trance, thereby recreating the sensation of reunion with God.

Sometimes, as we see, the congregation meets not from Sufi motivations but for very different reasons, such as life events, calendar events, or purely religious events. Most often, various forms of *Zikr* stages can be observed. The consistency in performance of Qur'an texts and Sufi poetry, ascending in emotional intensity from simple to complex, increasing in emotional expression by the end of the gathering – *Sama'* – could be expressed with reference to the classical musical tradition of Central Asia. This gradual ascent from quiet to excited stage, typical of mystical forms of Sufism, is very similar to genres of classical music called *Maqam* or *Hal.* So *Zikr* has in those cases a strong musical connection.[239]

The peculiar importance of using Qur'anic words and verses to remember Allah is derived from numerous Qur'anic injunctions, for example, 'So remember me and I will remember you.' Each Sufi order had a *Zikr* of its own, constructed by its founder. The women's *Zikr* in the Ferghana Valley is mostly based on the Yassaviya version, the so-called 'loud' *Zikr Jahriya*. After the climax, the *Otin-Oys* fall into silence. Everything else – daily life, problems and difficulties – seems to diminish and disappear, as if Eternity itself had come to this session. Emotionally, it is an extremely powerful and expressive ritual.

The *Murshid* is the one who selects the *Zikrs* for this spiritual stage. It is also believed that *Zikr* done without the guide's permission is practically useless.[240] The same happens among *Otin-Oys*. At the session described above the order and the method of performing the rites was dictated by the leader of the assembly, by *Otin-Oy* Mutabarak-hola. She was the person to whom everyone turned and she was the person to follow.

As mentioned, there are two types of *Zikr*: *Zikr-i-jali* or *Dashgariya* (loud recitation) and *Zikr-i-khafi* or *Hufiya* (performed with either low voice or silently). If in Naqshbandiyya the second type is used, in Yassaviya, as we showed, *Otin-Oys* follow the loud way. But the silence after the loud *Zikr* with *Otin-Oys* is remarkable. Some of the women were in a trance; others were weeping and repeating the name of Allah. The value and power of the *Zikr* is dependent upon the right level of concentration in body and mind. Only when these are achieved can the believer become identified with the *Zikr*, that is, the object and the subject are the heart illuminated by the divine light. It should be mentioned that the *Zikr* does not allow unity with God. It simply represents the means of purifying the heart.

Concerning the forms of mixed *Zikr*, where both men and women play an equivalent role, we should emphasise that in this region the practice of mixed *Zikr* has existed for centuries back in the history. The same can be seen in other Eastern countries such as Turkey.

An article by Troitskaya provides a very interesting piece of evidence about the existence of *Otin-Oys* in Tashkent at the beginning of the twentieth century. The description of the rite defines the most significant characteristics of this kind of women and of the kind of rituals they performed. For example, Troitskaya interprets the role of *Otin-Oys* as lying in directing *Zikr* with regard to the organisation of the interrelation between the dance rhythm and the rhythm of general cries and weeping.

Photo 15: *Otin-Oys* gathering in Gushtyemas village

However, nowadays this interrelation no longer exists in *Otin-Oy* activity. The *Otin-Oys* of today are content with singing and recital.

As it was mentioned above, each *Otin-Oy*, according to Troitskaya[241] had her very own style. Each performed in a different way. However, my own investigation reveals that a rather distinct similarity in the musical intonation of songs and tunes typical of various *Otin-Oys* can be distinguished within each region. For example, in the settlement of Gushtyemas in the south of Andijan district and in Butakora and Dudur in the north of Andijan region, the same songs based on texts by Mashrab and Uvaysiy are performed in a very similar manner.

And lastly, as Troitskaya points out, *Otin-Oys* covered their mouths with their hands and even with the holy books of Qur'an, trying thereby to decrease the resonance of their voice, relating it to the fact of general whirling in the dance.[242]

There are no analogous examples among modern *Otin-Oys*. At the same time, other new ways have developed. For example, *Otin-Oy* Sabohad from the village Gushtyemas carry out *Zikr* in a sitting position. However, the technique of her body movements is reminiscent of the previous dancing forms of *Zikr*. *Otin-Oy* Sabohad rocks her body smoothly from side to side, from the right to the left. She also uses circular rotational movements of the hands in time for each line, distinctively matching the singing to the character of the hand movements.

Many *Otin-Oys*, indeed, put the holy books to their mouths, but only in an outburst of feelings, in a kiss. An outburst of religious feeling is the more likely explanation for this action, rather than the acoustical moment of the sound regulation.

A number of questions arise when examining this unique phenomenon in the Uzbek culture, the most significant of which appear to be about the particular Sufi orders to which various *Otin-Oys*, and the various rituals carried out by them, belong. Note that in the present day it is quite common for either *Otin-Oys* or their followers to be unable to tell to which Sufi school or order they belong because they don't know the truth. Although this can be determined by the repertoire they use, it can be difficult to distinguish between the followers of *tariqah* of Ahmad Yassaviy, as for example in the Ferghana Valley, and the Naqshbandi followers who dedicate the songs to his name. However, many *Otin-Oys* use parts from both types of repertoire, therefore it is fairly impossible to determine their ritual forms as belonging to one distinct *Tariqah*.

An interesting fact is that similar forms of women's *zikr* are used in Islamic countries in wider Central Asia. So, for example, in Azerbaijan, the women of this kind are called *Marsiya*. Their repertoire depends in many ways on *Shiism*, to which they belong. Many rituals are dedicated to the image of Hussein, a tragic figure in Muslim history. With regard to the technical aspect of the *Zikr* as performed by them, the line of rhythm is strongly accented. Having positioned themselves by the walls and remaining still, the *Marsiya* clap the rhythm line with their right hand on the knee, simultaneously with all participants in the ritual. This method has not been observed in use among the *Otin-Oys* of Uzbekistan.

Similar forms of women's *Zikr* rituals are also practised in Turkey in different Sufi orders. For example, the Sufi rituals of the *Djafari* order, which I had an opportunity to observe in Istanbul in 1997, differ substantially from the women's ritual forms in Uzbekistan mentioned above. First of all, women of Sufi orders of *Djafari* take part in men's rituals too, although separately from men, on the top floor of a mosque. These rituals are carried out in the same building and at the same time, with both men and women simultaneously following the same order for each stage, directed by the Sheikh. Among the *Djafari*, however, the women do not spin in the dance, as men do. But the prayers are the same.

An altogether different picture can be seen in Uzbekistan. Here, women were totally isolated from men's religious practice in the last century, and fully concentrated on female forms of worshipping creating their 'own' space, and style.

38. CURRENT SITUATION: FEMALE
RELIGIOUS SCHOOL IN BUKHARA

The situation with regard to the state female religious education in Uzbekistan has changed. Whereas during Soviet times female students were not allowed to enter Madrasah, these days they are welcomed. In 2006, I visited the only Madrasah for girls' Islamic study in Bukhara. The Madrasah was an impressive building with a number of rooms where girls receive a high standard of education, not only in reading the Qur'an but also in sewing and computer skills. This is a new trend in the traditional form of religious education. Most of these girls obtained a scholarship to study a vocational subject. Girls there are obedient and friendly. They are lucky to have a chance to obtain a diploma at a prestigious academy. Most of them do not plan to take up Qur'an reading as a future profession but just enjoy the years of study before they get married. However, these first steps in official policy made towards Muslim education in Uzbekistan seems to be very successful.

After talking to the girls and staff from an official branch of Muslim education I met the most famous Bukharian Otin-Mullo (Bukhara's name for *Otin-Oy*), a remarkable lady called Rabiya Shukurova (b. 1932). She graduated from the Pedagogical Institution (1953), studied Persian and Arabic, and later even began to study for a PhD, but for some reason did not complete it and later gave it up. She used to be a member of the Communist party, and at one time held a position as a director of the House of Knowledge in Bukhara. In 1976, she retired as a 'personal pensioner' (a privileged form of retirement established in Soviet times). Her father was the famous Ota Mullo, who went to Mecca at the age of only fifteen years. Between 1992 and 2002 she went to the *Hajj* eight times and claimed that it was only possible to achieve this thanks to President Islam Karimov and Uzbek independence. She performed *Suras* from the Qur'an, *Na'ts*, *Mavludes*, *Marhabo*, and *Munojats* in the Uzbek language. She recited the local Sufi poetry but in the same narrative way common in the Ferghana Valley.

Outside state control, religious knowledge is still based on the Sufi repertoire. Therefore, as we can see, even today in Uzbekistan it is still widespread – a sign of its continuity.

10

Female Rituals

39. OTHER RITUALS LED BY *OTIN-OY*

At first sight, it would seem that Uzbek daily life follows standard Muslim forms of practice. For example, one can find that female religious rituals in Uzbekistan are based on well-established canons, echoing the rest of the Muslim world. So, for instance, in the morning prayers, Uzbeks begin with the sacred formula *Shahada*, expressing belief in a uniform God, Allah (*La-illaha-illa-Allah va Muhammadu-Rassulu-Allah*). Like all other Muslims, Uzbeks undertake *Namaz*, the practice of five daily prayers. On Friday, a special collective prayer known as *Djuma-Namaz* takes place in the mosque, accompanied by a sermon, *Hutba*. Following the attainment of independence by Uzbekistan and other neighbouring republics of Central Asia, it became popular once again to keep *Uraza*, a religious fast lasting thirty days, also known as *Ramadan*, the holy month, occurring every ninth month of the lunar calendar. Also, despite financial difficulties, many people have recently taken part in *Zull-Hajj*, the sacred pilgrimage to Mecca, which takes place in the first ten days of the twelfth lunar month. The end of *Hajj* marks the arrival of *Kurban-Bairam-Hait*, the main Muslim celebration and the equivalent of the European New Year. Likewise, the tradition of charitable acts made for the benefit of the community is highly regarded in Uzbek society. So, one could maintain that these common forms of religious practice correspond to the equivalent practice prevailing in the other countries of the Muslim East.

However, following the difficulties of survival underground during the Soviet era, the phenomenon in question gradually changed, developed, and acquired new features. Since rituals occupy an important place in the traditional life of the residents of rural areas of the region, they have become a daily occurrence among the agricultural population, which engages in a variety of ceremonies accompanying most of life's events. In urban environments, ritual is less noticeable, since the notion of collective and family bonds has always been less dominant compared with the communal and strictly hierarchical familial life in the village environment.

Nowadays, two predominant types of ceremony can be found:

1) Ceremonies to mark 'Rites of Passage'[243] in the transitional events of life such as birth, initiation into Islam, marriage, death.
2) Ceremonies tailored to the context of the occasion, whatever the content, but retaining some standard generalised form.

Thus the repertoire of ceremonies that *Otin-Oy* perform within the female community can be divided into three main categories:

1) Religious, quasi-Sufi rituals, built around religious events.
2) 'Rites of Passage': birth, circumcision, marriage, mourning.
3) Calendar events: pre-Islamic New Year Celebration, *Navruz.*

Before looking at religious, quasi-Sufi rituals, built around religious events, let us examine the background to all the rituals led by *Otin-Oy*. It is remarkable that such a system of rituals, typical of the inhabitants of the given region, fully reflects the world outlook of the Uzbek Muslims. For them, rituals have always represented a vital part of the school of life, along with the cosmological system and models of social hierarchies established by the word of Allah.

During Soviet times, however, since religion was seen as 'the opium of the people' its practice was banned by the Soviet state. In this context, the elaborate system of ritual practice essentially remained the exclusive medium, a cultural oasis in a way, which provided the strongest bonds between the present and the past by allowing people from different generations to interact and to pass historical knowledge down the family line. The true significance of this phenomenon and its impact is assessed in the socio-historical key below.

On the whole, each individual ritual represents a compound construction where obligatory pieces are alternated with derived variations. The common feature of all rituals performed by *Otin-Oy* is defined by a number of independent pieces strung like beads onto the thread of a particular subject relevant to the occasion. The similarity of content is maintained within the frame of the same cosmological idea of progression from characters inhabiting the Heavens to people on Earth (from Allah and the Prophet to Sufis, and further to heroes and accounts of exceptional human destinies) and then ascending back to the God. Thus, in essence, this performance structure projects all the complexity of the universe in a compressed form, focusing on its relevance to the persons concerned by involving them in this circle from God to Man to God, reflecting the hierarchy of values of Muslim culture.

Each individual composite piece is framed with *Bismillahir-Rahmanir-Rahim*, thus emphasising the link between the poetic and musical aspects from the beginning. This link encourages the transference of observers or participants from the reality of life's daily chores to the dimension of the spiritual world.

All kinds of eulogy are performed according to a predetermined order, following the established hierarchical structure. The opening reference to Allah gradually proceeds to praising the Prophet, then moving on to the sacred spirits, and so on. Finally, the subject of the event is addressed. The link between the subject, whatever it may be, and the main story line is made using an allegory, or simply by acknowledging the fact around which the event occurs via direct statements, such as 'Yes, let the newly-wed couple be happy! May their life be prosperous!' in the case of a wedding, or, in the event of death: 'Allah is great! There must be a reason He takes away the best people, close people.'

Use of standardised verbal expressions in these rituals is very common. The more skilled the *Otin-Oy*, the greater the ease with which she manipulates her repertoire, and the more natural is the transition between the past and the present event. Whatever the subject of the assembly, whether it is a religious holiday or secular event, the religious part of the ritual often reaches sizeable proportions and involves considerable complexity.

Essentially, religious fragments are followed by examples of high poetic skill and refined classical culture, rich in terms of philosophical heritage, followed by tales from the lives of the famous and then succeeded by educational stories from everyday life. Mythical text is very often used in the course of these rituals. For religion, there is a superabundance of material (hymns, prayers, myths, prescriptions for rituals) and virtually every kind of text has its religious elements, such as blessings invoked on the recipients of letters. For love, the quantity is much less, and much of the literary material is in fact concerned with religion: religious love poetry.[244]

The length of the ritual is determined by the significance of the event taking place, the time of the day and the number of guests involved. The above factors can be accommodated by the flexible nature of the ritual. However, the shortest variant of a performance lasts approximately one hour, while the longest rituals I have observed have continued for about twelve hours.

40. CLASSIFICATION OF RELIGIOUS RITUALS LED BY *OTIN-OY*

These rituals can be classified in two ways according to:

1) religious events around which they are built;
2) genres which are performed within them.

Religious Events

Religious events are common for the whole Muslim world, though some of them have specific local importance. They are:

Mavlyudi Sharif (**Holy Birth**)   The birthday of the Prophet Muhammad, which is celebrated with constant prayer and religious singing.

Ramadan (**or** *Uraza*)   This is the sacred month in Muslim history when the Qur'an was revealed. This is a month of fasting in the Muslim tradition. During this holiday, *Otin-Oys* are very welcome in every family, because they bless these families during the holy month. They pay particular attention to the oldest members of the neighbourhood, the sick, the disabled, orphans, and the less fortunate. Sometimes they set up *Zikr* rituals to commemorate this sacred month.

Laylatul Qadr (**the Night of Destiny**)   The twenty-seventh night of Holy *Ramadan*, when the Qur'an was revealed to the Prophet Muhammad.

Iyd-ul Ramadan (*Ramazon hayit*)   End of *Ramadan* celebrations, when Muslims go to the mosque for the final prayers of *Ramadan*, and visit their relatives, the sick, and people in need.

Qurban-Haiyt   The celebration of Sacrifice devoted to the story of Abraham, who was asked by God to sacrifice his son but was then given a ram by Allah to sacrifice instead. In this celebration at the end of *Hajj*, people slaughter lambs as an offering, while praying and singing religious songs.

Ashir-Oy (**Commemoration of the Imams' death**)   Imams are the descendants of the Prophet Muhammad, and Ali, his son-in-law. The sons of Ali, Imams Hasan and Hussein, were killed in the fight between different factions. Their death is considered a holy death and is commemorated especially by Shia Muslims.

Miradzh   A holy day, devoted to the ascension of the Prophet Muhammad to God's presence.

Hudoyi   This normally takes place to mark three, seven, and forty days, six months and one year of mourning. In modern Uzbekistan it is also the most common event for expression of any kind of gratitude to God. It takes place on a range of very different occasions indeed: a recovery after a long illness; a happy return from a long journey; return of a son from the military service; a child's enrolment at university, and so on. There are many such happenings both in the rural and in the urban areas. It is performed within female gatherings where the *Otin-Oy* conducts the event with prayer and recitations of the ancient poetry of Ahmad Yassavi, Mashrab, Alisher Navoiy, Nodira, Uvaysiy, or others to make the occasion as sacred, and to thank God.

Mushkul Kushod (**Sorting out complications**)   This female ritual can be performed at any time when a problem or a complication arises in someone's life. It could be to do with religious or daily life, but generally it is considered that the ritual itself is performed in an Islamic way, which resolves the problem by the grace of Allah.

Thus it can be seen that the system of rituals represents not a casual range of performances, but a harmonic space of songs and sounds, targeting every Muslim in the community, underpinning any important life event.

So Uzbek society, in keeping the tradition through the long years of different cataclysmic events, kept for itself the right to its own sounds and songs rooted in the past. They are still widely performed within the villages and various districts. Today one can 'book' a professional *Otin-Oy* for any family occasion even in Tashkent.

Genres   The *Otin-Oy's* range of ritual performance in the second dimension of our classification is very broad. It comprises different genres, but all of them commence with the same introduction

Bismilla-Ir-rahmanim-rahim and end with the formula *Allahu akbar*. This prayer-like frame is obligatory for any of the compulsory parts of ritual. According to my extensive field observations, many ritual sessions begin with *Fatiha* which are the opening *Sura* from the Qur'an.

Al-Hamdu Lillahi Rabbil Aalamin. Arrahmanir Raheem. Maliki yawmiddeen. Iyyaka naabudu wa iyyaka nastaiin. Ihdinassiratal mustaqueem. Siratal latheena anaamta aleihem gheiril maghdoobi aleihem walad dalleen. Ameen. It means 'Praise be to Allah the Lord of the worlds. Most Gracious. Most Merciful. Master of the Day of Judgement. Thee do we worship and thine aid we seek. Show us the straight way. The way of those on whom Thou hast bestowed Thy Grace. Those whose (portion) is not wrath. And who do not stray.'

Then they swiftly move to different stories from Islamic history and then to Sufi or mystic poetry. In general, the order of these chantings runs through from slow to more vivid and dynamic sections, ending up with short concluding chant. I would suggest that all rituals could be classified under different groups according to their poetic content and forms in following way:

1) **Classic poetic forms:** *Ghazals, Murabba, Muhammas,* and all the complex Sufi poetry of Ahmad Yassaviy, Mashrab, Uvaysiy (1779–1845), Nodira (1792–1842), and other poets. These forms sometimes include extracts from famous *Ghazals* by other poets like Hazini or Sufi Allahyor;

2) **Elegies:** *Arwah-noma, Musa-noma, Qiyomat-noma, Hikmats,* or wisdom from Ahmad Yassaviy;

3) **Epic parables:** A kind of rhythmic prose describing holy people or events, such as *Ser malyak, There lived a man in Bagdad, Dediyo,* including *Hazrat Imam* (a didactic story about the death of Imam Hussein);

4) **Original songs** created by the most remarkable *Otin-Oys* themselves. For instance, the song below, which could be called 'The lament of an infertile woman'. This song by Malika Asqarova comprises the features of all genres mentioned above, plus the private biography of her neighbour and friend, who is a barren woman.

Oh God, why did you create
Such a vagabond and stranger as I?
I am a gardener in the garden

Who has not taken into account
The number of pomegranates
I am the seedless one...

However, the main classification of those rituals I would suggest is based on the **order of different Islamic chanting and hymns**. In fact, there is no fixed set patterns for ritual development but a free style is used. It depends on the area of performance (so, in Ferghana Valley rituals are mostly based on local Sufi poems), the *Otin-Oy's* preference (the older the *Otin-Oy*, the wider the collection of *Ghazals* performed) or the reason for the ritual performance (for mourning, for example, the rituals are longer than for weddings and there are more genres involved). However, in general, rituals in my observations can be listed as follows:

1) **Songs or recitals of glorification**, an elaborate system of praise which includes all kinds of important characters in Muslim history at different levels and which renders to each holy person his due. These can be subdivided into separate subjects of praise or glorification:

   a) *Hamd*, praising Allah, which is the most important type of glorification. For example: *Qul hu allah subhan allah wird aylasam -a hu, biry borim diydoringni ko'rarmanmu?!* (Say he is Allah, holy Allah, if I meditate, can I see your face?), also introduced below *Antalho, Qulho Alloh*, etc.

   b) *Na't*, praises to the Prophet Muhammad and other Prophets such as Musa, Adam, Ibrahim. For example: *Bugun na'tingni aytarman...* (Today I shall glorify you, O our Prophet...), see below (*Assalavotu Vassalam, buguin ba'ttingni aytayin, Assalotun-Assalom*), etc.

   c) *Madh*, praises:
   for the followers and companions of Muhammad (Halifas Abu-Bekr, Umar, Usman, Ali);
   for Hussein, the grandson of Muhammad, who was tragically killed (see below: Dediyor, Ashur oy kissalari; Ser Malak);
   for the founders of the Mazhabs or commandments of Islam famous in Central Asia, for example, Ghavsul Aghzam Hanafi (see below 'Ghavsul Aghzam Hanafi');

151

for the leaders of the Sufi *tariqats* (orders) well known in Central Asia, people like Ahmad Yassavi, Naqshbandi, and so on (see Hojam Bahovaddindur);

for religious Sufi poets popular in that area, such as Mashrab (1657–1711), Sufi Allahyar (seventeenth century), and other poet-mystics, who wrote in Turkic (Chagatai) or in Persian languages.

Some of these chantings could be seen as songs or recitals of repentance and sorrow: *Tawba tazarru* (songs of repentance), *Arwahnamas* (pacification of spirit), *Qiyomat-noma* (description of the Day of Judgement), *Musa-noma* (adventures of Prophet Moses), and so on.

All these types of chanting and praises at such gathering, and singing, fall under the general term *O'qish*, and are ultimately dedicated to Allah.

41. *O'QISH* (READING) AS A RITUAL SESSION

All genres of religious rituals in Central Asia can be covered by this term. Since Islam is a religion based on the Word (the two most important sources of Islam are based on the Word – Qur'an is the Word of Allah, and Hadiths are Words of the Prophet Muhammad), so religious reading of these words is the main sacred function. First of all these texts, *Suras* from Qur'an and sayings of the Prophet Muhammad, are read to bless any kind of event. However, performance can take another form with poetry reading, such as a range of Sufi *ghazals, murabba' or muhammas*.

The main authors of these are Ahmad Yassavi (thirteenth century), Sufi Allahyor (eighteenth century), Mashrab (eighteenth century), Sadoyi (nineteenth century), Haziniy (nineteenth century), Uvaysiy (nineteenth century), and others. Each recitation is enclosed within the traditional frame called *Dua* – *Bismillah-i-rahman-i-rahim* and concludes with the formula *Allahu akbar*. This framing suggests the special religious purpose of the performed texts, devoting them to the ear and the name of the Almighty.

Here are some examples of the poems, read by *Otin-Oy* on different religious occasions. The *Hamd*, which I recorded in 1999 is *Murabba'* of the great Sufi saint and poet Ahmad Yassaviy which was also performed as the climax of a female Sufi *Zikr*.

Bismillohi rahmoni rahim!
Qul hu Alloh, subhon Alloh, vird aylasam, a hu!
Biri borim diydoringni ko 'rarmanmu?

Ellik yoshda cho 'llar kezib giyoh o 'rdim,
Tonglar chiqib toat qilib ko 'zim o 'ydim,
Diydoringni ko 'rarman deb, jondin to 'ydim,
Biri borim diydoringni ko 'rarmanmu?
Boshdin ayoq hasratingda vird aylasam,
Ellik ikki yoshda kechdim xonumondin,
Tark ayladim xonumon ne, balki jondin,
Biri borim diydoringni ko 'rarmanmu?
Ellik uchda vaqt topmayin ro 'za qildim,
Gumroh edim, yo 'ldin ozdim, yo 'lga solding,
Alloh dedim, labbay debon qo 'lim olding,
Biri borim diydoringni ko 'rarmanmu?

If I acknowledge in meditation, saying 'God is unique, God is holy'
Will I ever see your face, oh, the Almighty?
At fifty years of age I roamed the steppes, collecting grasses,
Praying at sunrise, tearing my eyes out,
Wishing to see your beauty, I felt satiated with life,
Will I ever see your face, oh, the Almighty?
If from head to toe I am struck with suffering in my wish to see you,
At fifty-two, having disowned myself,
Having let go of all my wealth,
And even leaving my life behind,
Will I ever see your face, oh, the Almighty?
At fifty-three I have devoted myself to the fast,
Despite the time I was lost, He showed me the right way.
I said 'Allah!' He replied 'I am here!' and took me by the hand,
Will I ever see your face, oh, the Almighty?
Will I ever see your face, oh, the Almighty?

Hamd *or Praise of Martyrs, Saints, Sufi Masters*

Hamd devoted to Hasan and Hussein are usually read during the month of *Ashura*, when they were martyred. The repertoire of the *Otin-Oy* is very rich in long poems devoted to that tragic event. For instance, the genre *Dediyo* (He said…) is in Uzbek a synonym for something infinitely long and monotonous. Here are some fragments, which I recorded in the Ferghana Valley.

Dediyo

Ul xuvorishlar imomni tiyra boron qildilar,
Otni uzra o'zin tutolmay qonsirab yiqildilar,
Yiqilib maydonda qoldi, o'rnidin turolmadi,
Zulfiqori ilkidin bir pecha yerga tushdi,

Holi yo'q borib qilichin qo'liga olgan imom,
Mehribonini ko'rdi, Duldurdin imom ayrildiyo,
Na'ra aylab yuz ila ko'zin bo'yab, faryod urub,
Vo Husseino, vo g'aribo, vo shahido dediyo,
Bu huvorishlar beki Abdul Umar sayid dedi:
Bu nechuk nola undir, na fig'on bu dediyo...

These *huvorishes* were subjected to an avalanche of stones,
He (Imam Hussein), failing to hold on to his horse, fell, covered in blood.
There, in the square, he remained motionless, unable to get up,
His locks touching bare earth
In his weakness, he lifted himself up and having taken his sword in his arms, oh, Imam,
Recalling the face of his loved one Mehribon,
He let the stallion Duldur go with his powerless hand...
And at this moment she wailed, full of tears:
'Oh, Hussein, oh wanderer, oh martyr, who died for his Faith!'

Below is a famous lament for the memory of martyred Hussein to be read in the month of *Ashura* to raise awareness of the facts of Islamic history.

Ashur oy kissalari (Anthems of the month of *Ashura*)

Bismillahi-r-rahmoni-r-rahiim!
Ketdi olamdin netay, ul vasli poki Mustafo,
Tomib bo'ldi bu jahondin nuri poki murtazo,
Hazrati Fotimaning, do'stlar, jigarbandi qani?
Kimga aytay bu alamni, naylayin, vo xasrato!
Bu ko'zim ko'r bo'lgani yaxshi edi, ey do'stlar,
Ko'rmagay erdim koshki bu holda, ey saido!
Yuragim afgor bo'ldi, vo Husseino, vo Husseino!
Naylayin, qismat, bu tanglikka bo'lubman mubtalo,
Dod etarman ul kuni yazidlar qo'lida yavmi jazo,
Hazrati Qahhorni oldida ul mahshar aro,
Vo imomo, vo Husseino, yoru jonim qaydasan,
Tashlabon ketding meni, ey shahidi Karbalo!

Bismillahi-r-rahmoni-r-rahiim!
He has left this world, the noble Hussein,
His clear light has left this world,
Where, my friends, is the flesh and blood born of Fatima's flesh and blood?
Whom can I tell of my unhappiness?
What can I do in this suffering?

I would rather go blind, my friends,
Oh, how I wish I could see him!
My heart is broken, Hussein, oh, Hussein,
What can I do, I am destined to live this fate,
I cry on this day when he suffered from the hands of his *yazids*.[245]
On the Judgement Day you will rise and stand next to your stern Lord.
Oh, Imam, oh Hussein, where are you, my soul?
You left here me and departed, oh victim of *Karbala*.[246]

The legend of *Ser Malak* (Seven Angels)

This is a popular story about the sacred dish *Ser-malak* which was served in the whole of Central Asia for the pre-Islamic New Year celebration *Navruz*.

Hasan and Hussein were once left hungry,
And Fatima-Zuhra put into the pot a bunch of grasses and pebbles.
Around the pot gathered angels:
And this is why The Prophet called this dish *Ser-malak*
Oh, the Prophet of both worlds and his *khalifs*,
I will devote my soul to God, to Prophets
and their faithful followers
and two princes Hasan and Hussein,
sons of Fatima and favourites of Muhammad.
Oh, the Prophet of both worlds
Muhammad and his *khalif* Ali threw a wedding feast for his children
and all the friends gathered round
Everyone stood with hands respectfully folded, bowing.
The prophet named this dish *Ser-malak*
It is made of a bunch of grasses and stones
all the birds that land on these grasses and stones turn into nightingales.
Oh, the Prophet of both worlds and his *khalifs*,
Whoever cooks *Ser-malak* is kind,
and whoever takes part in making it will go to heaven.

Hamd devoted to other saints and Sufi masters are read on different occasions, but mostly either during spiritual Sufi gatherings (*Gap*), or as an introductory part of Sufi *Zikr*, or during other religious rituals like *Hudoyi* (Remembrance), *Mushkul Kushod* (Sorting out complications), in order to ask for help and protection from those saints and Sufi masters. Here is an example of *Hamd*, recorded in Ferghana Valley, which is sung in a peaceful way and creates a very positive kind atmosphere. It is devoted to

Bahouddin Naqshband, the founder of the Naqshbandiyya Sufi order, asking his protection and help:

Bahovaddin piri balogardon
Bismillahi-rahmoni-r-rahiim!
Bismillahi-rahmoni-r-rahiim!
Ta'rif aylayman yozib, Xojam Bahovaddindur,
Avliyolar sarasi Xojam Bahovaddindur,

Olti oy yaratti jabbor Xoja Ahmaddin muhtor,
Qolgan qutgan baloga ham dardi bedavoga,
Xush kelibdur ochunga Xojam Bahovaddindur,

Hozir qilgan g'oyibni, tuzuk qilgan yomonni,
Maqsudiga loyiqdir, Xojam Bahovaddindur,

Haq yo'lini ko'rsatgan, botinini tuzatgan,
Lavhulqalamga yetgan Xojam Bahovaddindur.

To describe Hodja Bahovatdin...
He was the best of the holy men, Hodja Bahovatdin,
For six months God was busy creating the disciple of Hodja Ahmad,
To deal with all troubles and incurable diseases.
Welcome to this world, my dear Hodja Bahovatdin,
Revealing the hidden, turning bad into good.
Staying true to his aim, Hodja Bahovatdin,
The one who showed the righteous way and made hidden truths clear,
The one who has grasped the Heavenly Scriptures,

Hodja Bahovatdin...

Na't *or Praise of Prophet Muhammad*

Examples of *Na't* are usually performed during the *Mavlyud* ritual, which celebrates Prophet Muhammad's birthday. Usually *Otin-Oys* start with the meaning of the *Mavlyud.* They say that *Mavlyud* occurs on the twelfth of every *Rabbiul avval* month, when the Prophet Muhammad was born. He brought the light of Islam into this world and his *umma* should celebrate *Mavlyud* because of that. After the explanation of *Mavlyud's* meaning and importance *Otin-Oys* give an example of *Salavat* or hymn to praise the Prophet:

Bismillohu rahmonir rahim
Assalavotu vassalam alayka yo rasulullah,

Assalavotu vassalam alayka yo nabiullah;
Assalavotu vassalam alayka yo habibullah,
Assalavotu vassalam alayka yo shafi'ullah
Assalavotu vassalam alayka yo hayru halqullah.

Praise and peace upon you, O messenger of Allah
Praise and peace upon you, O prophet of Allah
Praise and peace upon you, O beloved of Allah
Praise and peace upon you, O closest of Allah
Praise and peace upon you, O blessing of people of Allah

Then *Otin-Oy* reads an Arabic prayer, which is followed once again by
another anthem *Salavat.*

Bugun na'tingni aytayin yo rasulu saidi barno,
Tufaylidin bino bo'ldi zaminu osmon barpo.
Mani hamdu na'ti sifoti mustafo qilmoq,
Xudo lutfi karam birla zabonim ayladi go'yo.
Anoning qornidin tushgan zamon yig'lab dedi ul mard:
Tamomi ummatimni mag'firat qil xudovando.
Tamomi anbiyo kelib ul kun salom qildi,
Kelib xizmatida turdilar Odam bilan Havvo.
Maloik birla g'ilmonlar saf-saf bo'lib turdi,
Etti qat osmonda hech maloik qolmadi aslo.
Yetib kelib Jabroil ham ayladi xizmat,
Bu olamni yaratti nuri poki ul habibulloh.

Today I will praise you, O Prophet,
From something you created Earth and Heavens.
Whereas me, o Prophet, in order to praise your virtues,
God has blessed me with a Tongue and Word.
As soon as he emerged from his mother's womb,
He said: guide my community to the true way,
O God, all the spirits of Prophets came that day to bow to him,
Adam and Eve stood ready to serve him.
All Angels and Archangels stood in rows and columns before him,
Not one angel remained in the Heavens.
Even Archangel Gabriel came to serve him,
And this day was lit up with a bright light.

Then the following hymn is usually sung by all participants in the gathering. After the chanting by the *Otin-Oy* has finished, the gathering ends with

the final prayer, which is also read initially in Uzbek but which concludes with Arabic verses.

> Salavat *Assalotun-Assalom*: Anthem devoted to the Prophet Muhammad
> *Assalomu, assalomu amini yo habibullo,*
> *Assalomu, assalomu amini yo rasulillo,*
> *Assalomu, assalomu amini yo sahihullo...*

> We pray and wish for peace, oh God's messenger,
> Pray and wish for peace, oh God's favourite,
> Pray and wish for peace, oh righteous one,
> Pray and wish for peace, oh king of love to people.

> Welcome into this world, oh, the leader of all forces of the world,
> The messenger of all living things,
> Welcome, the Ruler of the Universe,
> And of all views of the skies and the earth!
> Welcome, oh, the one who gives approval on behalf of God,
> One who can salute into the world of nothing!

Songs and poems of repentance and sorrow

Those poems as a rule are performed by *Otin-Oys* during funerals. Funeral rituals vary greatly in different areas of Central Asia and in Uzbekistan, but there are some elements which can be seen throughout the region. When a person dies, he or she should be washed by women, who weep while they do this, reciting poems. According to Muslim rules, the body must be buried as soon as possible before the sunset. Before burial, men take the body to the mosque, where *Janaza* or the Prayer for the Dead is recited and then the body is buried.

All this time, women in the house do not just weep but, led by *Otin-Oy*, read prayers for the dead, perform *Zikr* and sing songs of repentance, usually for three days and three nights. Therefore, this part of an *Otin-Oy*'s repertoire is particularly rich. They include first of all *Tawba-tazarru* (repentance) prayers.

Muhammas

> *Qodir Alloh', o'zing bo'lgil panohim,*
> *Rah'm ailagil manga qodri Alloh'im,*
> *Raqibimni yer ailadim, ilohim,*
> *Man nailayin, h'olim taboh' bo'ldimu?*
> *Man nailayin, bah'tim qaro bo'ldimu*
> *Kundin kunga dardim bo'ldi zieyda,*

Man nailain, etolmadim muroda,
Eyrsiz, eyrsiz yig'lab o'tsam dunyoda,
Va h'asrato, umrim ado bo'ldimu?

O'tkaribman yigitlikning chog'ini,
Kimga aitai eylg'izlikning dog'ini,
H'ason ailai umrim ohir bog'ini,
Man nailayinm ho'lim taboh' bo'ldimu?
Man nailayin, bah'tim qaro bo'ldimu?

Mungim aitur bu duneyda kimim bor,
Eylg'izliqdin maning yuz ming dardim bor,
Keng jahon ko'zimga sindopn kabi tor,
Man nailayin, h'olim taboh' bo'ldimu?
Man nailayin, bah'tim qaro bo'ldimu?

Oh Almighty God, Allah, be my protector!
Mercy me, oh Almighty Allah.
I made my friend my enemy, oh my God,
What am I to do, I find myself in an irresolvable situation?
What am I to do, have my happiness and luck turned black?

From day to day my troubles have multiplied,
What am I to do, I have not fulfilled my aim?
If I walk through this world of the loved one,
Oh, has my life really come to an end?
If I walk it crying in loneliness,
Oh, Almighty, has my life really come to an end?

My youth has flown away,
Whom can I tell about my loneliness?
Should I turn the garden of my life into Autumn,
What am I to do in this desperate situation?
What am I to do, has my happiness really been blackened?
Whom can I tell of my sadness?

In my loneliness there lurk a hundred thousand sufferings,
Has the big wide world turned into prison to my eyes?
What am I to do in this irresolvable situation?
What am I to do, has my happiness really been blackened?

Arwah-noma (Song of the Dead) The poem is performed on behalf of the dead person. According to local tradition, professional attendants called *G'assol* wash the body before it is taken to the cemetery for burial.

Och yuzim, g'assol, bu dam yorug' jahonni bir ko'ray,
Bu jahonda yaxshilik qilg'onlarimni bir ko'ray,
Necha yil, necha zamon bu dunyoda sayr ayladim,
Ro'zgor aylab o'zimni necha yor-yor ayladim,
Oqibat yotgan yerim shu bo'ldi nochor ayladim,
Och yuzim, g'assol, bu dam yorug' jahonni bir ko'ray.

Open my face, washing person, let me see the world for a moment,
Let me see my good deeds in this world,
I was walking around for years and years,
Busy with daily life,
But my final destination is here, I'm helpless,
Open my face, washing person, let me see the world for a moment.

Usually, poems which are recited on these sombre occasions are quite solemn. Their subject is Death, Hereafter, and the Day of Judgement and confessions, introducing emotional monologue addressed to God. I recorded some examples of this genre in the Ferghana Valley.

Qiyomat-noma (Song of the Day of Judgement)

Xudovando, gunohimdin man sharmandai rasvo,
Agarchi men yomonman, yaxshisan ey olimu dono,
Ishim doim gunoh bo'ldi, tilimda g'iybatu yolg'on,
Agar bo'lsa qiyomat kun, mani holimga dod ayla.
Xudovando, nechuk arzim qabul etsang qiyomat kun,
Qo'limda bo'lmasa bir zarra toatu taqvo.
Yotib g'aflat bilan doim tilimda sarbasar rohat,
Yana sandin tilar ko'nglim xazoro jannati ma'vo.

Oh God, I am ashamed of my sins,
Even if I am bad, You are good, You, all-knowing, all-learned.
My actions were always sinful,
On the tip of my tongue always gossip and lies,
When Judgement Day comes,
Please have pity on me, my sorry state,
Oh God, please accept my repentance,
On Judgement Day, will you forgive me
Even if I have no shred of decency?
I have been drowned in ignorance, although my tongue has always been in bliss.
And at the same time, my soul is left wanting from you a thousand heavens....

Here is another version by Malika Askarova from the village Dudur in Andijan Province:

Qiyomat-Noma (Judgement Day song)

Ayo do'stlar, qiyomat kun bo'lgonida,
Turli tuman alomatlar bo'lar emish.
Ul zamon mahshar tongi otkonida,
Ul oftob mag'rib sari botar emish.

Qiyomat kun bo'lgonini barcha bilgay,
Tog'u toshga boshin urib zor qilgay,
Yoqa ushlab, yig'lab yuz ming tavba qilgay,
Tavbam qabul bo'lmas debon aytar emish.

Avvaliga ketgay xalqdin mehru shafqat,
Hech qolmag'ay olam aro nozu ne'mat,
Andin so'ngra ko'tarilgay Qurondi xat,
Olam ichra yuz ming balo yog'ar emish.

Qurib qolg'ay yer yuzida shuncha daryo,
Arshdin bo'lak urib ko'char gunash yo,
Osmondin boron yog'mas, simas giyo,
Qudratidin pora-pora bo'lar emish.

Andin so'ngra yer yuziga o't yoqilg'ay,
Tog'u toshlar o'shal kunda titrab turg'ay,
Ikki olam bir-biriga hozir turg'ay,
Bihisht-do'zah anda hozir bo'lar emish.

Oftob kirgay o'shal kun turfa jo'shga,
Hmma hilqat ko'zi to'lg'ay qonli yoshga,
Qazo dasti jabru jafo solsa boshga,
Harna kelsa ojiz banda ko'rar emish.

When the Day of Judgement comes,
Various signs will reveal it,
When the morning comes, the sun will already be in the West.
Everyone will realise, it is Judgement Day.
They will throw themselves on the rocks, in repentance,
Clutching the collars of their robes,
Screaming cries, people will plead in repentance a thousand times,

Although in the knowledge that repentance then is of no value,
For mercy towards people will be gone,
And all beauties of the world will disappear,
And the letters of the Qur'an will rise.

Or another, poetic view of the same subject by Sufi Allahyor:

Gunoh'im bora-bora tog'din oshdi,
Qiyemat kun mani sharmanda qilma,
Boshim eystiqdayu, jonim ketarda,
Tanim, borim lah'aed ichra yetarda,
Sirot otliq guzargoh'dan o'tarda,
Qieymat kun mani sharmanda qilma.
Dudim qarosini oq ailagaisan,
Muhammaddin manga eyd ailagaisan,
Turar vaq'tdao'zing bandam degaisan,
Qieymat kun mani sharmanda qilma

The heap of my sins shadows mountain tops,
Do not disgrace me on the Day of Judgement!
When my head rests on the pillow, and my soul is about to leave,
When my body reaches the grave, when I cross the bridge called Sirat,
On the Judgement Day, do not shame me,
Make my black breathe white.
Remind me of Muhammad,
In the instance of Resurrection say yourself, my Lord,
Do not disgrace me on the Judgement Day:
'My sins are countless,
I came alone seeking your abode,
Please pity your poor slave',
Do not disgrace me on Judgement Day!

Didactic and Other Songs and Poems Read by Otin-Oy

These songs and poems may be read by *Otin-Oy* on different occasions, including those already mentioned, as well as all kind of religious festivities – *Qurban-Haiyt, Ramazan Hayit, Laylatul Qadr, Miradj*, and so on. Usually they are included in *Bayaz* (collections of poems) and are written by famous Sufi poets of different epochs. Here are poems by Ahmad Yassaviy, Sufi Allahyor, Mashrab, and female Sufi poet Uvaysiy. Other examples are given in the Appendix.

Hikmat Ahmad Yassaviy

Endi adashdim do'stlar, kelgan yo'limdan.
Endi adashdim do'stlar, kelgan yo'limdan.
Turgan davlatlarim ketdi qo'limdan
Ayrildim do'stlar yolg'iz gulimdan
Hechkim qutilmas dod faryod o'limdan,
Hechkim qutilmas dod ushbu olimdan

Dunyoni harqiz poyoni yo'qdur
Ishqsiz kishilami imoni yo'qdur
Omonli qo'llar o'lgani yo'qdur
Hechkim qutilmas dod faryod o'limdan
Hechkim qutilmas dod ushbu olimdan

Now I have lost my way, oh friends!
Now I have truly lost my way, my friends!
All my wealth and riches have fallen through my fingers,
I have parted, my friends, with the one and only flower – my Rose,
No one can avoid or save themselves from their death,
There are no thoughts of light,
No faith in people, without love.
Believers do not perish
No one avoids their death!
Realise every day of your life is fleeting,
Because in the world is such suffering…
Death has not even spared Adam.
All Prophets, kings and paupers –
No one avoids death!

Ghazal Sufi Allahyor

Teshdi ko'ksim, ezdi bag'rim,
Teshdi ko'ksim, ezdi bag'rim,
Dog'i h'ijronim manim,
Bu alamda muncha g'amda
Chiqmagan jonim manim.
Dardda ulsam, g'amda so'lsam,
Telba bo'sam ishqida,
H'asratida bundai bo'lsam
yo'qdur armonim manim.
H'asratim bor, h'asratim, behad fig'onim beadad,
Qil madad mandek yiqilgan qulga sultonim madad,
G'ussaeydur g'ussaye, mushkulga qoldim ei vali,
Obi gil ichra hijil qolgan tab'u jonim manim

The suffering of parting has stepped on my chest and crushed me,
In this suffering there is so much sadness,
The soul has not left me.
If I die in suffering, if I wilt away in my sadness,
If I go mad from my love for him,
If in longing for him, I become like that,
I have no regret.

I have yearning, suffering,
My moans are countless and eternal,
My cries are countless and eternal,
Help your slave, oh my Sultan!
I made a move towards difficulties,
My heart and soul remain trapped in the net.

Ghazal Mashrab

Yi'glasam vaqti duo bo'lgaymukin?
Ko'z yoshim dardi gado bo'lgaymukin?
Bodai oshiq muhabbatdin ichib,
Shavkati dunyo judo bo'lgaymukin?
Bosh ura keldim saning dargohinga,
Bir madadkorim xudo bo'lgaymukin?
Yig'lamoqdin o'zga imkon qolmadi,
Yordin manga nido bo'lgaymukin?
Qaysi bir dardimni aytay, do'stlaro,
O'lmayin dardim ado bo'lgaymukin?
Yoro kuydirdi mani, holim xarob,
Arz etarga dod etib bo'lgaymukin?
Telba Mashrab yig'lab o't yori bino,
Rabbiul-avval desam bo'lgaymukin?

If I cried, would the time of my prayer descend upon me?
Would my tears be the suffering, the pain of a pauper?
Having tasted the wine of love, would I lose the glory of this world?
I have come to You, bowing low
Will God help me, comfort me?
There is nothing left to do, but cry,
Will I receive a reply from my beloved?
Which one of my troubles should I start telling you about first, my friends?
Will all my sufferings end before the day I die?
My beloved burnt me, together with what little I possessed,
Could I still complain to the one who listens to complaints?
Cry, crazy Mashrab, seeing your beloved.
Maybe you should shout out 'rabbii-ul-avval'!
So that a new Prophet is born and your dreams are fulfilled.

Ghazal Uvaysiy

San dunyo, san dunyo,
Sanga kelib kimning ko'ngli shod bo'ldi?
Ma'buding yo'q, kundin kunga badtarsan,

Sanga kelib kimning ko'ngli shod bo'ldi?
Hazrati Odamni hayron aylading,
Havvoni Chashmi giryon aylading…

Oh, world! Oh, world!
Having come to you with an open heart
I have not found anyone, in you, oh world,
Whom I could worship,
Every day you turn increasingly worse to all
And to me, the one who has come to you with an open heart.
You surprise me, oh, the world of the Adam, our Great father,
You, the world, which made Eve cry.

42. PRE-ISLAMIC PRACTICES: *MUSHKUL KUSHOD*

The Boisun settlements still follow traditional mode of life revealed in oral poetry, epics, folk handicrafts, national dress, games, and music, as well as in ancient style rituals. In 2001, UNESCO awarded the district of Boisun with a title of 'Masterpiece of Oral and Intangible Heritage of Humanity'. While conducting regular fieldwork there, I gathered significant material on the local traditional customs of pre-Islamic practices led by women.

There in Boisun, I met a remarkable Uzbek woman Ruhsatoi Agzamova (b. 1930), who had spent her entire life in the same village, with its population of around 80,000 people (Photo 16, p. 166). Married to the local government representative (the local Secretary of the Communist Party) and having brought up eleven children, Ruhsatoi-opa is a typical local woman. Her primary concerns were to raise her children and support her husband in each of his actions. After he passed away, her interests turned towards raising and educating her grandchildren. Her sharp mind, eloquence, and wit, enriched with idiomatic languages (Uzbek and Tajik, typical for the area), give her the ability to create epic style parables for every life situation she faces. Her wisdom and generosity are the reasons why people are so attracted to her. She is familiar with many local traditions and customs and is able to set up any ritual at home on her own. For her family, her grandchildren, she is able to perform rituals of *Beshik-Toy* (Photo 17) and *Mushkul Kushod* at home.

On one occasion, when I was visiting Boisun (Photo 17), Ruhsatoi-opa performed the *Beshik-Toy* ritual. Surrounded by a handful of family members, neighbours, and friends she opened the ritual with a prayer. Sitting

Photo 16: Lady of Boisun Ruhsatoi Agzamova

around a beautifully arranged tablecloth on the floor of her guestroom, she continued with *Suras* of the Qu'ran and then invited the mother (her daughter-in-law) to come over with her baby who was just 40 days old. This was accompanied by collective prayers and protective sayings. The baby was solemnly put into the *Beshik* (cradle), and the baby's sisters sang lullabies over the cradle, while the mother breastfed the baby.

The main accessories of the *Beshik-Toy* ritual on the tablecloth were items from the recent harvest: *qovun* (melon), fruits from her garden, *non* (bread) freshly baked in *Tandyr* (clay oven in the yard), and *kok chai* (green tea). Cutting the melon precisely, arranging it piece by piece on the tablecloth, she invited the guests to share it. It all had a special meaning, and every participant shared her concern to protect her grandson from evil eyes. The guests joined in with prayers, songs, and protective sayings. Everyone was pleased and satisfied.

Indeed, in Boisun, if there is need, and the will, any woman can perform rituals like Ruhsatoi-opa Agzamova. It reminds us of the Shamanic saying that everyone can Shamanise!

Photo 17: Ritual *Beshik-Toy* (first putting Baby in the Cradle)

The ritual of *Mushkul Kushod*

The structure of the ritual *Mushkul Kushod*, which I recorded on my visit to Boisun in April 2004, consists of many parts. The event developed step by step, built up from the initial preparation, through the introduction, beginning, the ritual itself (with solo and chorus singing), climax, to the conclusion, ending with conversation, tea drinking, eating, then parting.

All the women gathered together as usual on a Tuesday for this day of ceremony. The purpose of that occasion was simple: the ritual-holder Nasiba Azimova's son had obtained a job as a policeman. Such success! Twenty-six ladies, neighbours and relatives from Boisun village, came to celebrate with the family and (as happens at such events) to ask for the assistance of the Goddess to help with other matters (the daughter-in-law of one of these ladies had not given birth for a long time and was mentioned as a person for consideration). The ritual took about two- and three-quarter hours.

In preparation for the ritual, the women, one by one, gathered together in the biggest room of the household. They sat comfortably around the *dastarkhan* on the floor, greeting each other as usual with polite questions like, 'How are you? Are you in a good health? How is your family, children, mother-in-law, father-in-law, your husband? How are your parents? How is your job (if there is any!)', asking questions, exchanging news. They all spoke in low voices awaiting the arrival of the local *Otin-Oy*. Her voice was subdued but anticipated the mood of the occasion. All conversations stopped. The *Otin-Oy* prepared forty candles (by wrapping cotton wool on wooden sticks) to set alight later. Everyone had brought food for a meal, and laid it on the *Dastarhan*. Everything was ready for the ritual to commence.

The *Otin-Oy* began reading the first *Sura* from the Qur'an (*Fatiha*). Then she progressed to the proper story of *Bibi-Seshanba* (a pre-Islamic Goddess, whose traces as a helper still exist within the Islamic frame-work), alternating with religious and educational stories. The women all kept their heads bowed during the reading, collectively adding the end-ings *Allahu-Akbar*. Everyone appealed to the Goddess *Bibi-Seshanba* who is believed to be the protector of women all over the world. The story of her miracles, her good will and good deeds was told. She was praised and asked for help. The *Otin-Oy* put out the candles, and the room grew smoggy and dark.

All worries were shared as those assembled appealed to the goddess for intercession and support in collective prayer, made in low whispering voices. There was silence at the culmination of the ritual. Everyone was in a deep trance for almost an hour and a half.

At the conclusion, the women slowly started moving and talking. They were offered tea and a meal. They felt relaxed and refreshed. They looked happy and encouraged. They chatted, then some of them left.

On different occasions when I witnessed the same ritual, some other ele-ments were observed. The primary purpose of this ritual is to help people to cope with problems. These could be associated with some misfortune in the family, but there could also include some other worrying circum-stances. In such cases, the *Otin-Oy* leading the ritual will start the session with a prayer. After this, the process of 'healing' begins, highlighting its significance, calling the attention of the saints to the place where the ritual is taking place, asking for their help and, finally, expressing a hope for a change of circumstances. All of this is accomplished in conditions which are not usually typical of Muslim rites. Seven items are required, the avail-ability of which is crucial to performing the ritual:

- Water or tea
- Bread

- Sweets: honey, sugar, bonbons, or all of these
- Flour
- Oil (liquid)
- A mirror
- Fire

The ritual assigns specific significance to each item, the symbolism of which originates from Zoroastrian rites rather than Muslim ones. Hence, fire is the symbol of faith in Zoroastrianism, the mirror is the symbol of contained and open space, flour is the symbol of purity owing to its white colour, honey is the symbol of intended sweet bliss, bread stands for fertility, water is the symbol of the flow of time, and oil is a substance of energy.

Furthermore, special food called *Bibi-Mushkulkushod* is prepared for this ritual. As a rule it consists of seven kinds of dishes, which include:

Shir Guruch – rice soup,
Palov – pilau rice,
Umach – corn soup,
Khalvaytar – sherbet,
Bogursak – pastry balls,
Kulcha – little breads.

This collection of dishes plays an especially important role in the organisation and performance of the ritual. In such a case, it is performed on a Tuesday, as it is supposed to be addressed to *Bibi-Seshanba*, that is, Lady Tuesday. The very name of the ritual means an appeal to Mother-Mushkul Kushod, 'the lady who solves problems'. The **ritual** *Mushkul Kushod* comprises a distinct succession of stages.

First, the *Otin-Oy* herself lays all the necessary things on the tablecloth, blessing all her preparations. She carefully divides them into portions for everyone present, so each will, in a way, share part of the responsibility for the bad luck of her subject. *Otin-Oy* then appeals to the authority, asking them to help, attracting their attention by lighting the fire.

The main part of the ritual includes a predetermined sequence of songs and texts chosen by the *Otin-Oy*. She is the one who performs the holy texts. The *Otin-Oy* in the Boisun area was Muhtaram Nazarova, who was at this time 85 years of age, together with an *Otin-Oy* called

Mukarram-bi who assisted her. These holy texts are sung with long pauses between each part. The sequence of transition from one text to another rises in pitch before the culmination and after that eventually falls into silence.

Finally, the sacred meal is eaten and tea is drunk, while the women chat and share the latest news.

Thus, it can be seen that the system of rituals represents not a casual range of performances, but a harmonic space of songs and sounds, targeting each and every member of the community. Being part of the basic code of Muslim life, these rituals involve a system of religious recitations which have religious meaning. This local tradition underpins any important event in life.

So, one can suggest that this ritual form is based on a similar idea and structure, that of a 'long journey' or the Way – *Tariqat*. In open-form rituals, repetitive patterns of performance combine recitation from the Qur'an, Sufi poetry and singing and dancing with short conversations, drinking tea and eating. The most important part is the climax, a culmination with singing, which can be repeated several times depending the purpose of the event.

43. FEMALE RITES OF PASSAGE

Rituals in their general forms, irrespective of where they are performed, resemble chains of patterns containing predetermined basic elements joined in combinations of contrasting or similar types of building block. According to our observations, female rituals in Uzbekistan typically tend to involve a fusion of changing and static parameters such as:

Space: this is often an unchanging dimension characteristic of the ritual, defined in Uzbekistan by the boundaries of the sitting room in the house.

Time: the ever-changing feature, also defining the underlying event.

Event: the nature of which determines the ritual and the time of its performance.

This was shown in the case of Sufi and quasi-Sufi rituals. The same features apply to life-cycle rituals.[247] In comparison to Sufi and quasi-Sufi rituals these rituals are widely performed today. The leaders in these ceremonies are always *Otin-Oys* (in most parts of Uzbekistan) or *Halpa* (in the Khorezm area) – those who possess special ability and knowledge and experience to organise such ceremonies.

Life-Cycle Rituals
- Birth (cradle) rituals – *Beshik-Toy*
- Circumcision – *Sunnat-Toy*
- Wedding rituals – *Toy*
- Mourning rituals – *Aza, Motam, Hudoyi*

Beshik-Toy (Birth ritual)
This is a small festival for a woman who has recently given birth. For the first forty days after the baby is born the mother is not allowed to go out, or to introduce her baby to outsiders, whether they are neighbours, friends, or relatives. On the fortieth day after the birth she announces the Day of Official Laying of the Baby in the Cradle (in Uzbek, *Beshik*). She invites many women who celebrate the appearance of a new member of the Uzbek community. Actually, *Otin-Oy* here is the main person. She starts to introduce the baby to the visitors by singing a joke song. She asks the people present:

> 'Shall I put this Baby across the cradle?'
> 'No!' they answer.
> 'Shall I put a baby under the cradle?' –
> 'No!' they reply.
> 'Shall I put this sweet baby into the Cradle?' –
> 'Oh, yes!' shout the women merrily, and so on.

Though it would be far-fetched to connect this ritual with Sufism, in some religious families the whole atmosphere of the birth, of the first lullabies sung, are full of hints towards the long Way, which lies ahead of the newcomer to this world, and many of these lullabies could be read as Sufi-related poetry.

> *Alla aytay jonim bolam*
> *Uhlab qolgin – alla,*
> *Bahtimga sen katta bo'lgil*
> *Shakar qo'zim, alla*
> *Asalmisan, qandmisan,*
> *Ghazal muhabbatmisan*
> *Men qarigan chogimda, bolam,*
> *Belimga Quvvatmisan, alla*
> *Oyni olib beraymu,*
> *Gullar terib kelaymu, alla*

Atrofingdan ailanib, bolam
Shamol bulib, yig'laimu?
Bugun tun ham osuda
Hammalaryo uiquda, alla
Mehrim tog'day ketti, bolam,
Alla aytkim kelar juda.
Onang kabi sho'rlik bulma,
O'ynab o'skin, alla
Alla aytay, alla…

I 'll sing a lullaby,
Sleep my sweet child.
Grow up for my sake and happiness,
My sweet lamb, alla.
Are you honey or sugar,
Are you *ghazal* of love?
When I get old
Are you strength of my stature, alla?
Shall I give you the moon,
Or shall I pick up flowers for you?
Or wandering around you
Shall I blow as a wind, alla.

Today the night is quiet,
Everything is sleeping,
My love is like a mountain, which is broken,
I want to cry very much, alla.
Don 't be helpless like your mother,
Grow up joyfully and playfully, alla.

Sunnat-Toy (Ritual of circumcision)

This celebration, the initiation of a boy (usually when the boy is 3, 5, or 7 years old) into the Islamic community, demands the invitation of a huge number of people and can sometimes be as large as a wedding party. It is very expensive and because of that it demands long preparation. The event takes place in two different locations: one, attended by the men, where child has the operation, and the other for the women who gather together to join the child 's mother. *Otin-Oy* here is the person who has to support the weeping mother and a whole community of sympathetic women. She says a prayer as the mother of the child begins to cry because the operation has started. She reads poetry, examples of which have been given above.

The religious and Sufi connotations of this poetry lie in the fact that the boy gives up a part of his body in order to achieve a spiritual unity with the *Umma* or Islamic community and through it, ultimately, with God. Hamid Ismailov in the final chapter of his novel *The Railway* describes the whole ritual of circumcision from the boy's perspective.[248]

Toy (Wedding reception)

Toy is the name for the main kind of celebration in Uzbekistan, of which there are many different kinds. These events take place at the most important points in Uzbek life, as above. Sometimes other events could be counted as *Toy* as well, like the end of the holy month of *Ramadan* (*Ramazon Hayit*), or a small *Toy* could be arranged for a close friend as a thanksgiving to God after overcoming some particular difficulties (*Hudoiy*). But the principal *Toy*, meaning wedding celebration, merits a special explanation.

Toy as a Sufi phenomenon is described below in section 44.

Aza (Mourning ritual)

This series of rituals has been analysed above in the section devoted to Song and Poems of Sorrow and Repentance. As stated, the *Otin-Oy* is the key person who is really able to support the relatives of the deceased. She sings endlessly and recites stories, which are supposed to console people. She sits near the widow, or the mother of the deceased and encourages the women to cry, because it gives them relief. If women cry, it means things are getting easier for them. Reaction to the tragic event passes through stages, from inconsolable grief to more and more expressive despair and, after that, resignation and humility. Here the *Otin-Oy* plays the main role.

Here is a *Ghazal* of the great Sufi poet Mashrab, which is often read on these sad occasions:

Ko'rsat jamoling mastonalarga,
Ishqingda kuygan parvonalarga.
Mendan duoyo, sendan ijobat,
Jonim tassaduq jononalarga.
Mashrab sani deb
Kechdi jahondan,
Boshini qo'ydi ostonalarga.

Ey kungli qattiq rahm aylamaysan,
Qilgil nazora bechoralarga.
Kuygan g'aribman shavqat qil ohir,
Kuyingda yurgan devonalarga.
Mashrab sani deb
Kechdi jahondan,
Boshini qo'ydi ostonalarga.

Show your beauty to blinded with love people
To those who are burnt in your love.
A prayer is mine, salvation is yours,
My soul is sacrifice for beauties.
Mashrab has denied the world for you,
Putting his head onto the thresholds.

Hey ruthless, you don't care about me,
Give a glance to poor us.
I am a burnt stranger, pardon finally
Those vagabonds, who wander around you.
Mashrab has denied the world for you,
Putting his head onto the thresholds.

44. *TOY* (WEDDING CELEBRATION) AS A SUFI FEAST

Toy as the main Sufi and ritualistic phenomenon in traditional life deserves a separate chapter. As the Uzbek saying runs *Toy bo'lsin* (May celebration happen in your life!) expressing the highest value of such an occasion for a human being. Nothing is more important for Uzbeks as a *Toy*!

This is a grandiose performance involving hundreds of people. Once I was invited to a wedding in Samarkand, which was attended by about five

Photo 18: Mourning ritual in Boisun

hundred people, but people agreed that was not the biggest wedding in the modern history of the city. The *Toy* concentrates all features of social life such as the hierarchy of different social levels, which demand different forms of respect, different styles of permitted or accepted behaviour, and so on.

One can say that the essence of Uzbek society is present here. Men and women sit separately. The most respected people sit at the best places – quiet and comfortable, far away from the entrance, near the bride and groom. They are the first to whom the food is offered. They are the first to give congratulations to the bride, groom, and parents at the climax of the wedding. Among them are the *Otin-Oy*, who is involved in, and has a very important role in the wedding itself. For example, the *Otin-Oy* has to introduce the bride to the groom, at the so-called 'first sight' (as is necessary following traditional custom). They sing a song of benediction in order to make this moment sacred.

The Sufi poem *Husn va Dil* (Beauty and Heart) by Muhammadniyaz Nishoti, mentioned earlier, ends with the scene of a great feast, where all characters, which personify human features and capacities, meet and combine. Here is the piece:

This passionate *Bazm* (ball) developed,
There the sky and the earth were indistinguishable,
After forgetting their name,
They found themselves spectators
On the scene of a mysterious show
And the sun descended with them.
Mouths were opened like gates,
To the favour of coming kings and paupers:
Above them the night shone as dawn,
Or the dawn of eclipse requested
Disappearance of the word "force',
So everywhere just beauty would remain,
Where Night with her sister Dawn
Were matched in excellence in the sky,
Radiant, clean, glad and passionate
Were those two, unnamed royals
Thanks to God were forever connected.
God's grace is to connect the thread of two fates.
So, should we pray,
To give Beauty to the suffering Heart, as I did?
Thus, the ball flowed, like wine over the brim,
And the two unnamed royals were drinking

The source of life from the very mouth,
As I drank my sorrow and melancholy,
Breaking the calculation of those who served cups.
And Beauty, a queen, moon-like,
Floated in celestial clothes,
And servants swam after her, as the blood swims into the Heart.
And the Heart opened wide the door
Into that place where friends united:
Hope with Kindness, Mind with Occasion,
Sight with Bliss, Doubt with Tenderness.
There Joyfulness awaited Patience among all,
And here Fate gave a desired Embrace to Waste.
Everything desired was given to everyone,
And the only curse to me: to know who is worthy of whom,
Like a general who knows which soldier is worthy of battle,
Of heroism and, also, possibly, of death…
And God….

That is the image of the *Toy* in Uzbek culture: a symbol of merging, unification, togetherness. For *Otin-Oys* the wedding is their world: the scene, the audience and even the source of their livelihood. In Soviet times, weddings were neglected by official policy, which considered such events to be relics of the old feudal system, but the *Toy* was, and still is, the most important element in life in Uzbekistan and Central Asia. It reflects the traditional concept of life and keeps many ancient customs and rituals alive.

The wedding celebration has a certain fixed structure involving the whole community in a networking process, from meetings with future family members to farewells to friends and relations. The parties can differ from place to place, but these common elements can be found:

1) *Sovchi solish/ Unashish,* the process of matching;
2) *Non ushatish* (dividing bread), the engagement, when the relatives of the bride and groom divide a small loaf into two parts
3) The wedding *Toy* itself, which has its own structure:
   - *Ertalabgi osh* – morning pilav (the main Uzbek meal);
   - *Qiz chaqiriq* – meeting of women with the bride;
   - *O'g'il chaqiriq* – meeting of men with the groom;
   - *Nikoh* – registration by the Mullah and the authorities;
   - *Bazm* – the culmination, climax; the musical party;

4) Events for the second day of the wedding, popular in some areas of Uzbekistan, are:
- *Kelin salom* – (welcoming the bride), performing songs and dances for the bride's relatives
- *Chorllar* – a meeting for old people.

The conduct of wedding celebrations assumes separate spheres of activity for the men and women. This means that the *Otin-Oy* represents the main participant and is the ritual leader within the female half of the celebrations. Her singing of good wishes, which is a religious element, accompanies every important stage of the wedding: the arrival of the bride, the arrival of the groom, the 'first glance' of the bride by the groom (according to old Asian tradition, the groom must not have seen the bride chosen by his parents before the wedding; although this may no longer be applicable in all cases, this stage of the celebrations remains), and so on. Hymns *Assalomu*, Sufi poetry of philosophical nature as well as other folk genres are commonly used in this repertoire.

Music plays an exceptionally important role at the *Toy*. It serves as a mirror of the social and political situation, a symbol of happiness; a means to pay tribute to the social system, as the young couple enter society in a traditional, joyful way; a means to respect the religious system; and a way to please the ancestors, as did the previous generation. It is a mixture of many different aspects of culture – court culture, market art, mosque rituals, pop music – and it is a uniting instrument, which maintains feelings and provides a sense of wholeness to the event.

This is reflected in the huge variety of types of music performed at the *Toy*: solo and ensemble songs; instrumental music (e.g. as an interlude between different acts); prayers and praise for the parents, advice to the young, religious poems (performed by *Otin-Oy*), and songs as dialogue in form of questions and answers (*Otin-Oy* and all guests).

Toy performances include various combinations of instruments like *Tanbur, Dutar, Rubab, Ghidjak, Tar, Saz* along with a vocalist. The choice of instruments depends on the area involved. In the Ferghana Valley, *Toy* used to have *Karnay* (a long trumpet) as the main instrument for the announcement of a feast. In the areas of Khorezm, Samarkand, and Bukhara, the same function is performed by *Surnay* (a short wooden trumpet). In the Khorezm region, the main *Toy* is *Qurly-Toy*, which can involve between two and five thousand people. These *Toys* have been served by fighters/wrestlers, comedians, artists, and musicians (both men and women) and

Surnay players. Sometimes, in the Ferghana Valley, musicians used to play the violin in folk style instead of *Ghidjak*. In the Khorezm area, influenced by Azery culture, it could be *Tar* or even *Saz* instead of *Rubab*.

Each *Toy* represents the most important cultural and ethnic features common to a certain area. But some characteristics are the same for *Toy* in different parts of Uzbekistan. In rural areas, musical performance is divided into two parts: that for daily life and that for family celebrations (*Toy*). In daily life, amateurs used to play delicate instruments like *Nay* (wooden flute), *Chang-Qobus* (timbales). Sometimes, the long and sad sounds of *Nay* were heard in the early morning meaning that someone had died. Very often even each community meeting is accompanied by songs and *Doira*.

Toys differ in size and local origin. In areas like Surkhandarya and Qashkadarya where there is a strong nomadic influence, the main musical performance of *Toy* is given to *Baqshis* – hereditary bards – for the male community and *Otin-Oy* for the female. *Baqshis* perform epic genres (*Alpamysh* and *Kyor-Ogly*) and *Terma* (short songs, improvisations), which are a kind of wedding blessing and dedication. Only *Baqshi* can introduce the bride to the great number of guests by carefully lifting her white veil with the head (peg box) of the *Dombra*.

In the Khorezm area, *Baqshi* performs the epic genre *Dastan* with an ensemble of *Dutar, Bulaman, Ghidjak*, and *Doira*. But for the main part of *Toy* performance, people invite small teams of instrumentalists (*Ghidjak, Nay, Doira*) who play folk music together with a singer. So, the range of instruments in urban and rural *Toys* is almost the same, but the repertoire is different: a wider one, with essential parts of classical music, in urban *Toy*, and a narrower one, moving on to simple folk tunes, songs, and dances, in rural *Toy*. *Doira* is the typical main instrument of entertainment, with groups like *Mavrigikhon*, a male ensemble with five or six *Doiras* plus singers in Bukhara, or *Sozanda*, a female ensemble with two or three *Doiras*, but who sometimes add *Zang* (bells) or *Qayroq* (castanets).

The wedding music differs according to the place and time of the performance. The music in the bride's house is mostly religious, whereas in the restaurant pop music or folk music with a modern interpretation is commonly played. The order of performance is pre-determined. One section at the bride house is sacred in type and function, another one at the restaurant is ordinary, secular. In the first stage the music includes joyful, inspiring songs, as well as the 'protective' ones. Only performance at the restaurant includes popular songs and music with dance rhythms, but without special lyrical content.

Different parts of the wedding are celebrated at the houses of the bride and the groom. For example, in 1992, I attended a wedding that took place partly in Samarqand (the ritual part of the wedding) and partly (the secular party) in Tashkent. The music followed the progression of the event itself, from the groom's house, to the bride's house, to a restaurant. It involved very different genres, from the mystical poetry of medieval Sufi poets like Navoiy, Mashrab, and Djami, to local pop hits. All those genres are appropriate for particular stages of the wedding. For example, the song-signals *Yor-yor* (Beloved, beloved) and *Toylar muborak* (Congratulations on the wedding) are performed at the beginning of the event to proclaim the wedding. The whole event can take from two to ten hours. The wedding I attended in 1992 in Samarqand was twelve hours long with more than 500 guests and visitors.

The female part of the *Toy* was called *Ru binon* (Open your face). It was the celebration of the first appearance of the bride to the female community. This celebration witnessed the moment of the acceptance of the bride as an equal member of the society. After having been concealed behind the curtain, the bride came into the view of the assembled women. Queuing one after another, they kissed the bride, giving her presents and praising her beauty. During this process, two *Otin-Oys* sang the *Ghazal* by Mashrab, blessing the bride. Alternating between the lines of poetry, the audience sang the phrase *Hasoraalei* (One thousand times) which meant that they wished all blessings to materialise one thousand times. It should be mentioned that the *Ghazal* was sung in Uzbek, while the salutations and wishes of well-being were exclaimed in the Tajik language. This is explained by the historically bilingual nature of the Samarkand area. The rest of the ritual was carried out quietly and towards the end became rather monotonous.

Generally, in the countries of Central Asia, apart from the phenomenon of the *Otin-Oys* and their leadership, there exists the so-called 'Grandmothers' school of life', an outlook on life which is passed particularly strongly down the female side of the family from the older generation to the younger. So, should an important event involving numerous guests, such as a wedding, be celebrated publicly without the implementation of ancestral ways, the participation of older generations and the deployment of things generally connected to the past, it is considered to be doomed to attract the attention of evil spirits and the evil eye. For this reason, the role of head of the event is usually given to a representative of the older generation. This also explains the ostentatious display of household and personal items, like clothes, jewellery, and dishes, which, although subsequently mostly unused, illustrate accordance and peace with the world of the ancestors' spirits, and ensure a problem-free future. Maintaining this balance between the two worlds is very important. This way of things is firmly established in the mentality of the modern-day local population, be it rural or urban, carrying forward the weight of the traditions accumulated through centuries.

Around 90 per cent of the urban population follow traditional approaches, since their family roots often lie in the rural areas. Even though they may not wish to keep to the traditional ways of 'grandmothers' schooling', they are obliged to do so, in order to keep the peace with their relatives and maintain favourable public opinion. Large families, with strong links between their members and the societal communal mentality of Central Asian peoples, are thus partially responsible for this strong propensity to follow tradition. These include following the wedding rules regarding ancestors and elders mentioned above, in order to protect the bride and groom from the evil eye, as well as playing ancient traditional music alongside modern pop. Occasionally, these popular modern tunes played at weddings even boast inserts of ancient religious songs of Islamic essence, sung by local grandmothers along with *Otin-Oy*.

Who are the heroes of this performance? Certainly the groom and his bride. But their role in the Uzbek wedding is passive. The relatives and guests from both sides are more active. They are the producers of this performance. They are involved in all its stages. However, a compulsory feature of the wedding is segregation by gender. Thus, women have to represent the environment of the bride and men that of the groom. They even separate themselves physically. The bride's visitors are seated in one place and those of the groom in another. They join together only at the end when the *Bazm* starts.

Each ritual has a 'beginning, middle, and an end' (Aristotle). It is a piece of drama that proceeds through various stages. The *Toy* has gradually developing parts with the most important and dynamic section, called *Bazm* (Festivity), at the culmination. The *Bazm* is the climax of the performance and it is here that the professional musicians arrive on stage and all participants (bridegroom, bride, performers, and audience) mix and unite in the process of performance.

We have much evidence of *Bazms* in medieval times at the courts of the Timurids. In Alisher Navoiy's fifteenth-century series of epic poems *Hamsa* (Five poems) or in the book *Babur-name* (Diary of Babur) of Zahiriddin Babur (sixteenth century) one can find accounts of lavish festivities with music. Closer to our times, a great Uzbek writer Cho'lpon, in his novel *Kecha va Kunduz* (Night and Day) gives a picture of a *Bazm* at the start of the twentieth century:

> When two women entered the door, with faces shining like stars, Zebi's song "My black hair" was sweetly tickling the ears... That was the night when a drop turned into a sea. All girls of the *kishlak* [village] and young ladies were gathered here. Even the grannies of neighbouring houses came to join them. Two other *dutar* players apart from Zebi, and several dancers, caused all of the guests not to look at all at the table, but to be busy with *Bazm*, forgetting themselves. Everyone turned into children. When a trio of girls was supported by the voices of others and the song flew into the sky, even the lads of the village started to gather at places beyond the reach of the lamplight. They were sitting breathlessly in the darkness.[249]

I also remember a *Komsomol*, or young communists' wedding, from my childhood, when our most traditional Uzbek neighbours invited our family to the nearest canteen, where the brass band was playing marches of Dmitryi Dunayevski (a well-known Soviet composer), celebrating the marriage of two *Komsomols*. But stronger still are memories of numerous *Bazms* with Sherali Juraev as the main singer of the event. In a way, the very word *Bazm* is for me intertwined with the name of Sherali.

So, what can we conclude from the wedding as a musical performance? Such a performance consists of many parts characterised by developing continuity. The participants play different roles. The main function of the performance is to celebrate the process that unifies people through the joining of bride and groom, which represents a sacred ritual. The structure of the wedding reflects more generally the universal structure of a Sufi ritual. As in a Sufi rite, *Zikr* is a mystical way for a person to unify with God, so the structure and the stations or stages of the wedding develop as a process of the joining of two separate parts into one, of two separate lives merged into another single new life. Just as the culmination of Sufi *Zikr* is *Sama'* or ecstasy, when all participants fall into a trance, at a wedding, the celebrations lead to the climax of the *Bazm*.

An Uzbek singer at a wedding has an archetypal role. There are hundreds of myths, anecdotes, and stories associated with who said what, or sang what, at this or that wedding, and these stories are passed from generation to generation. I would like to relate here a story told about the death of Mamurdjan Uzakov.

In the summer of 1966, several friends came to the wedding party of Mamurdjan's neighbour. The day after the *Bazm*, when some of them were struggling with hangovers, Mamurdjan invited them to the *choxona* (tea house) of the city park. There, by a pond with a number of white swans, he told his friends of his dream the previous night. 'I dreamt of swans, who took my soul to heaven,' he said sadly, and started to sing. As the song reached its climax, the birds in the pond started to show signs of impatience. They were noisy as never before, and suddenly took off into the sky. At the same moment, Mamurdjan's head dropped onto his chest. His friends thought for a moment that he was teasing them, but then they discovered that he was dead.

Such myths, containing a strong Sufi, mystical element, are typically associated with the great Central Asian musicians of the past. How striking, and how indicative of the continuities underlying the change, to find the same type of myth told of a Soviet-era singer whose songs praised the comrade collective farmers. These myths fly on the wings of those swans across the generations.

Like Mamurdjan Uzakov, many *Otin-Oys* and singers love to end the *Toy* as a Sufi feast with the famous *Ghazal* of the great female Sufi poet Uvaysiy. I have decided to include this poem here. As Uzbeks say, 'If I spoke out, my tongue would burn: if I didn't speak, it would burn my soul.'

> If I ask for the symbol of the meeting (vasl) from the people who love, they kill me,
>
> If I don't ask I die
> If I build a shop of love for the suffering people, they kill me
> If I don't build I die.
>
> Don't put me to torments of jealousy, O death, if my beloved is sitting with another,
> If I bark unceasing like a dog at his door he kills me,
> If I don't bark I die.
>
> There is no other way but to be patient if I want him till the dawn of day
> If I wander like a vagabond hither and thither, he kills me,
> If I don't wander I die.
>
> If I was absent while I was far away, it was because my beloved said, forbear:
> If I go today to see the flower of his face, he kills me,
> If I don't go I die.

He avoids me, intimidates me, my soul leaves this ephemeral world,
If I stay with this wan face, strange Uvaysiy, he kills me,
If I don't stay I die.

45. CALENDAR RITUALS LED BY *OTIN-OY*

Along with Sufi, Sufi-related and life-cycle rituals there is a class of
Calendar rituals, which are also led by *Otin-Oys*. Here also their role as
leaders of the ritual is paramount. Readiness to perform alone or with
friends (not necessarily in public, but in front of members of their peers),
the ability to act, and an acute mental focus combined with a relaxed state
of mind represent the essential factors for the task of ritual performance
by *Otin-Oy*. The artistic capacity to sing, read melodically, memorise large
amounts of text, and the ability to involve the audience in the process of
performance and capture their attention are also vital for this task. The
skill of creating a spiralling upwards in the emotional development, with
one repetition following another, bringing the performance to a climax,
provides evidence that all their ritualistic performances have their roots in
Sufism.

Indoor celebrations: *Navruz* (New Year Celebration: a relic from pre-Islamic times)

This festival takes place on 22 March. It is one of Central Asia's most
favourite holidays, associated with the renewal of nature and the arrival
of the warm days of spring. *Navruz* is associated with the magical importance of the cult of Nature and the Earth. Its history goes back to ancient
Mesopotamia and Babylon, giving rise to many traditions rich in rites,
amusements, and performances.

Outdoor celebrations: *Suz Hotin* (Call for rain)

This ritual involves a procession of women who climb a hill nearest to the
village and appeal to the Goddess Suz Hotin with incantations. According
to local traditional belief, the performance of these songs brings forth
clouds and heavy rain.

Sail – Lola Sail (**Tulip-trip**) This involves a group of people going to the
steppes to gather tulips. They enjoy themselves, cooking, eating, singing,
dancing, and offering thanks to God for the spring, which is seen as a
symbol of returning life.

Qovun (**Melon-trip**) This outdoor celebration with a feast of ripe melons is a summer festival with singing and dancing.

Hosil Bairami (**Harvest celebration**) This celebration, usually associated with the end of the cotton-gathering season, fell victim to state ideology and was forcibly transformed into public events for celebrating the 'strength of public will in collecting the harvest and exceeding quotas' and celebrated with concerts, fairs, and food markets.

Qor Yog 'di (**Snow celebration**) This occurs on sighting the first snow, when the person seeing the snow puts a letter announcing it (*Qor hat,* a letter of snow) into the pocket of a friend or relative, who is then obliged to throw a party. Jokes, dialogues, and songs are involved in organisation.

46. *OTIN-OY* IN UZBEK POP CULTURE

Speaking of traditional culture represented by females – very often an elderly population – one might ask: What about the youth culture in that country? How important is 'granny's school' for Uzbekistan? In fact for Uzbekistan, the country where more than half of the population is under 25 years old, this is a very important question.

Uzbek pop music in the twenty-first century is remarkable for the rich variety of genres, languages, symbols, and styles where female cosmology is present. There are a number of interesting examples but I would like to give particular attention to the group D J Pilgrim, founded by Ilhom Yulchiev and Dmitryi Levin. Established in 1998, this group depicts in their multilingual songs the experience of the former Soviet Union's blend of 'Estrada culture' which is 'a staged performance built from a variety of entertaining genres' (Akbarov 1987: 416; Keldysh 1990: 659). The band's music was described as 'a new genre of Uzbek-style Europop from upstarts' (*New York Times*; 18 October 2000). In the video clip of the song *on i ona* (He and She), the plot of unrequited love is shown in two alternating images. In one, the boy is in love and the girl does not share his feelings, driving the boy to commit suicide. In the other, a local old lady, appears as symbol of the universe or as goddess who comforts all broken hearts. The boy (performed by Ilhom Yulchiev) tells his story; the old lady recites a medieval Sufi poem that has deep symbolic meaning.

Boy's story
Он её любит а она его нет,
Он ей пишет а ей даже дела нет!
Он её ищет но нигде её нет,
Она красива но глупа,
А он любовью слеп!

He loves her, She does not love him at all He writes her letters – She ignores them!
He is longing to see her – But cannot find her anywhere! She is beautiful but silly!
And he is blinded with love.

Old lady's monologue
Qoshigni qarosiga hol bo'lay arosiga
Saning rahming kelmaydiyo doday
Birovning bolasiga qoshing bilan ko'zinga
Oshno bo'ldim o'zinga
Aytolmayman yuzingayo, doday, Insof bersin o'zingga

To the blackness of your eyebrows, Let me be a beauty spot between them
You have no pity for the child of a stranger.
To your eyebrows and eyes, I became a friend to you, I can't say it to your,
Let God grant you fairness

Here, the distinctive language of the text is reinforced by the difference in music style. Though both songs have a similar melodic framework the Russian lyrics come in brief phrases with simple rhythm, emotionally explicit sentences in the style of rap music. In contrast, the Uzbek song is characterised by long phrases, ornaments on vowels and a melancholy melody.

Spiritual depth and an eternal subject turn the clip into a picture with a dual vision of earthly and cosmic love. Here we see an elderly woman who has become a symbol of Eternal Wisdom trying to protect an unhappy boy, to keep him away from the tragedy. However, her image is heavily transformed: with her clouded eye, hoarse voice, and rotten teeth, she looks like a beggar. The common image of the well-respected 'granny' is being mocked here in response to the teasing/defiant nature of the pop music style. Pop music comes together with the old ritualistic singing style of the female *Otin-Oy* repertoire. Two different languages – Russian and Uzbek – represent two levels of narrative: Russian is used to describe the love story, and Uzbek, deeply rooted in old poetical Sufi symbolism with its mystical *Ghazal* poetry, is used to add a philosophical stance. If the teenage boy's story and action evoke the grotesque tragi-comic style of famous Arlecchino-related image (popular comic servant character from the Italian Commedia dell'arte), the old Uzbek lady introduced in a 'granny-style' nagging appears as a symbol of Eternity.

As one can see, in Uzbekistan, *Otin-Oy* are believed to hold the power over time and space, bringing together images of the past, present, and future, life and death, solar and lunar features, Islamic and pre-Islamic traditions.

For Uzbeks it is enough to see a woman singing an old-fashioned ritualistic song to associate themselves with the universe, safe and protected as another pattern in the embroidery of life.

11

Similar Female Rituals in the Turkic-Speaking World (in Tatar, Azeri, Turkish, Cypriot, and Afghani Traditions)

47. TURKIC RITUALS AND CEREMONIES

> If the sky above did not collapse and if the earth below did not give way,
> o Turkic people, who would be able to destroy your state and institutions?
> (inscribed on *Orkhon-Yenise Tigin* seventh-century funerary tablets).

These tablets are the earliest known surviving written monuments of the Turks in their own language. Along Orkhon-Yenisey, Turkish stelas from the eighth century remind the world about their early civilisation. Further evidence is provided in the eleventh-century documents: the *Compendium* of Kasgarli Mahmut and *Kutadgu Bilig* of Balasagunlu Yusuf. Turks were famous for their passion for ceremonies and sacraments.

This chapter is devoted to the description of female ritual and culture among settled Turkic peoples, which differs radically from that of nomadic peoples. The culture of the wide area of the Turkic-speaking world, stretching from Siberia to the shores of the Mediterranean and increasingly present today in diasporic locations elsewhere, is composed of the art and music of numerous different ethnicities, among them Yakuts, Tuvans, Hakassyans, Kyrgyz, Kazakhs, Uzbeks, Uyghurs, Turkmens, Karakalpaks, Azerys, Tatars, Bashkirs, and Turks.

Etiquette, in particular, is reflected in a system combining ritualistic behaviour that is rich in symbolism, and attributes specific meaning to objects and events that that inhabit every aspect of the average Uzbek's daily life. How can you explain to a foreigner the true significance of attending to your morning toilet and carrying out your ritualistic wash early in the morning? If you have failed to do so, after you emerge from the house, you will find your host's whole family busy doing their chores in the yard, the people you will come across will act as if you did not exist in metaphysical space and certainly not in their field of view. Once you have visited the toilet (normally located outside the house) and have washed your hands and face, you will be warmly and loudly greeted by the hosts, as if you had just come out of the house and they had just seen you![250]

According to the existent theory, 'the ritual system maintains the main parameters of the collective life.'[251] So, what is a ritual from the aspect of its symbolic content? 'Ritual is a symbolic act, carrying no obvious practical meaning and representing a symbol of a certain social relationship.'[252] In this sense, the rituals of the *Otin-Oys* belong precisely to this type, connecting events of daily life with Heavenly and Earthly purpose.

'In order to relate to the ways of the world prescribed by the sacral example, the act of creation has to be reproduced in Ritual. This reproduction represents the dominant element of every ritual, if seen from the aspect of mechanism responsible for smooth running of life used for corrective purposes in case of deviations from the norm. For this reason, the ritual recreates the image of Chaos, from the composite parts of which the conductor of the ritual orchestrates the integration of a highly ordered cosmos, according to a set of stringent rules.'[253]

Thanks to the rituals, all the main stages of the life cycle are maintained within the framework of a higher order, relating the events to the cosmic/universal perspective.

In order to be fully recorded and perceived in reality, the event is transposed into other dimensions, emphasising its significance in this world by measuring it against the historical and mythical realms, where the event's multiple meanings are synchronically combined. It is as if all the possible forms of existence, ranging from everyday life to the cosmic scale of events, are combined in a focused projection into the current time frame, and represented in a ritual.

The phenomenon of ritual among Turkic people is known for its power to stabilise charge and harmonise the psychological environment shared by a group of people.[254] For instance, talking about celebrations as a widespread form of ritual, one would note that Medieval celebrations always possessed a deep significance and philosophical content.[255] 'The categories of laughter and tears in the world perception of Turks...is broader than the existing modern perception of what is comical and tragic... Apart from celebration ceremonies, researchers have noted the fact that the burial ceremonies of the Turks in Central Asia, as well as South Siberia were notorious for the remarkably dramatic expression of the tragedy of the event.'[256] It is not without reason that local tradition maintains that a singer (*Haidji*) should be invited to attend to the family for the whole time prior to the funeral, which takes place before the sunrise. It is believed that the singer 'helps alleviate the pain of loss experienced by the relatives, which becomes worse by night, giving the chance to the people present at the house during the night to overcome sleepiness and remain alert, to attend to the funeral at the right time'.[257]

The repertoire itself (the epic, the singing), performed within the usual frame of the burial ritual, represented a cleansing plea, substituting for a sacrifice, made for the sake of the departing soul. The poet played the role of the medium in this case. Singing at the funeral was equivalent to the actions of Sayano-Altai Shamans.[258]

As V.N. Toporov recalls, 'this state of things is maintained predominantly in cultures where the language retains its ritualistic function,' and 'where each saying carrying a ritualistic function is essentially aimed at performance'.[259] Therefore, reality was created through the word, which carried the deeper meanings of the objects and subjects brought to life by the higher thoughts of, the ritual performers. In describing the possibilities of the world in prayers and poetical improvisations, the Shamans and storytellers recreated the world for their audience using the power of words and imagination. Often, the beginnings of the image drawn by the words would hark back to the very beginning of this world, thus relating the current event to that starting point.[260]

The Shamans and storytellers were the protagonists of this ritualistic performance, since 'they possessed the experience of the preceding generations; they were the carriers of the history of culture. The historical happenings were preserved not in books, but in tales, legends and fairytales, where every new event leads to birth of a new story. Just as the book is illustrated, given a new lateral meaning, enveloped in a different artistic form, so does he decorate his tales of life with the pearls of his fantasy: responsible for the emergence the fluidity and malleability of a myth.'[261]

Not only the words, but also the song, serve as a means of communication between the two worlds. Turkic peoples have always been renowned for their love of song and music. According to folk tradition, a person's gift or ability to poeticise and sing has been received through divination, through an encounter with an ancestor spirit or through a blessing from a deceased folk hero. This source of inspiration is expressed in a person's ability to make music. The Tatars believe that the power of words and wisdom are stronger that the power of a steel sword, as the heroes of their tales depart to faraway lands seeking wisdom and good advice, and more often than not the strong protagonists are defeated by the wise word of a weak woman. It is noteworthy that, according to Tatar beliefs, a song represents the highest expression of wisdom, and that there is no creature in the world able to resist it.[262]

The image of the universe, brought to the public through the performer's effort, relates to the act of creation. The singer himself takes on the role of creator. The music and poetry here form a bridge linking reality to the mythical world. Reflection of the links with the mythological image of the world in the performance enables the idea of the beginning of creation to be realised through rhythm, music, and song in a dramatic-symbolical form. Strings and percussion, instruments closest to the human voice and the rhythmic heartbeat, are commonly used as an accompaniment, especially in Shamanistic practice.[263]

So, the Turkic culture has remained for centuries the main means of preservation and propagation of a rare historical heritage and knowledge. Some other considerations regarding the nature of Central Asian rituals are mentioned by the German scholar Karl Reichl, who suggests that 'Although in some traditions (notably in India) oral epics are performed as part of a religious ritual, there is no overt ritual function of the epic in most oral traditions known today. However, even in a purely secular and seemingly non-ritual context, the performance of oral epics can have ritual dimensions. This is discussed with reference to the oral epic poetry of the Turkic peoples of Central Asia. It is argued that the performance of oral epics is a particular type of communicative event, of which the comparatively rigid act sequence can be seen as being on a par with the patterning of ritual. A second important aspect linking epic performance to ritual is that both events are meaningful in a similar way. It can be shown that in the performance of heroic epics tribal and cultural origins are explored and that hence the primary function of epic is not entertainment but the search for ethnic and cultural identity.'[264]

This background helps us to understand how Islamic beliefs, brought to Central Asia by Arabs, merged with the local Shamanic beliefs to created Sufism.

Being deeply involved in researching female religious rituals and music in Uzbekistan, I was also interested in comparing the role of the *Otin-Oy* with that of their counterparts, if they exist at all, in other neighbouring countries of Central Asia and some other Muslim countries. Here is a brief account of what I found in my field research.

Afghanistan: female music making in Uzbek diaspora

A comparison between mainland Uzbeks and Afghani Uzbeks is highly important as historically those people were closely connected. There is a strong notion of tribal identity and a sense of some things being 'essentially Uzbeki' in aspect or attitude. However, my research has uncovered the way in which a sense of authentic identity was constructed within the societies themselves. The first is based on what people think of as their original culture, before it became overlaid with nationalism, Soviet influence, the restrictions of the Taliban, and so on. Of course, this appeal to an original, clearly defined and apparently homogeneous past is itself something of a fantasy particularly since there must have been a rather different Uzbeki culture before the arrival of Islam in the seventh century, for example – but it is one strongly held by many older members of the population. This is particularly interesting in relation to the position of women in the Afghan Uzbeki communities where the recent Taliban traditions may have masked or obliterated certain female roles as compared with traditional activities in Uzbekistan itself.

Today the population of Afghanistan is estimated at more than 31 million, up to 5 million of whom are considered to be Uzbeks, who for centuries have lived in the northern part of Afghanistan, just across the river, Amu Darya. My documentation is based on fieldwork conducted in the northern part of Afghanistan, making recordings with Uzbek musicians in Mazar-i-Sharif, Shobergan, and Akcha.[265]

I went to Afghanistan in October 2006 at the time of *Ramadan*, during the very last days of that celebration which is so important in Muslim life. Female communities were bustling with many social activities. People paid visits to family members, relatives, friends, and neighbours, bringing presents and sweets, cooking the most fabulous dishes, visiting on their way to holy and famous places. As in Uzbekistan, I saw large groups of women with their children gathering together for celebrations around the table-cloth in the sitting room. They were dressed in brightly coloured clothes. Songs, jokes, teasing, and songs were in the air. This festive mood was

Photo 19: Eid celebration in female community of Shobergan, Afghanistan

shared by everyone. Music sounded from the streets, from radio and TV. Staying in Shobergan, on the first day of Eid (*Hayit*), I attended a female gathering celebrating the end of *Ramadan*. I was invited to join the family in the living room where about forty women with children were enjoying the celebration.

The gathering lasted for more than three hours. Different styles of music, teasing and religious songs were performed during the festivities. Sitting on the floor, women accompanied themselves playing on *daf* (frame drum) and *chang-qobuz* (Jews' harp). This performance took place in a relaxed, free atmosphere and excitement was in the air. The joke song *Noi-Noi* alternated with comic sung couplets *Taralalai*, later followed by the purely religious *Qambar* and *Marhabo*. Special attention was paid to the *Salavat* (hymn) *Hush keldingiz* (You are welcome!). A middle-aged lady Hanipha Mullomuhammad Niaz covered by a white scarf (identical to that worn by the Uzbek *Otin-Oy*) and girls were singing glory to the Prophet.

Lailatul mehrojiga qilmak uchun siz rohbaror
Quddisiro diydasiga to'tiyo hush keldingiz

Kishvari izzat aro mahzanishini podishoh
Shahsuvori korigari kibriyo hush keldingiz

Welcome, you panacea to the eye of Jerusalem
In kingdom of respect you owe a king.
Welcome, you superior cavalier.
To ascend to *Miraj* at night

I also had a rare chance to visit professional female singer Sabzy-gul, famous for her distinguished style. Today Sabzy-Gul (Red hair flower), local icon and local myth, is the only living professional female wedding singer, and is very popular in the Northern part of Afghanistan. Sabzy-Gul turned out to be a tiny, simply dressed, shy-looking woman, with the most casual appearance I ever expected to find. I caught up with her at home in Akcha, in the early hours. 'I have just returned from General Dustum's [the local military ruler's] party last night. He doesn't hold any parties without my performance,' she boasted. 'I go there regularly.' During our interview she constantly cracked jokes and made ironic comments. During the day we spent together she sang one song after another, first on her own and then together with her husband, the *Nay* player. Lyrical and joyful, they were all love songs. What was even more interesting (and I could not believe my eyes!), sometimes in the middle of a song she whistled dashingly – she was playful and mischievous, like any star. Sabzy-Gul still performs in the Northern part of the country where Uzbeks have lived for centuries: in Andhoi, Shobergan, Maimana, and Kabul, a 14-hour drive away. Like any professional musician, Sabzy-gul had a famous Usto-teacher, Marjun-Hola from Bukhara, who was famous for her *Halpa* (female wedding performers in Uzbekistan) skills and activity. So, this demonstrates the continuation of *silsilah* practice – the transmission of oral knowledge – which is widespread among professional musicians from Central Asia.

During my fieldwork in female communities in both Uzbekistan and Afghanistan, I witnessed gatherings of female artists – weavers of Suzani – weaving pattern after pattern, each seemingly unrelated to the other. Those patterns are usually associated with the sun and with the moon, the sky, stars, birds, flowers, and many other objects reflecting age-old myths and beliefs. When the work was finally complete, those seemingly unrelated patterns would suddenly come together into a coherent picture. So, now, will this book. It is now time to draw the threads together into a conclusion that will make of this work a picture that ultimately makes sense.

Female communities both in Uzbekistan and Afghanistan maintain deeply-rooted traditional cultural beliefs, which combine Islamic faith with elements of the pre-Islamic mythological beliefs of a Zoroastrian, Manichean, or Shamanic nature. Rituals at their gatherings are mostly musical and their structure follows the elements of cosmological concepts, developed over the centuries. The main elements of this cosmology is based on a dualistic understanding of divinity where, despite a predominantly 'male' understanding of Islam, a strong image of pre-Islamic female goddesses is offered, along with mystical features of Sufism, where the macrocosm (universe) equals the microcosm (human soul).

There are significant differences between the practices of female gatherings and rituals in Afghanistan and Uzbekistan. If in Afghanistan the Islamic tradition has never been broken over the last two to three centuries, in Uzbekistan 'the land was ploughed' by the Socialist revolution and by 70 years of Russian rule. Therefore, female rituals of the mainland Uzbek population worked out a complex 'hidden underground art', with a wealth of different elements, including Islamic and pre-Islamic celebrations like *Bibi-Seshanba*, while Afghani Uzbek female communities formed predominantly Islamic rituals with Quranic reading as the main functional element in those gatherings.

Azerbaijan

Female religious activity is widely spread in Azerbaijan. Religious festivities are performed by women *Marsyia*. I had a chance to witness a rare but typical Shiite ritual called *Ashir-Oy*. Held every year, this event commemorates the Prophet's grandson Hussein who was killed in Karbala. Gathering at home together with relatives, neighbours, and friends, the women sit around the room singing and rhythmically clapping hands. In between, they drink tea and eat sweets. Their performance is very emotional. As it reaches its climax they are in tears, singing expressive chants about the dramatic history of Islam more and more rhythmically and dynamically. Women and girls, of all ages, are involved in those rituals, whereas men are not allowed to participate.

> Open your eyes, Mother Fatima
> Tell me what is your pain?
> Open your eyes, look at me,
> Tell me, what do you suffer from?
> My wounded Mother, what is your pain?
> My lovely Mother, tell me what is hurting you?

Lady Fatima opened her eyes,
She kissed her daughter Zeyneb,
And said: 'Have patience, my daughter,
I have broken my ribs very badly.
I have a lot of misfortunes
My wounds hurt'.
My hurt Mother, what is your pain?
My mother, tell me what is hurting you?

....

'Look at your Hassan as he is pale,
Look at your heart Hussein as he sobs.
He said dear mother what hurts?
My hurt mother, what do you suffer from?'

.....

'My mother, you're only eighteen years old,
Do not leave me Mother,
Don't abandon your daughter,
Tell me, what do you suffer from,
My wounded Mother, what is your pain?
My lovely Mother, tell me what hurts you?'

....

'You sleep so peacefully,
You should be tired,
You're alive, you're not dead.
You sleep forever in the arms of your daughter.
My Mother, you're alive, you're not dead.
Lai, lai, lai my mother, lai'.

Turkey

Every time I visit Istanbul it seems to be wintertime. Snow brings purity to this stunning city which, with its beauty and high spirits, is always associated in my memory with the voices of the *Marsyias*. The city, glamorous in a covering of white snow, with the heads of minarets and cupolas rising above, is a vivid reminder of the local *Marsyias* in their white shawls. Looking for these ladies, longing to meet them at last, I heard all kind of excuses from the local 'intelligentsia', whose members are usually proud of their secular upbringing: 'They are not from educated people... They are very, very simple women...'

Covering themselves in the same white shawls, sitting around the tables, the *Marsyias'* singing is similar to that of their Uzbek counterparts, a repertoire of songs transmuting into slow and rhythmically undulating chanting on the same eternal subjects, whilst they hold tiny notebooks of poetry written in Arabic script in their hands.

Marsyia Fatima Turker, with whom I was working, is a young woman with three children and husband Arif. In her house, in small, tidy simple rooms she began her session. Her repertoire varied from the *Suras* of the Qur'an to *Mavluds, Suleiman Cheleabi Allah Oidyn,* Yunus Emre's *Sordum sary chichege,* also his *Sahar Vakti bed-bular, Shukur Olsyn Allah, Tekbir,* and many other genres. Her rich voice began in a low register and then became higher when she chanted more developed Sufi poetical verses.

The tunes and melodic patterns of her chanting were of Turkish origin with a decorative style of pronunciation on every single syllable and sophisticated ornamentation. The style of singing was also very much Turkish with characteristically open vowels, and a slow 'sliding' at the end of each phrase.

> *Sordum sary chichege*
> *Anen baban varmidur*
> *Chichek aydur dervish baba*
> *Anam babam toprakdur*
> *La ilaha il Allah*
> *Allah, La ilaha il Allah*
> *Sordum sary chichege*
> *Kardashlarin varmidur*
> *Chichek aydur dervish baba*
> *Kardeshlarim yaprakdur.*
> *La ilaha il Allah*
> *Allah, La ilaha il Allah.*
> *Sordum sary chichege*
> *Nedan benzin sarydur*
> *Chichek aydur dervish baba*
> *Olum bena yakindur.*
> *La ilaha il Allah*
> *Allah, La ilaha il Allah.*
> *Sordum sary chichege*
> *Size olum varmidur*
> *Chichek aydur dervish baba*
> *Olumsiz yer varmidur*
> *La ilaha il Allah*
> *Allah, La ilaha il Allah.*
> *Sordum sary chichege*

Sen beni bilirmisin
Chichek aydur dervish baba
Sen Yunus Emramisin
La ilaha il Allah
Allah, La ilaha il Allah.

I asked a yellow flower
Do you have a mother and a father?
The yellow flower says, O, dervish,
My mother and father are soil.
There's no God except Allah,
Allah, there's no God except Allah.
I asked a yellow flower
Do you have brothers?
The yellow flower says, O, dervish,
My brothers are leaves.
There's no God except Allah,
Allah, there's no God except Allah.
I asked a yellow flower:
Why do you look yellow?
The yellow flower says, O, dervish,
Because death is close to me.
There's no God except Allah,
Allah, there's no God except Allah.
I asked a yellow flower:
Is there any death for you?
The yellow flower says, O, dervish,
Is there any place without death?
There's no God except Allah,
Allah, there's no God except Allah.
I asked a yellow flower
Do you know me?
The yellow flower says, O, dervish,
Are you Yunus Emre?
There's no God except Allah,
Allah, there's no God except Allah.

Female Mullah in Turkish part of Cyprus

Middle-aged Aisha is a *Marsyia* from a tiny village near Lefke in the Northern Turkish part of Cyprus. As she has a disabled husband, she makes her living by performing her repertoire for family and friends. I watched her cover herself in a white shawl she started her performance with *Salavat*, as do her counterparts in all the Islamic areas mentioned above. Her high-pitched voice seemed unusual, in my experience, but her pure chanting with its sincere devotional strength was very convincing. Her way of vocalising in a high register was more like that of an opera singer. Sometimes, an un-metred section of sung verse alternated with spoken greetings. She asked my mother's name and recited a hymn in her honour.

Allahdan zikr edelim ve fena
Vojib oldu har bir ishde har kuno
Allahdan har kim aylar har ishi
Oson etar Alloh har ishni ango.
Allaha har bir nefes dem-dem etem,
Allaha deyinda olur har ish tamom.

Let's remember Allah and Hereafter,
It's necessary to do so everyday.
Who acts with the name of Allah,
Allah makes easy his acts and actions.
I take my breath with the name of Allah,
When you say Allah, every act is fulfilled.

She was singing and I thought once again how musical these rituals with their flexible structure are. The chanting style of performing devotional poems incorporates increasing and diminishing waves of dynamics, repetitive, monotone, and pulsed rhythms, an alternation between improvised and planned sections, with the tempo increasing towards the end of the rituals. This style is common to female performers in all these countries. This music fulfils not just an aesthetic but also a social and religious function, reflecting the female role in preserving the folk culture.

Female leaders among Tatars in Russia

There is an Uzbek saying: 'Studying the world I found myself.' In researching female rituals and religious music I discovered that my Tatar Granny Fatima-obi, who lived all her life in Orenburg on the banks of the Ural River in Russia, was herself an *Abystai*, or what the Uzbeks call *Otin-Oy*. I remember once, when I was a child, hearing women crying outside our house in Andijan and being told that our next-door neighbours had lost their father. I was frightened by the thrilling sound made day and night by the chorus of weeping women. 'Why are they doing it?' I asked my mother. 'They lost their Daddy, the head of their family. They are grieving,' she said. 'Only simple uneducated women weep this way,' she, the best Maths teacher in the best city school, observed, adding, 'Your Granny is like that.'

In summertime, we used to go to see my granny in far-away Orenburg. I remember her whiter-than-white tablecloths, her unbelievably tidy house. She was very strict. She wanted us to speak only the Tatar language at her house (coming from Uzbekistan we easily switched to Uzbek or Russian to talk to each other when she was not around). As children, we were scared by her rather strict and formal character though, at the same time, we were charmed by her extreme beauty and image.

She used to read old books. Neighbours would come and invite her to gatherings which our parents would not allow us to attend. But, following the death of my Orenburg Granny, several of her books and notebooks were recently passed on to me, carefully wrapped in white tissue. Here is an example of what I found:

Urol Bo'yi – Tatar to'yi

Ural shores – Tatar wedding
(Poetry of Shakir Muhamedov)
Bizning Ural buylari
Semiz buladir quylari,
Biygrak zur bula tuylari,
Nadir onday uylari.
Yilqini kup suyalar,
Qimizni mechkalab quyalar
Oshob ichib tuyalar
Bizning Ural buylari.

On our Ural shores
Fat are our sheep,
But even bigger and greater are the festivities,
Why is it so?
They slaughter many horses,
Qumys is prepared in sacks,
They eat and drink till they are full
On our Ural shores.

This is a didactic book about weddings, which, it asserts, should not happen in an atmosphere of complete luxury and splendour, but should be modest. It is typical of *Jadid* literature from the beginning of the twentieth century, which is usually recited at the female gatherings.

Guide book on *Mavlyud*

This starts with a poem on *Mavlyud*

Bismillahu rahmani rahim
Jer yuzinda ahli Islom,
Nega shod jahon bukun?
Qayda borsang onda shodliq,
Jer juzinda ahli Islom

All over the world people of Islam,
Why is the world so happy today?
Wherever you go you see the joy,
All over the world people of Islam.

Then the book continues with the meaning of the *Mavlyud*. It relates that *Mavlyud* occurs on the twelfth of the month *Rabbiul avval*, when the Prophet Muhammad was born. He brought the light of Islam into this world and his *Umma* should celebrate *Mavlyud* because of that. After the explanation of *Mavlyud*'s meaning and importance, the guidebook gives an example of *Salavat* (hymn) to praise the Prophet:

Bismillohu rahminir rahim
Assalavotu vassalam alayka yo rasulullah,
Assalavotu vassalam alayka yo nabiullah;
Assalavotu vassalam alayka yo habibullah,
Assalavotu vassalam alayka yo shafi'ullah
Assalavotu vassalam alayka yo hayru halqullah.

Praise and peace upon you, O messenger of Allah
Praise and peace upon you, O prophet of Allah
Praise and peace upon you, O beloved of Allah
Praise and peace upon you, O close of Allah
Praise and peace upon you, O blessing of people of Allah

This is followed by an Arabic prayer, devoted to *Mavlyud,* which is followed once again by *Salavat.*

It continues with Tatar words, which follow the reading of the Qur'an and *Salavat* during the gathering devoted to *Mavlyud,* which states that all blessings of the gathering should go to praise Muhammad and save his *Umma* in both worlds. This Tatar prayer, with some Qur'anic inserts, is followed by a Tatar verse:

> *Allahning dustisan sen, ey mustafo Muhammad,*
> *Bizga shafoatchisan sen, ey mustafo Muhammad.*
> *Sami' Allah alayka, yo mustafo Muhammad,*
> *Yedi qad ko'k kechding sen, arshga-da ashding sen*
> *Alloh ilan surashding sen, yo mustafo Muhammad.*

> You are a friend of Allah, O sincere Muhammad,
> You are our saviour, O sincere Muhammad,
> Allah listens to you, O sincere Muhammad,
> You passed seven layers of heaven, you reached the throne of Allah;
> You spoke to Allah, O sincere Muhammad.

This hymn is usually sung by all participants at the gathering. After the chanting by the leading person has finished, the gathering ends with the final prayer, which is also read initially in Tatar but which concludes with Arabic verses.

48. HOW MUSICAL ARE FEMALE RITUALS?

During the course of 20 years, studying female rituals, I often asked myself the following questions: What is the nature of this phenomenon? Is it music or reciting poetry? Is it song or a speech phenomenon? Are rituals a part of a musical liturgy? Can we apply to their study some methods of ethnomusicology, which is a study of music as a cultural process, a social act, and as a sonic structure?

Poetry, historically, was very often connected with music because 'texts when sung or chanted have more power to impress the listener'.[266] It has a very special meaning to the Eastern, and particularly to Central Asian, culture. The tenth-century Central Asian scholar Al-Farabi said that 'the most perfect is a melody united with verse. This is what can move a man and change his morals.'[267]

Central Asian classical poetry from early times used to be chanted in a 'singing' way. One reason for that could be because the metrical system of classical poetry, based on an alternation of well-developed long and short syllable combinations lends itself to this treatment (*Aruz*). It produces a fundamental rhythmical design making the pronunciation of every poetry line sound like a musical performance.

Indeed, female rituals are all built on a combination of music, poetry, and words, interspersed with silence. Rituals may be distinguished by their different genres, ways of performance, and of the poetic forms from which they originated, but all of them are chanted. Representing a mix of poetry: folk (narratives and legends) and classical (*Ghazal*-related genres) these rituals, based on a variety of poetics metres, took shape as chanting rites.

It is difficult today to understand how this has developed through the centuries, how it was taught and transmitted, but everywhere these rituals have been performed as a singing poetry. It was my aim to document, that is, to prove the current practice of these phenomena. It is worth mentioning that these female religious leaders themselves – by whatever name they are known by – *Otin-Oys, Marsyias, Abystays* – called the process of performance *O'qish* (reading) meaning 'reciting'.

Music plays a very important role, portraying along with dramatic acts the essence of the ritual, through the use of historical parables, poetic metaphor, and so on, transferring the audience into a surreal dimension. The music of those rituals is not borrowed from other genres and being a composite part of the rite, is fully realised only in the process and context of its performance.

Music helps to sustain the participant's attention over extended periods of time aiding the ritual representation of the encounter between divine and terrestrial. The power of a ritual lies in the reach of its appeal and grip on the audience. Usually it happens in the community gathering, where all distinctions and boundaries between the two groups – the audience and the performers – are lost in the process, with everyone becoming an active participant. A true ritual spans a vast common ground, filling it with shared feelings and emotions. The collective participation in the performance all contribute to the ritual, combining it into a glorious whole, which reflects the Wholeness of God and Universe. Here the microcosm and macrocosm are united and the famous formula of the great Sufi Master Mansur Al Halladj (c. 858–922) – 'God is me!' – comes to life, bringing to mind a famous saying that 'it is women…who reproduce nations, – biologically, culturally, symbolically.'[268]

Conclusion

Female involvement in the religions and culture of Central Asia is evident in the facts emerging from this book, which is based on nearly twenty years' fieldwork and examination. Music is the thread which led to this discovery: singing voices heard exclusively within closed female communities helped me to recognise that, despite the winds of political change and turbulent historical transformations, female life continues to follow the full compass of various religious practices and beliefs.

Being a female researcher was an extra advantage for me as it opened a door to life 'behind the walls', behind bans and political restrictions, proving that real life is richer that any scholarly theories and assumptions.

I am happy to share with my readers what I was privileged to witness: how the sacred knowledge of a thousand years is transmitted orally from older to younger females, confirming the fact that the world belongs to women.

APPENDIX:
FEMALE POETRY

GHAZAL MASHRAB

Dame bu dunyodin o'tti jam'I beku sultonlar,
Qaro yerga fano bo'ldi hamma kokil parishonlar,
Na mardonlar fano bo'ldi bu dunyoda, musulmonlar,
Qaro yer ostiga kirdi hamma xon birla hoqonlar,
G'animatdur, birodarlar, ki bizga ushbu davronlar.

Ajalning bodai g'arqi umrlarni hazon qildi,
Ko'ngulning bulbuli ushbu alamlardin fig'on qildi,
Jami' ahli alamni ko'rung bag'rini qon qildi,
Ne odamlarni, ne mardlarni ul bexonumon qildi,
Ajalning dastidan hech kim qutulmas, ey musulmonlar.

In one instant have passed all the lords and kings,
All dishevelled beauties gone into the black earth
Oh Muslims, people who have left for the eternal world,
Into the black earth went all the khans and sultans,
Temporary has their time been, my brothers, and so is ours.

The drowning wine of death has turned into autumn leaves of life,
The nightingale of the heart began to cry from this suffering,
Look at the inhabitants of this world, their hearts are awash in blood,
Those people, this death has made weak,
No one can avoid their death, oh, Muslims!

GHAZAL SADOII

Yoronlar, Qosim shahzoda o'sa yig'lamasmanmu?
Bu g'urbat dashtida qoni to'kulsa yig'lamasmanmu?
Tilida "al" tashlab tashna ketsa yig'lamasmanmu?
Aziz jismi xassiz zahmlansa yig'lamasmanmu?
Ki dushman tig'ida bo'g'zi kesilsa yig'lamasmanmu?
Aning ahvoliga bag'rim ezilsa yig'lamasmanmu?

My friends, would I not cry, if Prince Qasim dies?
If in this steppe of suffering spills his blood, would I not cry?
Would I not cry, if having said "All…" he leaves thirsty

Would I not cry if his precious body turns to dust?
Or if the blade of the enemy's sword cuts his throat?
Would I not cry?
If my heart was filled with his suffering, would I not cry?

GHAZAL HAZINII

Kimki Haqqa bandadur, paymonidin ayrilmasun,
Kecha kunduz toati subhonidin ayrilmasun,
Barcha umrin rahmati rahmonidin ayrilmasun,
Piri rahmat shafoat konidin ayrilmasun,
Jahonda dur gavhari imonidin ayrilmasun.

Hafta adoida do'stni chun sahar bedorini,
Va'da qildi onalarga jannat bilan diydorini,
Haftiyak qilsa sahobat banda harna borini,
Rahmatidin benasib etgan chu dilozorini,
Tanga rohat istagan ehsonidin ayrilmasun.

Let the believer not lose their love for their Lord,
Let him never part from the object of his worship,
Let him never part with the Merciful through his short life,
Let him never part with the spring of kindness and mercy,
Let him never part with his faith, which is the pearls and diamonds of his life.
Like to a friend, sleepless in his vigil during the holy week

He promised to mothers the gardens of heaven and his image.
If a person sacrifices everything they have,
He (Allah) will not make him hapless,
So one, who seeks comfort for himself,
Never does part with his own kindness.

GHAZAL HUVAIDO

Qayu ishga qadam qo'ydim manga andin ziyon bo'ldi,
Manga ey betole' dostlar anda ko'p imtixon bo'ldi,
Qo'lim sho'ru, yo'lim qattiq, erurman turfa betole',
Hammaga mehribon bo'lsam, manga nomehribon bo'ldi,
Suyub jonu dilimdan kimga qildim oshnoliq,
Uzib ul oshnoliq oqibat manga yomon bo'ldi,
Hamma el baxtidin elga olsa xoki zar bo'ldi
Maning ilkimdagi zar shul zamon tuproqsimon bo'ldi,
Gulistonlar aro kirdim, ilik sundim olay deb,
Hah, ko'ringki betole'im, xorlar manga nishi chayon bo'ldi,

Huvaydo aytadur zolim falakning dastidin sad dod,
Manga yetkanda ul zolimning charhi ravon bo'ldi.

Whatever business I pursue, I end up only with losses,
I have experienced many of life's trials, my friends,
The hand of Destiny, sour; life's track, harsh,
Unfortunate is my fate.
I was kind to all, but they were unkind in return,
Loving with all my heart, I befriended a great many people,
But torn are the bonds of friendship, and I have felt pangs of pain
at the happiness of my friends.
Even ashes would turn into gold for the people,
But in my hands, gold turned into ashes.
I walked into flower fields, stretched my hand out, reaching for a flower,
But from my misfortunes, all would turn into scorpion's stings.
Huvaido, screams a thousand fold from the hands of the cruel heavens.
What can I do, if its sharp spikes have crushed and ground me?

Notes

1 HISTORICAL OVERVIEW

1   Zoroastrianism is the pre-Islamic Persian religion founded by the Persian prophet Zoroaster in the sixth century BC, and still practised by the Paresees in India. The Zend – Avesta is the sacred scripture of the faith. The theology of this religion is dualistic, *Ahura Mazda* or *Ormuzd* (the good God) being perpetually in conflict with *Ahriman* (the evil God), but the former is assured of eventual victory. There are theories that Zoroaster lived in Khorezm (modern Uzbekistan).

2   Tengrianism is a common faith of ancient Eurasian people. Originating in the most ancient land of the world – Sumeria – about 6,000 years ago, Tengrianism is considered to be the basis for all other religions of the world: Zoroastrianism, Buddhism, Christianity, and Islam. But only in the Turkic-speaking world do people today still believe in Tengrianism.

3   Manichaeism is a dualistic religion which originated in Iran at the time of the Sasanids (third century). Manichaeism fast developed within the vast area from the North of Africa to India and China, absorbing features of different local cultures. From the very beginning, Manichaeism was considered to be universal, absorbing transformed elements of such religions as Zoroastrianism, Christianity, and Buddhism. According to Manichaeism, there are two independent, opposed and conflicting foundations/substances, Light and Dark, associated with Good and Evil and divided by empty space. The Kingdom of Light possesses a harmony, peace, wisdom, grace, truth, and justice. It is spiritual. In the Dark kingdom are disharmony, chaos, arguments, evil, malice, madness, disgust, death, and so on. It is material. The highest deity is Light, which is, at the same time, the Great Father whose representatives are shining deities. Dark brought over in the image of Matter, which creates numerous evil demons to fight Light (Religovedenie. Enziklopedicheskyi slovar' (Theology, Encyclopaedic dictionary), Eds: A.P. Zabiyako A.N. Krasnikova, E.S. Elbakyan, Akademicheskyi Proekt, Moskva, 2006, p. 609.)

4   Zhainadarov, 2006, p. 245.

5   According to the secret history of Mongols, written in 1240, Chingiz Khan used to say: Tengry (God) opened the gates and handed us the reins indicating that Chingiz regarded only himself ruling by divine order. (Paksoy H., Sun is also fire: Central Asian Monuments, Istanbul, Isis Press, 1992, p. 3).

6   Schurman (1962, 249, n. 51) reports that the term *Tanggri* still appears in the phrase *Tanggri ta' ala'*, used in the present Ghorat region of Afghanistan to describe the omnipotent God of Islam.

7   Snesarev, 1969, p. 78.

8   There are many publications in Central Asian and Western historiography devoted to this question, which demonstrate various approaches and views. In general, in the Soviet Central Asian works, this period is considered as aggressive and very negative for local cultures. At the same time, scholars mark dual consequences of the conquest in the further historical development of the region.

9   There are several important studies devoted to the influences of Muslim music and science on European theory and practice. See, for instance, the well-known classical works of Henry George Farmer.

10   The same text, with some differences, is found in the work of another historian of this time – Hafiz-I Abru. For more on this text see the following publications: Alexander Djumaev. Hudojestvennye tendentsii i esteticheskie idealy v muzyke. – In: Amir Temur v mirovoi istorii. Izdanie vtoroe, dop. i pererab. Tashkent, 2001, p. 179. And also: Jung Angelika. Quellen der traditionellen Kunstmusik der Usbeken und Tadshiken Mittelasiens. Untersuchungen zur Entstehung und Entwicklung des sasmaqam. – Beitrage zur Ethnomusikologie. Band 23. Hamburg: Verlag der Musikalienhandlung Karl Dieter Wagner, 1989, p. 14, with references to previous mentionings, and so on.

11   There is a huge literature devoted to the theme of Russian conquest and colonisation policy in Central Asia published in the USA, Western countries, the former Soviet Union, and new independent Central Asian countries. They reflect different (in most cases – opposite) positions and views. See, for instance, some of the last Western books about it: Russia's Orient: Imperial Borderlands and Peoples, 1700–1917. Daniel R. Brower and Edwards J. Lazzerini, editors. Bloomington and Indianapolis: Indiana University Press, 1997; Daniel Brower. Turkestan and the Fate of the Russian Empire. London and New York: RoutledgeCurzon, Taylor & Francis Group, 2003. See also: Ishakov Faizulla. Natsional'naia politika tsarizma v Turkestane. 1867–1917. Tashkent: FAN, 1997; Rossia, Zapad i musulmanskiy Vostok v kolonial'nuyu epohu. [Sbornik statei]. St.-Petersburg, 1996; Gluschenko Evgeniy. Geroi Imperii. Portrety rossiyskih kolonialnyh deiatelei. Moscow: Izdatelskiy dom 'XXI vek – Soglasie', 2001; Ziyoev Hamid. Turkistonda Rossia tajovuzi va hukmronligiga qarshi kurash (XVIII – XX asr boshlari). Tashkent: 'Sharq', 1998, and many others.

12   Jadids' activity and the Jadid movement in Turkestan and Central Asia became one of the most popular themes in the new national historiography in Central Asian independent states. See, for instance: Sharipov Rustam. Turkiston jadidchilik harakati tarihidan. Tashkent: 'Uqituvchi', 2002; Qosimov Begali. Milliy Uigonish: Jasorat, ma'rifat, fidoyilik. Tashkent: 'Ma'naviyat', 2002; Ismoil Gasprinskiy va Turkiston. Tashkent: 'Sharq', 2005; see also: Adeeb Khalid. The Politics of Muslim Cultural Reforms. Jadidism in Central Asia. Berkeley and Los Angeles: University of California Press, 1998; Sartori, Paolo. Altro che seta: Corano e progresso in Turkestan (1865–1917). Pasian di Prato (UD), 2003, and many others.

13   Akiner, Shirin (1995), 'The Struggle For Identity', in. Jed Synder ed. *After Empire: The Emerging Geopolitics of Central Asia* (Washington: National Defence University Press), p. 7.

14   Martha Brill Olcott.

15   Ahrari, M. and Beal, James (1996), The New Great Game in Central Asia, McNair Paper, No. 47 (Washington: Institute for National Strategic Studies), p. 23.

16   *Pravda Vostoka*, 9 July 1933.

17   Mironov, 'Musyka Uzbekov (Music of the Uzbeks)', Samarkand, 1929, p. 9.

18   K. Alimbayeva and M. Ahmedov, 'Narodnye muzykanty Uzbekistana' (Folk Musicians of Uzbekistan), Tashkent, 1959, p. 53.

19   *Izvestia*, 24 August 1932.

20   Kabulov, 'On the Results of the Regional Cultural Congress', *The Bolshevik of Kazakhstan*, 1935, No. 6, p. 39.

21   Gavrilov, 'The Tasks of the Young Communist League on the Cultural Front', *The Bolshevik of Kazakhstan*, 1936, No. 4, p. 4.

22   Resolution of the Regional Communist Party Committee, *The Bolshevik of Kazakhstan*, 1935, No. 5, p. 94.

23   Nurnpeisov, 'On Mass Political and Cultural Work in Villages', *The Bolshevik of Kazakhstan*, 1935, No. 4, p. 18.

24   Resolution of the Regional Communist Party Committee, *The Bolshevik of Kazakhstan*, 1935, No. 4, p. 94.

25   *Pravda Vostoka,* 24 June 1933.

26   The Bolshevik of Kazakhstan, 1935, No. 3, p. 61.

27   *Folk Art*, Moscow, 1939, vol. 3.

28   *The Bolshevik of Kazakhstan*, 1939, No. 4, p. 94.

29   'Musical Culture of Kazakhstan', *Folk Art*, 1938, No. 12, p. 36.

30   Iyas Akbarov, 'Junus Rajabi', M 1982, pp. 7–8.

31   N.G. Melik-Shahnazarova, 'The National Tradition and Composition', doctoral thesis syn., M 1988, p. 31.

32   *Pravda Vostoka*, 18 July 1934.

33   Vakhidov, 'Uzbek Soviet Song', *Tashkent*, 1976, pp. 50–51.

34   Ibid., p. 58.

35   Akbarov, 'Junus Rajabi', M 1982, p. 6.

36   *Anthology of Turkmen Poetry*, M 1949, p. 358.

37   Liberated Kazakh woman. In: *The Bolshevik of Kazakhstan*, 1938, No. 3.

38   *The Bolshevik of Kazakhstan*, 1938, No. 5, p. 57.

39   Ibid., No. 55.

40   Esmagambet Ismailov, 'The Akyns', Alma-Ata, 1957, p. 187.

41   *Folk Art*, 1939, No. 4, p. 24.

42   Relations between the new independent state and Islam, attitude to politi-
      cal Islam in Uzbekistan and other matters are the subject of many scholarly
      studies published in USA, Western countries, and former USSR in 1990s
      and up to the present day. See among them, for instance: Abduvakhitov
      Abdujabar. Islamic Revivalism in Uzbekistan. – In: Russia's Muslim Frontiers.
      New Directions in Cross-Cultural Analysis. Edited by Dale F. Eickelman.
      Bloomington and Indianapolis: Indiana University Press, 1993, pp. 79–100;
      William Fierman. Policy toward Islam in Uzbekistan in the Gorbachev Era. – In:
      Nationalities Papers, Vol. 22, No. 1, 1994; Reuel Hanks, The Islamic Factor
      in Nationalism and National-Building in Uzbekistan: Causative Agent or
      Inhibitor. – In: *Nationalities Papers*, Vol. 22, No. 2, 1994; Babajanov B.,
      Komilov M. Razvitie religioznoi situatsii v Ferganskoi doline: problemy i per-
      spektivy izucheniia. – In: Obschestvennoe mnenie. Prava cheloveka, Tashkent,
      2000, Nos 1–2, pp. 95–102; Babajanov B., Komilov M. Domulla Hindustani
      and the Beginning of the 'Great Schisme' among moslems of Uzbekistan. – In:
      Stephan Doudiangion and prof. Hisao Komatzu ed. Politics and Islam in
      Russia and Central Asia. London-New York-Bahrayn, 2001, pp. 195–220;
      Babajamov B. Vozrojdenie deiatelnosti sufiyskih grupp v Uzbekistane. – In:
      Sufizm v Tsentralnoi Azii (zarubejnye issledovaniia). Sbornik statei pamiati
      Frittsa Maiera (1912–1998). St.-Petersburg, 2001, pp. 333–59, and many
      others.

2   SHAMANISM IN NOMADIC CULTURE

43   Basilov, Vladimir, 1997, 'Chosen by the spirits', In: Marjorie Mandelstam Balzer
      (ed.) *Shamanic Worlds: Rituals and Lore of Siberia and Central Asia, A North
      Castle Book* (originally published in New York: M.E. Sharp, 1990), p. 30.

44   Sidky, H. Shamanism in Afghanistan, p. 277.

45   Krader, 1963, p. 131; Car 1959, pp. 109–10.

46   Car, 1959, p. 114.

47   Sidky, H. Shamanism in Afghanistan, pp. 276–301.

48   Krader, 1963, p. 132.

49   Ashirov, p. 23.

50   Ibid.

51   Laufer, 1917.

52   Eliade, 1972, pp. 4–5.

53   Burke, 1973.

54   Gilberg, 1984, pp. 21–27.

55   Basilov, p. 43.

56   Ibid., p. 30.

57   From Popov A. A., 1936, 1948, posthumous: Nganasany: sotsial'noe ustroistvo
      i verovaniya (Leningrad: Nauka, 1984), p. 46.

58   'How Sereptie Djaroukin of the Hganasans (Tavgi Samoyeds) became a Shaman,
      Popular Believes and folklore tradition in Siberya', Utal-Altaic Series 57,
      Bloomington, 1968), p 34.

59   Kharuzin, 1988, p. 39.

60   Troitskaya, p. 195.

61   Basilov, 1997, p. 6.

62   Ibid., p. 44.

63   Ibid., p. 45.

64   Ibid., p. 46.

65   Basilov, Vladimir, 1997: 'Chosen by the spirits', In: Marjorie Mandelstam Balzer
      (ed.) *Shamanic Worlds: Rituals and Lore of Siberia and Central Asia, A North
      Castle Book* (originally published in New York: M.E. Sharp, 1990), p. 46.

66   Jirmundskyi Narodnyi Heroic epic, M-L 1962, p. 282.

67   Reichl, Karl, The search for origins: Ritual aspects of the performance of epic.
      Journal of Historical Pragmatics, Volume 4, Number 2, 2003, pp. 249–67(19).

68   Evgenyi Bertels, Roman ob Alexandre, M.-L., Izd Ac Nauk SSR, 1948, s 137.

69   Manas – geroicheskyi epos kyrgyzskogo naroda, Frunze, 1968, s 94.

70   Samar Musaev, *Epic Manas*, Academy of Science of Kyrgyzstan, Frunze, Ilim,
      1979, p. 47.

71   Yunusaliev, B., Manas, Kirish Sez, Frunze, 1958, c IY.

72   Ibid., p. 41.

73   From the point of gender issues, one remarkable fact mentioned in Manas is the
      ritual *Ok Attoo*: if a virgin woman steps over an arrow wound the wound will
      heal!

74   Roza Amanova. Kurmanbek Eposu. Bushkek, 4CDs, 8B4404.

75   Aitmatov, Chingiz. Jamilya. Telegram, 2007, pp. 66–67.

76   Harshahi M. Tarifa Bukhoro, Tashkent, 1897, 63 bet.

77   Social'no-utopicheskie idei v Srednei Azii, Tashkent, Fan, Uzbek SSR, 1983, p. 32.

78   Hultkrant, 1978, p. 52.

79   Krader, 1963, p. 121.

80   Basilov, p. 36.

81   Ibid., p. 35.

82   Ibid., p. 39.

83   Ibid., p. 40.

3   **SUFISM IN CENTRAL ASIA**

84   Sufii. Voshoghdenie k istine (Sufi: an assessment to the true), Moscow, EKSMO-Press, 2002, Evgenyi Bertels, pp. 477–80.

85   Ibid., p. 482.

86   See, for instance: Bodrogligeti, Andras J.E. The Impact of Ahmad Yassavi's teaching on the cultural and political life of the Turks of Central Asia. – In: [*Dili Arastirmalari Yilligi*. Belleten, 1987]. Ankara, 1992, pp. 35–41; and especially the various publications of Devin DeWeese.

87   Sufii. Voshoghdenie k istine (Sufi: an assessment to the true), Moscow, EKSMO-Press, 2002, Evgenyi Bertels, p. 510.

88   Ibid., pp. 510–11.

89   *The Oxford dictionary of Islam.* John L. Esposito (ed.), Oxford University Press, Sufism, pp. 302–3.

90   Abul Muhsin Muhammad Boqir ibn Muhammad Ali, Bahouddin Balogardon, Tashkent, Yozuvchi, 1993, p. 5.

91   Ibid., p. 9.

92   Ibid., p. 10.

93   Ibid., p. 11.

94   Ibid., pp. 12–13.

95   Ibid., p. 13.

96   Ibid.

97   Ibid., p. 14.

98   Ibid., pp. 14–15.

99   Ibid., p. 84.

100 Sadriddin Salim Buhoriy, Dilda Yor, Tashkent, G'afur G'ulom nashriyoti, 1993, p. 46.

101 Najmiddin Komilov, Tasavvuf, Tashkent, Yozuvchi, 1996, p. 117. What differs here is that in comparison with the main stages, which we mentioned earlier in our general overview, there are other stages Qanoat – satisfaction, Uzlat – seclusion, Tavajjuh – contemplation, and Rizo – acceptance.

102   Ibid., p. 118.

103   Ibid., p. 119.

104   Fuad Koprulu, Turk edebiyatinda ilk mutasavvifler, Ankara, 1993, p. 98.

105   Ibid., p. 99.

106   D.S. Margoliouth, 'Kâdiriyyâ'. *The Encylopaedia of Islam*, 2nd edn, vol. IV, p. 381.

107   To study the question of religious rites in male society in Central Asia it is neces-
       sary to have a male companion. I was accompanied by my husband.

4   FEMALE SUFISM

108   Bertels, p. 485.

109   Charles Upton, *Doorkeeper of the Heart: Versions of Rabi'a* (Putney, VT: Threshold
       Books, 1988), p. 36.

110   Camille Adams Helminski (ed.), *Women of Sufism: A hidden treasure,* Shaambhala
       Publications Inc., 2003, p. 83.

111   Ibn 'Arabi, *Sufis of Andalusia,* tr. R.W.J. Austin (Sherborne, Gloucestershire:
       Beshara Publications, 1988), pp. 25–26.

112   Camille Adams Helminski (ed.), *Women of Sufism: A hidden treasure,* Shaambhala
       Publications inc, 2003, , p. 96.

113   Ibid., p. 52.

114   Annemarie Schimmel, *Mystical dimension of Islam,* Chapel Hill: University of
       North Carolina Press, 1975, p. 432.

115   Ibid., p. 433.

116   Ibid., p. 429.

117   Camille Adams Helminski (ed.), *Women of Sufism: A hidden treasure,* Shaambhala
       Publications Inc., 2003, p. 207.

118   Ibid., p. 85.

119   Bakhtiyor Babajanov. 'O zenskikh sufiskikh centrakh-mazarakh v Srednej Azii
       XVI-XVIIvv'. *Srednyaia Azia i mirovaja civilizacija.* Tashkent: 1992: pp. 17–18.

120   Aleksander Djumaev. 'Turkestanskij Starec Hodzha Akhmad Yassavi i musul-
       manskye dukhovnye pesnopenia'. *Musykalnaja Akademija* 3–4 (1996), Moskva.

121   Troitskaya, 1928, p. 174.

122   Ibid., pp. 176–77.

123   Ibid., pp. 178–82.

124   Ibid., p. 183.

125   Ibid., p. 194.

126 Ibid., pp. 192–93.

127 Shemeem Burney Abbas, *The Female Voice in Sufi Ritual*, University of Texas Press, Austin, 2002, pp. xx–xxi.

128 A great poet of the fourteenth century, who wrote poems about love to women and God.

129 Hamid Ismailov, Razia Sultanova, K poetike klassicheskoy uzbekskoy gazeli, in Hamid Ismailov 'O'zbek ongi chizgilari', Tashkent, 1996, p. 41.

130 Great Persian Sufi poets of eleventh–twelfth centuries.

131 Hamid Ismailov, Razia Sultanova, 1996 pp. 41–42.

132 Great Muslim Sufi philosophers of the tenth–twelfth centuries.

133 Hamid Ismailov, Razia Sultanova, 1996 pp. 53–54.

134 Ibid., p. 43.

135 Ibid., p. 44.

136 Ibid., p. 49.

137 A great Sufi poet of the sixteenth century. Belonged to the court of great Mughals, founded by Babur-shaikh, who was himself a great Uzbek Sufi poet.

138 A famous Uzbek Sufi poet (seventeenth century), whose *ghazals* became the most popular Sufi songs.

139 Abdurauf Fitrat, Tanlangan asarlar, Tashkent, Ma'naviyat, 2000, 17, 82 betlar.

140 Razia Sultanova, *Rhythm of Shahsmaqam*, Tashkent, Yana, 1998, p. 28.

141 Bertels, p. 518.

142 Nodira she'riyatidan, Tashkent, FAN, 1979, 3–6 bet.

143 A cup, in which you could see the world.

144 Different poetic forms.

145 For more on Anbar-otin and her works see: Kadyrova Mahbuba. Svetoch vo t'me. Tashkent: Izdatel'stvo 'FAN' Uzbekskoi SSR, 1980.

146 Translation by Azam Abidov.

5 TRANSMISSION OF SACRED KNOWLEDGE IN ITS CONNECTION TO SUFI TRADITION

147 Koshifiy, Husayn Voiz, 1991, 'Ahloqul solihiyn' (On Ustad (Master) and his conditions), Dushanbe, Adib, pp. 48–56, translated from Persian by Futuvatnomai Sultoniy.

148 Kandiyoti Deniz, 1998, Rural livelihood and social networks in Uzbekistan: Perspectives from Andijan, in *Central Asia Survey*, 17(4), p. 562.

149 Ibid., p. 572.

150 Ibid.

151 Turkestanskyi ustav-risola zeha artistov D340/3II Materialsy po ethnografyi. T III vypusk vtoroi Izd Gosudarstvennogo Russkogo Muzeya Leningrad, 1927 (s 115) A. Samoilovich: Kukol'nyi teatr v Turkestane Izd Russ Muzei Ethnograficheskyi Otdel), translated by Razia Sultanova.

152 Alexander Jumaev, Kambar-ata (Kambar, Baba-Gambar) I musykal'nye tradizyi narodov Srednei Azii, 2004: Kurak, Beshkek, No. 6, p. 9.

153 Begmatov Soibjon, Tradizyi Iskusstva Hofizov Ferganskoi Doliny. Avtorefeerat dis na soiskanie uchenoi stepeni kanddiddata iskusstvovedeniya, Tashkent, 1995, UDK 78:03(09); 781, 7, p. 10.

154 Ibid., p. 8.

155 Ibid., p. 14.

156 Ibid., p. 13.

157 Ibid., p. 15.

158 Ibid., p. 18.

6 MUSIC AND FEMALE SUFIS

159 Pir-o-Murshid Inayat-Khan, 1914, 'A Sufi Message of Spiritual Liberty', London, p. 47.

160 Ibid., p. 48.

161 Huccetul-Islam Imam Gazali, Ihyau ulumid-din, Bedir, Istanbul, 1985, cilt 2, p. 751.

162 Ibid., pp. 744–51.

163 Ibid., p. 722.

164 Ibid., p. 720.

165 Pir-o-Murshid Inayat-Khan, 1914, p. 47.

166 Regula Qureshi, 'Indo-muslim Religious Music: an Overview', Asian Music, 1972, no. 2, p. 16.

167 Echard Neubauer, 'Islamic Religious Music', New Grove, vol. 9, pp. 342–49.

168 Regula Qureshi, 'Popular Religious Music, Muslim', New Grove, p. 145.

169 Ishoq Rajabov, Maqomlar Masalasiga doir, Tashkent, Fan, 1976, bet 8.

170 See Karomatov F., Elsner Jurgen. Maqam i maqom. – V knige: Muzyka narodov Azii i Afriki. Vypusk chetvertyi. M. 1984, p. 95.

171 Hamid Ismailov, Razia Sultanova, K metodologii izucheniya pyaterich-nogo kanona v hudojestvennom tvorchestve Vostoka (na primere Hamsy i Shahshmakoma). M, Izd. Nauka, 1990: 227.

172 Ibid., pp. 233–34. Connections of Shashmaqam and in general Uzbek and Tajik maqamat with Sufi ideas and Islam values are considered by several scholars in Uzbekistan and Tajikistan. See Oqil Ibragimov, 2006, Fergano Tashkentskie makomy, Tashkent, UNESCO, p. 170.

173 Levin, Theodore and Sultanova, Razia, 'The classical music of Uzbeks and Tajiks'. In: *The Garland Encyclopedia of World Music,* Volume 6, *The Middle East,* Routledge, pp. 913–14.

174 Here also one can see a correlation between this structure and famous saying of the Prophet Muhammad: 'I loved most of all women, fragrances, but more than that praying', which according to many theologians relates to the physical, virtual, and spiritual worlds.

175 Otanazar Matyoqubov, Maqomot, Tashkent, Musiqa, 2004, p. 92.

176 From my personal interviews with Berta Davydova in 1997, 1999, 2007 in Tashkent.

177 From my interview with Kommuna Ismailova taken in Tashkent on 12 April 2007.

178 A. Semyonov, K istorii uzbekskoy klassicheskoy muzyki, Rukopis', Bib-ka Instituta iskusstvovedeniya im.Hamzy, Tashkent, 1950, s.3. For more about *Khanaqai,* see: Alexander Djumaev, Sredneaziatskaya hanaka, sufyiskye predpisaniya o slushanyi (*sama*) i tradiziya duhovnyh pesnopenyi (honakoi). In: Transoziana, Istorya i kul'tura. Cbornik statei. Tashkent, 2004 (Seria: Kul'tura Srednei Azii v pis'mennyh istochnikah, dokumentah i meterialah). S 314–321.

179 Rustambek Abdullaev, Zhanr Katta Asula i ego nositeli, Tashkent, 1982, pp. 9–10.

180 Otanazar Matyoqubov, Maqomot, Tashkent, Musiqa, 2004, pp. 94–95.

181 My interview wth Munojat Yulchieva, recorded in May 1997.

7 INTERACTION OF SHAMANISM AND SUFISM IN CENTRAL ASIAN FEMALE PERFORMANCE

182 Azemoun, Youssef, Halinin Sunduğu Bazi Dil ve Müzik Kavramlari 'Some Linguistic and Musical Concepts which Carpets Present', Harvard, 2007, pp. 120–26.

183 Soren Neergard, Oriental Carpet and Textiles Studies IV, Milan 1999, p. 232.

184 Kutadgu Bilig, II: Tercume (Ankara, 1959). Resid Rahmeti Arat, p. 15.

185 Heike Owusu, Inca, Maya and Aztecs, translation by R. Andreeva, Ilya, Izmir, p. 27.

186 Y. Azemoun and Brian Aldiss, Songs from the Steppes of Central Asia, UK, p. 9.

187 Ibid., p. 9.

188   Today the second title is used for the wife of the Aga Khan, the leader of the Ismaili sect as 'Begum Aga Khan'.

189   Uspenskyi, V.V. Belyaev Turkmenskaya musica; 'Turkmenistan' publisher, Ashgabad, 1979, pp. 61–62.

190   Ibid., p. 10.

191   Ibid., pp. 11–12.

192   Elemanova, Saida 2009, A Brief Comparative History of Musical Shamanism and a Contemporary Kazakh Example: Galiya Kasymova's Phenomenon. In: Sultanova Razia (Ed.), *Sacred Knowledge: Schools or Revelation? Master-Apprentice System of Oral Transmission in the Music of the Turkic Speaking World.* Koln, Lambert Academic Publisher.

193   Suharyeva, Olga. Syuzani: sredneaziatskaya decorativnaya vyshyvka, Vostochnaya literatura, RAN, Moskva, 2006. Some similar connection between carpet design and music are explored in: Inna Naroditskaya, Mugham and Carpet: Cross-Domain Mapping, in Ethnomusicology Forum, Volume 14, No. 1, 2005, pp. 25–57, Routledge.

8   MUSICAL INSTRUMENTS AND DANCE IN FEMALE COMMUNITIES

194   *Kobuz* is the most ancient Central-Asian bowed lute.

195   Pre-sounds (overtones), which play an important sacral role in the timbre of *Kobuz* are produced because the strings and the bow of this instrument are made of bunches of straight horsehair (strings – of 40–50 hairs, the bow – of 30–40 hairs). The friction between the bow and strings involuntarily produces partial tones – overtones and adjoining tones.

196   The task of *Kobuz's* participation in *baiga* is complicated by the fact that this instrument is tied to the mighty oak. Nevertheless, *Kobuz* pulls out the oak from the ground and brings it together to the finish.

197   Alektorov writes about Bakshi Suimenbai to whom genies declared that they chose him as their master, that is, Bakshi. 'At that time, the father's *Kobuz* started to play by itself and approached me from the wall near which it lay'. Baksa. Izvestiya of the Society of Archeology, History and Ethnography under the Kazan University. 1900, v. XY1, edition 1, 34–35.

198   V. M. Zhirmunsky, *Turkic Heroic Epos.*

199   Razia Sultanova, O vzaimosvyazyah usulya i ritma melodii v vocal'nyh chastyah Shahshmakoma, Tashkent, Yana, 1998.

200   The principal cities of Khorasan were Nishapur, Herat, Merv/Mary, and Balkh. The Khorasani *tanbur* is described in treatises by al-Farabi (d. 950).

201   For further organological information, see Baily and During 2001.

202   For background information about musical traditions of Uzbekistan, see Levin and Sultanova 2001.

203   Nodira, 1980.

204   Voljinski's photo appears in Cagatay, 1996: 52–53.

205   Qadiry, 1974.

206   Cholpon, 1991.

207   Many male Sufi songs were, and are, performed with the accompaniment of *Tanbur*. For instance, famous Sufi singers brothers Sufikhanovs perform nearly all their Sufi songs with *Tanbur*. See: Otanazar Matyoqubov, Maqomot, Tashkent, Musiqa, 2004, p. 95.

208   Interview: Tashkent, 1999. This sort of legend is current in musical circles.

209   Plato and Aristotle are considered in Muslim tradition as Prophets, and in Sufi tradition as the Great Masters of Sufism.

210   Uspenskyi, Victior and Belyaev, Victor: Turkmenskaya Musika, Ashhabad, 'Turkmenistan', 1979.

211   Ibid., pp. 112–13.

212   Djumaev, Alexander, 2004, *Kambar-ata (Kambar, Baba Gambar) I muzykal'nye tradizyi narodov Srednei Azii*, Kurak, Bishkek, p. 12.

213   Uspenskyi, Victior and Belyaev, Victor: Turkmenskaya Musika, Ashhabad, 'Turkmenistan', 1979, pp. 112–13.

214   Uvaysiy's text comes from a *ghazal* (a well-known poetic form often performed in sung versions). The Uzbek text is (Uvaysiy 1981).

215   The text in Uzbek is (Cholpan 1991).

216   Compositions set to poetry include the following: Lutfihonim Sarymsakova: *Uzgancha, Tanovar*, and *Ferghancha Jonom* by Mukimy. Mehro Abdulaeva: *Ruzi tanovar* and *Tanovar* by Mukimy. Bashorat Hojaeva: *Isma-Hush* and *Kalandar-5* by Mukimy. Mavluda Akzamova: *Chully Irok* and *Yghitlar* by Toshmapulat, and *Korashidur* by Furkat.

217   The *balalaika* is a three-stringed Russian plucked lute, with a characteristic triangular body. Early representations of the *balalaika* show it with anywhere from two to six strings, which resembles certain Central Asian instruments. See: Blok, V. Orkestr russkikh narodnykh instrumentov – Moscow, Sovetskyi kompozitor, 1986.

218   Interview with Ilyas Akbarov, 1989, Tashkent; also see Sultanova 1993.

219   For more biographical details, see Sultanova 2001. For a musical example, see Sultanova 1998.

220 From my interviews with Turghun Alimatov, April 2007, Tashkent.

221 One should not, however, confine dances just to Sufism. Gods and goddesses who revealed doctrine through dance are met everywhere. In the Gnostic gospel Acts of John, even Jesus danced and said to his disciples, 'To the Universe belongs the dancer. He who does not dance does not know what happens. Now if you follow my dance see yourself in Me'. (*The Woman's Dictionary of Symbols and Sacred Objects.* Barbara G Walker. Pandora, 1988, p. 176.)

222 Mary Masayo Doi, 2002, *Gesture, Gender, Nation: Dance and Social Change in Uzbekistan,* Greenwood publishing group.

9   FEMALE FOLK SUFISM

223 As the *Sura* of Qur'an says, 'Men are the protectors and maintainers of women because Allah has given the one more (strength)', Sura Al-Nisa (IY), 34.

224 Seclusion in general terms did not permit women to go out of the house, to move freely in the streets or to visit relatives without men's permission. Thus, all that was connected to the outside world became the responsibility of men. Restricted to the four walls of their homes, seclusion condemned women to degradation, led to stagnation of their mental potential, suppressed their individuality, lowered their self-esteem and social value, led to physical exploitation and to them being treated like child-bearing machines. Nevertheless, women brought up in the Muslim tradition largely accepted this without question, restricting their lives to the realm of home and family.' M. Tokhtakhodjaeva, p. 38.

225 Ursula Reinhardt, The Veils are Lifted. Music of Turkish Women.: Intercultural music studies, in which she describes many common situations of Turkish women.

226 This discrimination against women leads to awful consequences like the self-immolation of Uzbek women. As Marfua Tokhtakhodjaeva mentioned: 'in 1970–1980 a trend of suicides among women developed; in despair, denied even the possibility of complaining about their situation, and not finding protection among their parents and their nearest, they took this extreme step' (p. 93). It is still ominously popular among Uzbek women. About 300 Uzbek women die almost every year from self-immolation.

227 Dodkhudoeva, Larisa Cultural leadership in Central Asia: Ancient and medieval epoch.: The Institute of History, Archaeology, Ethnography after A. Donish, the Academy of Science of Tajikistan, Dushanbe, 2003. p. 60.

228 Exactly this aspect, having first caught my attention in 1990, resulted in series of special field investigations and expeditions, which I conducted in the following order: 1990 – Namanghan and Yazavan village; 1991 – Shakhimardan settlement in the Ferghana district; 1992 – Ferghana Valley: Andijan and its surroundings, Dudur and Butakora villages of Andijan district. Also Namanghan and Osh with their surrounding settlements Eski-Noukat, Chashma-Say, and others. The

cities of Tashkent and Samarkand. 1996 – Ferghana district, Andijan district, Surkhandarya district, Boysun. 1997 – Tashkent city and surroundings, Hodjent and surroundings (Tadjikistan).

229 There are special studies devoted to *Otin-Oy* by French anthropologist Habiba Fathi. See: Habiba Fathi. *Otines*: the unknown women clerics of Central Asian Islam. – Central Asian Survey, 1997, 16(1), pp. 27–43; Le pouvoir des *otin*, institutrices coraniques, dans l'Ouzbekistan independent. – In: Cahiers d'Asie Centrale, No. 5–6. Boukhara-la-Noble, Tachkent – Aix-en-Provence, 1998, pp. 313–33; Femmes d'autorite dans l'Asie centrale contemporaine. Quete des ance-tres et recompositions identitaires dans l'islam postsovietique. Paris: Maisonneuve & Larose, Institut Francais d'Etudes sur l'Asie Centrale, 2004.

230 See: Abdurahmoni Jomi. Osor. Dar hasht jild. Jildi hashtum. Nafahat al-Uns. Dushanbe, 1990, pp. 129–32.

231 'Amir Temur in world history', Paris, 1996, p. 153.

232 In the 1930s, Victor Uspensky noticed this remarkable musical character of reli-gious chanting within local communities. He made comments on different genres of worship performed by male performers: 'Even the cantillation of the Qur'an was called "reading" rather than singing although both melody and vocal ornamentation are beautifully presented there and to a lesser extend in the Azzan or call to Prayer.' Among genres performed by religious performers were Yakka-honlik – solo singing; genre dedicated to Allah – Hamd; to the Prophet – Na't; to his fellows – Ilhon; rulers and warriors – Mad'ya' 1. As one can see, female religious chanting were not introduced to the academic reader. (Uspenskyi Viktor, 1980, Nauchnoe nasledie, vospominaniya sovremennikov, dokumanty, pis'ma. Tashkent, Gafur Gulyam.)

233 Similar situation with the rite of initiation occurred within the circles of Bukharan Sozanda (female entertainers). See Djumaev, Alexander, K izucheniy ritualov 'arvohi pir' i 'kamarbardon' v gorodskyh tzehah muzykantov Srednei Azii, in: Obshetvennye nauki v Uzbekistane. Tashkent, 1995, No. 5–8, p. 163–70.

234 Razia Sultanova. *Pojushchee Slovo Uzbekskikh Obrjadov.* Almaty: Konzhyk, 1994.

235 Ibid., pp. 68–69.

236 Razia Sultanova Qadiriyya Dhikr in Ferghana Valley in *Journal of the history of Sufism,* Paris, volume 1–2, 2000, p. 535.

237 Ibid., p. 537.

238 Nikolay Lykoshin, 'A half of lifetime in Turkistan', St. Petersburg, 1916.

239 There is an interesting observation that proper/pure Sufism was denying the ritu-alisation as an act bringing a mystical side-effect to the pure faith. Even 40 days' fasting, vagrancy, begging, public Sama' with music, songs, dances, and also loud Zikr-Jahriya have been regarded as actions distracting from pure Muslim wisdom.

240 Alexander Djumaev, 'Turkestanskyi Starets' Hodja Ahmad Yassavi i musulmanskye duhovnye pesnopenia'. Musykalnaya Akademia, Moskva, 1996, No. 3–4.

241 Troitskaya, 1928, p. 193.

242 Ibid.

10 FEMALE RITUALS

243 Van Gennep, Arnold, *The Rites of Passage*, Chicago: The University of Chicago Press.

244 W. G. Lambert, 'Devotion: The Languages of Religion and Love', In: *Figurative language in the Ancient Near East*, SOAS, University of London, 1987, p. 25.

245 Enemies.

246 The place where Imam Hussein was killed.

247 Strictly speaking, some of those life-cycle rituals are also part of the previous element of classification: so, Mourning rituals are mostly held in a Sufi and quasi-Sufi way, which were analysed in this chapter 10 earlier in the sub-chapter 41, devoted to Songs and Recitals of sorrow and repentance.

248 Hamid Ismailov, The Railway, Harvill-Secker/Random House, 2006, p. 299.

249 Cho'lpon, Kecha va Kunduz, G'afur G'ulom, Tashkent, 1991, 49 bet.

11 SIMILAR FEMALE RITUALS IN THE TURKIC-SPEAKING WORLD (IN TATAR, AZERI, TURKISH, CYPRIOT, AND AFGHANI TRADITIONS)

250 According to tradition, a woman during the days of her period is not allowed to perform the rituals, since she is physiologically 'unclean'. So her ability to be transformed into the mythological teller has its physical limits.

251 Baiburin, A.K. *On Ethnographic Research of Etiquette: Etiquette of the peoples of Asia Minor*, Moscow, 1988.

252 Ibid., p. 17.

253 Ibid., p. 27.

254 Sagalaev, A.M., Oktyabr'skaya I.V. *Traditional world outlook of Turkic peoples of South Siberia. Sign and Ritual*. Novosibirsk, 1990, Ch: Laughter and Tears, p. 160.

255 Bahtin, M.M. *Creations of Fransua Rable and folk culture of Middle Ages and Rennaisance*, Moscow, 1965, p. 1.

256 Sagalaev, A.M., Oktyabr'skaya I.V. *Traditional world outlook of Turkic peoples of South Siberia. Sign and Ritual*. Novosibirsk, 1990, Ch: Laughter and Tears, p. 167.

257 Ungvizkaya, M.A., Mainogasheva V.E. *Hakassian poetical folk creativity*. Abakan, 1972, p. 57.

258   Ibid., pp. 166, 167.

259   Toporov V.N. *About some assumptions in the formation of category of possessiveness. Slavic and Balkan linguistics: Problems of Dialectology, problems of possessiveness,* May 1986, p. 146.

260   Ibid., p. 169.

261   Verbitski, V.I. *World perception and folk creativity of Siberian indigenous tribes* (Ethnographic materials). Literature compilation, SPB, 1885, p. 338.

262   Kastren M.A., Trip to Lapland, North Siberia and Russia, *Journal of geography and travels: Geographical compilation,* Moscow, 1860, vol. 6. Part II Compilation of old and new travels, p. 388.

263   Ibid., p. 179.

264   *Journal of Historical Pragmatics.* Volume 4, No. 2, 2003, pp. 249–67.

265   My fieldwork was made possible by the grant I received from the Committee for Central and Inner Asia at the University of Cambridge.

266   The Oxford companion to music, 2002, Alison Latham (ed.), London: Oxford University Press, p. 1044.

267   Razia Sultanova, Rhythm of Shashmaqam, Tashkent, Yana, 1998, p. 28.

268   Yuval-Davis, Nira, 1998, Gender and Nation, in *Women, Ethnicity and Nationalism,* Robert Miller and Wilford Rick (eds), Routledge, p. 24.

Glossary

All definitions are provided according to the Uzbek language's transliteration.

A

Adab – (Arabic) rules of behaviour

Adat – (Arabic) compilation of traditional regulations particularly among nomadic people of Central Asia

Agy – Turkmen lament songs, means 'weeping'

Ahawan – gift, in Kubraviyya school of Sufism stands for the colour blue

Ahvol (Arabic *ahwal*) plural for *Hal* – state, a cornerstone of Sufism, meaning a state of belonging to God

Akyn – traditional nomadic storyteller, singer

Alla – a lullaby

Alpomish – a mythic hero from the Uzbek epic poem of the same title

Antalho – a religious genre

Armans – Kyrgyz songs of complaints, regrets

Aruz – (Arabic *Arudh*) – a system of poetry based on short and long syllables

Ashir-Oy – a month, when Prophet Muhammad's grandson Hussein was killed, commemorated by Shia Muslims

Ashula – a traditional Uzbek, Tajik song

Awj – culmination of instrumental piece or song

Ayak-lale – a dance in Turkmen Sufi *Zikr* performed with jumping from foot to foot and intense body movement

Aytys – a nomadic genre of poetry, dialogue – competition between two poets

Azayimxon – fortune-teller and healer woman

B

Bacha – a boy, used for entertainment by men

Baiga – a horse race

Baqo – (Arabic *baqâ*) a term in Sufism, means 'eternal world'

Baqshi/y – a nomadic singer-healer with shamanic qualities

Baraka – (Arabic *Barakah*) – bounty, blessing

Barmoq – a system of Turkic poetry, based on accents

Barmoq qirsillatish – finger snapping in Uzbek dancing

Bastakor – a traditional composer in Uzbek and Tajik music

Bayaz – a collection of traditional poems

Bayt – two lines in a *Ghazal*

Bazm – the culmination, climax; the musical party of the *Toy*

Bedilhonlik – readings of Bedil's poetry

Bek – usually a military commander in the history of Central Asia

Bektoshiya – a branch of Sufism, which is widespread in Turkey

Beshik – a traditional Central Asian cradle

Biligi – a voice technique in Uzbek classic singing

Bir-depim – a form of Turkmen Sufi *Zikr*, means 'once step'

Bismillo – beginning of all Muslim prayers, means 'in the name of Allah'

Bosmachi – (Russian and English Basmachi) means 'assaulter' – a freedom fighter against the Bolshevik rule

Botin – (Arabic *Batin*) – a term in Sufism meaning 'hidden'

Buzruk – a part of Shashmaqam, means 'great'

C

Chahor kitob – means 'Four Books', introductory books in Central Asian madrasahs

Chang – Uzbek, Tajik musical instrument

Chang-qo'buz – Kyrgyz/Kazakh musical instrument

Chertmak (flip) – *Dutar* musical piece, which includes striking strings and flipping the belly of the *Dutar*

Chishtiyya – a branch of Sufism widespread in India, Pakistan

Chor zarb – rhythm of *Doira*, consisting of four beats

Chorllar – a meeting for old people as a part of *Toy*

Choxona – a tea house, a place of public gatherings

D

Daf – a round percussion instrument

Daromad – an introductory part of musical pieces in Shashmaqom, means 'introduction'

Dashgariya/Jahriya – a loud form of *Zikr*

Dastarkhan – a traditional Central Asian tablecloth

Dediyo – a genre of *Otin-Oy's* narration meaning 'he said'

Devon – a collection of *Ghazals* in Arabic alphabetic order

Doira – a round percussion instrument

Domla – a teacher, master

Doppi – Uzbek male traditional hat

Dastan – an epic poem

Dugoh – a part of *Shashmaqam*

Dunasr – a development in the musical pieces in Shashmaqom, means 'double prose'

Duo – a prayer

Dutar – an Uzbek/Tajik/Turkmen/ Uyghur/Afghan musical instrument, means 'two strings'

Duzarb – a rhythm of *Doira*, means 'two beats'

E

Ertalabgi osh – morning pilav (the main Uzbek meal) as a part of *Toy*

Eshon – a Sufi master, comes from Persian 'they'

Ey dilbari jononim (O, my Beauty) – classic Uzbek song, *katta ashula*

F

Fano – (Arabic *fana'*) – this ephemeral world

Farz – a religious obligation in Islam

Faqiriani – women singers at Indian Sufi shrines

Faqirs – poor people, people at a certain stage of Sufism

Faqr – poverty, one of the stages of Sufism

Folbin – a fortune-teller

Furaward – a part of the musical piece

G

Gashtak – a social gathering of men and women, held separately in Uzbekistan

G'assol – local professional attendants called to wash the body before it is taken to the cemetery for burial

Gap – a social gathering of men and women, held separately in Uzbekistan

Gavda tibranishi – body movements in Uzbek dances

Göl – the main design of Turkmen rugs

Guligi – a vocal technique in Uzbek classic singing, characterised by ornaments

Ghazal – a traditional classic form of poetry

Ghazalxonlik – reading of Ghazals

Ghidjak – an Uzbek/Tajik, Uighur musical instrument

H

Hadis/Hadith – sayings of the Prophet Muhammad or stories of his life, the second main source of Islam after the Holy Qur'an

Haftiyak – an introductory religious book, based on the Qur'an – means 'one seventh'

Halfa – a religious woman in Khoresm, leading the rituals, the same as *Otin-Oy*

Halifa – Caliph, representative of Allah or of a prophet

Halol/halal – allowed in Islam, opposite of *harom* – disallowed

Hamd – praise to Allah before the prayers, or genre of glorifying Allah

Hamsa – means 'five' in Arabic, a literary form, comprising five epic poems

Hang – vocal ornaments in Uzbek, Tajik, Uighur singing

Haqiqat – means 'truth' in Arabic, the ultimate stage of Sufism

Harom/haram – disallowed in Islam

Hasan and Hussein – martyred grandsons of the Prophet Muhammad

Hat – a letter, way of writing

Havf – fear, a stage in Sufism, means 'fear of God'

Hayajan – means 'trembling' in Arabic, a stage in Sufism

Hayrat – means 'surprise' in Arabic – a stage in Sufism

Hazrat – sir, religious master

Hijra – according to Hijra calendar, Hijra is the date when Prophet Muhammad escapes from Mecca to Medina

Hikmat – Wisdom, the title of Ahmad Yassaviy's Sufi poem

Hizb – (Arabic *hidhb*) army

Hofiz – a person memorised the Holy Qur'an

Ho'ja/hodja/khodja – a descendent of the first four Caliphs, a respected Muslim

Hol/Hal – a state in Arabic, a stage of Sufism

Hufiya – a silent *Zikr*, Sufi meditation

Hundi – a Turkmen lullaby

Hutba – an Islamic sermon before the Friday prayers

I

Ichkari – the inner part of the Uzbek traditional household, where women and children live

Ijod faoliyat – a stage of perfection, meaning 'creativity'

Ilm – science, knowledge, in Islamic context means 'the religious knowledge'

Imon – faith, belief, one of the preconditions of Islam, a stage in Sufism

Imam – an Islamic priest leading the prayer

Imtinan – faith, a stage in Sufism

Irfan – knowledge, a stage in Sufism

Iroq – a part of Shashmaqam

Ishqi majoziy – symbolic love, earthy love of women in Sufi literature

Ishqi mutlaq – absolute love of God in Sufi literature

Istighfar – asking forgiveness, a stage in Sufism

Itmanina – peace of mind, a stage of Sufism

Iyak h'arakati – chin movements in Uzbek dances

Iyd-ul Ramazon – day of celebration at the end of Ramadan

J

Jadid – means 'new' in Arabic, a reformist movement in Islamic world at the end of the nineteenth century

Jahriya/Dashgariya – a loud form of Sufi *Zikr*

Janoza – a mourning prayer

Jir – a nomadic song

Jirau – a nomadic singer and musician

Jomok – a nomadic narrative of the past

Jo'ranavoz – a form of a duet, singing in a couple with a partner singer

Juma-namoz – a Friday prayer in the mosque

K

Kalamkash – a female artist, drawing the ornament of Suzane

Kara olen – a genre of Kazakh song, means 'black song'

Karnay – an Uzbek/Tajik/Uighur musical instrument, 2-m-long brass trumpet

Katta ashula – a form of an Uzbek professional song

Kelin salom – (welcoming the bride), a performance for the bride's relatives

Kereez – a nomadic genre means a statement of the will

Kilim – a rug in Turkmen

Kinanchi – a traditional healer, mostly fighting 'an evil eye'

Kirish – an Uzbek word for an introduction

Kobuz – nomadic spike fiddle

Kom – a shaman in Turkic languages

Komuz – kyrgyz plucked lute

Ko'r-og'li – a famous epic poem, traditional for many people of Central and Minor Asia

Koshok – a Kyrgyz folk song

Koshuk – an Uzbek folk song

Kowuz – a Turkmen musical instrument, the same as *Kobuz*

Kubraviyya – a school of Sufism founded by Najm ad-din Kubra (eleventh century)

Kulliyat – a complete work of certain poets

Kushtdepie – a form of a Turkmen Sufi *Zikr*

L

Lapar – a folk song

Larzon – trembling, movement in Uzbek dances

Latif – tender, a quality in Sufism

Layale – a musical genre with a modest, simple tune

Laylatul Qadr – the Night of Destiny at the end of Ramadan, when the Holy Qur'an was first revealed to the Prophet Muhammad

M

Madh – genre of praise and glorification

Madrasah – a religious Muslim school

Majlis – usually poetic, artistic, musical gathering

Makhv-isbat – hidden/proven, an opposition in Al-Ghazali's philosophy

Makruh – undesirable in Islam

Manas – famous Kyrgyz epic, which is considered to be the world longest epic

Manaschi – teller, narrator of Manas, usually a person of a shamanic nature

Marhabo – a religious genre of welcoming

Ma'rifat – a stage in Sufism meaning Enlightenment

Marsyia – religious women leading the rituals in Azerbaijan and Turkey, the same as *Otin-Oy* in Central Asia

Mashrabhonlik – public reading of Mashrab's Sufi poetry

Masnaviy – a great poem by Mavlyana Rumiy

Maqom/Maqam – means 'station', a stage in Sufism, a genre of professional music of Sufi nature

Mavlud – birthday of the Prophet Muhammad, religious rituals devoted to it

Mawlaviyya – a school of Sufism, founded by Mavlayana Rumiy (twelfth century)

Mazhab – a legal school in Islam

Mehtarlik – professional guild in Central Asia

Meroj – ascension of the Prophet Muhammad to the celestial worlds

Misra – a line in *Ghazal*

Miyonxona – a middle part of a professional musical piece

Monjukatdy – a Turkmen fortune-telling song

Muboh – (Arabic *mubah*) admissible in Islam

Muhabbat – means 'love', a stage in Sufism

Muhaddis – a connoisseur of Hadises

Muhammas – a genre of poetry, with stanzas, consisting of five lines

Mukammallik – perfection, a stage in Sufism and in learning the skills (e.g. musical)

Mukashafot – discovery, a stage in Sufism and in learning the skills (e.g. musical)

Mulla – religiously educated person

Munojat – a prayer to God, a genre of song

Muqomlar – capricious movements in Uzbek dances

Murabba – a genre of poetry, with stanzas, consisting of four lines

Murid – a Sufi apprentice

Murokaba – closeness, a stage in Sufism

Murshid – a Sufi Master, Teacher

Musa-noma – a religious poem about the life of the Prophet Musa (Moses)

Mushahada – contemplation, a stage in Sufism

Mushkilot – instrumental parts of Shashmaqam

Mushkul Kushod – a religious ritual for untangling difficult situations

Mustahab – beneficial in Islam

N

Nag'ma – a tune, melody

Namoz – a Muslim prayer

Nasr – a vocal part of Shashmaqam

Naqshbandiyya – a school of Sufism, founded by Bahoutdin Naqshband (fourteenth century)

Na't – religious genre of glorifying the Prophet Muhammad

Navo – a part of Shashmaqam, means 'melody'

Navruz – a New solar year celebration of equinox, which is of pre-Islamic nature, means 'New day'

Nay – an Uzbek/Tajik/Uighur/Persian/ Turkish musical instrument, flute

Nido – music heard in vision (inspirational)

Nikoh – registration of matrimony by the Mullah and the official organisation

Nog'ora – an Uzbek/Tajik/Uighur drum

Nohun – a metallic plectrum to play *Tanbur*

Non ushatish – (breaking bread), the engagement, when the relatives of the bride and groom divide a small loaf into two parts

Noy-noy – a genre of folk music in northern Afghanistan

O

Obi Hayot – a mystical source of life

O'g'il chaqiriq – meeting of men with the groom as a part of *Toy*

Ohun – an educated person

Olami kubro – macrocosm in Islam

Olami sugro – microcosm in Islam

O'qish – religious reading

Oq rumol – a white shawl covering *Otin-Oy*

Ornau – a didactic genre of nomadic poetry

Orom – 'Meditation' – an Uzbek dance

Otinbuvi – religious women leading the rituals in Central Asia, the same as *Otin-Oy*

Otincha – religious women leading the rituals in Central Asia, the same as *Otin-Oy*

Otin-Oy – religious women leading the rituals in Central Asia

P

Parandja – a kind of Central Asian *hijab*, veil

Pari – a fairy

Parihan – a sorcerer, who is considered to deal with fairies

Pir – a religious, Sufi master

Q

Qadiriyya – a school of Sufism, founded by Abdulqadir Giloniy (eleventh century)

Qambar – a genre of religious songs among Uzbeks of Afghanistan

Qanoat – satisfaction with existence, a stage in Sufism

Qarsaklar – clapping, movements in Uzbek dances

Qiroat – a professional reading of the Holy Koran

Qiyomat-noma – a religious genre about the Day of Judgement

Qiz chaqiriq – meeting of women, with the bride, as part of a wedding ceremony

Qobuz – nomadic spike fiddle

Qori – a reader of Qur'an

Qul – Indian music which creates feelings (emotional)

Quldasta ailanish – wrists turning, a movement in Uzbek dances

Quldasta titrama – hands trembling, a movement in Uzbek dances

Qulub – plural of *Qalb* – means 'heart' in Arabic

Qurb – closeness, a stage in Sufism

Qurban Bayram/Haiyt – Islamic commemoration of Sacrifice (Prophet Ibrahim's/Abraham's intended sacrifice of his son)

Qyig'ir bo'yin – neck movements in Uzbek dances

R

Rabbiul avval – a month, when the Prophet Muhammad was born

Radif – a repetitive word at the end of *Ghazal*

Raga – Indian music which appeals to the intellect (Gnostic)

Raja – hope, a stage in Sufism

Risola – a treatise

Rizo – acceptance, a stage in Sufism

Rost – a part of Shashmaqam, means 'true'

Rubab – Central Asian musical instrument, a lute

Rubinon – means 'seeing the face', a stage in the wedding ceremony, when the bride shows her face to the relatives of the groom

Ruboi – a genre of poetry, a quatrain with the rhyme scheme a-a-b-a

S

Sabr – tolerance, a stage in Sufism

Salavat – genre of glorification of the Prophet Muhammad

Salmoniy – a professional guild of cleaners

Samo – (Arabic *sama*) – means listening, Sufi extasis

Sanaat nasiyat – nomadic didactic songs

Sarahbor – the main part of every *Maqom* in Shashmaqam, means 'main message'

Savt – music in the abstract (celestial) sense

Sayfiy – a professional guild of military people

Sayid – descendant of the Prophet Muhammad

Segoh – a part of Shashmaqam

Ser malak/sumalak – a sweet halva cooked from fresh offshoots of grain, for Navruz

Sezarb – a rhythm of *Doira*, means 'three beats'

Shahada – a formula of belonging to Islam, consisting of the words: 'There is no God, but Allah, and Muhammad is His Prophet'

Shariat – code of Muslim regulations, at the same time one of the stages of Sufism

Shashmaqam – Uzbek and Tajik musical cycle, consisting of six *Maqoms*

Shavq – passion, a stage in Sufism

Shayx/sheikh – a religious, Sufi master

Shogird – an apprentice

Shu'ba – a part of Maqom

Shukr – acceptance, a stage in Sufism

Silsilah – a chain of masters–apprentices both in Sufism and in professional guilds

Sovchi solish/Unashish – the process of matching

Sozanda – a musician, instrument player

Sozlanish – to tune, term in Sufism and in apprenticeship

Sunnat – Islamic code of behaviour taken from the life of the Prophet Muhammad

Sunnat-Toy – a circumcision party

Sura – a chapter in the Holy Qu'ran

Surnay – a Central Asian musical instrument, a conical oboe

Suvora – a genre of an Uzbek/Tajik classic song

Suzane – Uzbek/Tajik traditional wall-hanging embroidery

Syut-Gazan – a Turkmen ritualistic song calling for rain

T

Tabib – a traditional healer

Talqin – commentary, a musical part of Shashmaqam

Tanbur – Central Asian musical instrument, long-necked plucked lute with three strings

Tandyr – a clay oven for baking bread

Tanovar – an Uzbek dance and tune

Tarab – music which induces motion of the body (artistic)

Taralalai – a folk song genre among the Uzbeks of Afghanistan

Tariqat – a Way, used for distinguishing different schools of Sufism (different *Tariqats*), at the same time the second station of Sufism after *Shariat*, before *Ma'rifat* and *Haqiqat*

Tarona – instrumental pieces of Shashmaqam

Tasavvuf – Sufism

Tashqari – the outer part of the Uzbek traditional household, where men are allowed

Tavajjuh – contemplation, a stage in Sufism

Tawakkul – hope, prospect of God, a stage of Sufism

Tawba – (Arabic *Tawba*) – confession, repentance, an initial stage in Sufism

Tawba tazarru – a religious genre of repentance songs

Tayawwun – the theory of 'colour' of the soul according to Kubroviya Sufi school

Ta'ziyya – mourning, compassion, a genre of ritualistic, religious songs

Tazkira – a treatise

Terma – Uzbek folk songs of a joyful, playful nature

Tolgau – a nomadic genre of song

Tor/Tar – Central Asian musical instrument, a lute with wire strings

Toy – an Uzbek/Tajik/Uighur party, celebrating different events (birth, circumcision, marriage, etc.)

U

Ufor – a musical piece from Shashmaqam

Ufori chillyaki – 'Fragrance of ascetic 40 days'

Ufori Qalabandi – 'Fragrance imprisoned in the castle'

Umma – global Islamic nation

Uns – friendship, a stage in Sufism

Urfan – knowledge, enlightenment in Sufism

Ushshoq – means 'lovers', musical pieces in Shashmaqam

Ustad/Usto – a master

Usul – rhythms of *Doira*

Uzlat – seclusion, a stage in Sufism

V

Vird – whirling, Sufi dance

Voiz – a person who delivers the Islamic sermon

Y

Yakkahon – a solo singer

Yakzarb – a rhythm of *Doira*, means 'one beat'

Yalla – an Uzbek/Tajik song with dance

Yaqin – confidence, a stage in Sufism

Yaremezan – a Turkmen festivity song

Yassaviya – a school of Sufism founded by Ahmad Yassaviy (twelfth century)

Yassaviyhonlik – reading of Yassaviy's poetry

Yelka qoqish – shoulder movements in Uzbek dances

Yelka titrama – shoulder shaking, movements in Uzbek dances

Yor-yor – a genre of wedding songs

Yovvoyi – wild, a mode of singing

Yurta – a nomadic tent

Yusufiy – a professional guild of craftsmen

Z

Zikr – a Sufi meditation, remembrance of Allah

Zikr Jahriy – a loud *Zikr*

Zohir – obvious, apparent, opposite to *Botin* – hidden

Zuhd – temperance, a stage in Sufism

Bibliography

Abduvakhitov, Abdujabar (1993) Islamic Revivalism in Uzbekistan. In: Dale F. Eickelman (ed.) *Russia's Muslim Frontiers. New Directions in Cross-Cultural Analysis.* Bloomington and Indianapolis: Indiana University Press, pp. 79–100.

Abdullaev, Rustambek (1982) *Zhanr Katta Asula i ego nositeli,* pp. 9–10.

Abul Muhsin Muhammad Boqir ibn Muhammad Ali (1993) *Bahouddin Balogardon,* Tashkent; Yozuvchi, 5 bet.

Ahrari, M. and Beal, James (1996) *The New Great Game in Central Asia,* McNair Paper, No. 47, Washington: Institute for National Strategic Studies, p. 23.

Aitmatov, Chingiz (2007) *Jamilya.* London: Telegram, pp. 66–7.

Akbarov, Ilyas (1982) Junus Rajabi, Tashkent: Gafur Gulyam, pp. 7–8.

Akbarov, Ilyas (1987) Музика лугати, Tashkent: Gafur Gulyam.

Akiner, Shirin (1986) *Islamic peoples of the Soviet Union,* London: KPI.

Akiner, Shirin (1995) The Struggle For Identity. In: Jed Synder (ed.) *After Empire: The Emerging Geopolitics of Central Asia.* Washington: National Defense University Press, p. 7.

Alektorov, Baksa (1900) *Izvestiya* of the Society of Archeology, History and Ethnography under the Kazan University, v. XY1, edition 1, pp. 34–35.

Alimbayeva, K. and M. Ahmedov (1959) *Narodnye muzykanty Uzbekistana* (Folk Musicians of Uzbekistan), Tashkent, p. 53.

Amanova, Roza. *Kurmanbek Eposu.* Bishkek, 4CDs, 8B4404.

Amir Temur in World History, Paris: United Nations Education Science And Culture Organisation (UNESCO); 1996.

Antologia Turkmenskoi poezii (*Anthology of Turkmen Poetry*), (1949), Hudozhestvennaya literatura, Moscow.

Arabi, Ibn (1988) *Sufis of Andalusia,* trans. R.W.J. Austin Sherborne, Gloucestershire: Beshara Publications, pp. 25–6.

Ashirov, Adhamjon (2008) *Drevnie religioznye verovania v tradizionnom bytu uzbekskogo naroda (po materialam Ferganskoi doliny).* (Ancient religious beliefs in Uzbek traditional life [Ferghana Valley's case].) Avtoreferat dissertazyii na soiskanie uchenoi stepeni doktora istoricheskyh nauk, Academiya Nauk Uzbekistana, Tashkent.

Azemoun, Youssef (2007) *Halının Sunduğu Bazı Dil ve Müzik Kavramlan* (Some Linguistic and Musical Concepts which Carpets Present), Harvard, pp. 120–26.

Azemoun, Youssef and Aldiss, Brian (1995) *Songs from the Steppes of Central Asia,* UK: The Society of Friends of Makhtumkuli, p. 9.

Babajanov, B. (2001) Vozrojdenie deiatelnosti sufiyskih grup v Uzbekistane. In: *Sufizm v Tsentralnoi Azii (zarubejnye issledovaniia). Sbornik statei pamiati Frittsa Maiera (1912–1998).* St. Petersburg: Nauka, pp. 333–59.

Babajanov, Bakhtiyor (1992) O zenskikh sufiskikh centrakh-mazarakh v Srednej Azii XVI-XVIIvv. In: *Srednyaia Azia i mirovaja civilizacija.* Mezhdunarodnaya Konferenziyya 'Srednaa Azia I mirovaya zivilizaziya', Tezisy dokladov, Tashkent, Izdatel'stvo Akademyi Nauk Uzbekistana, pp. 17–18.

Babajanov, B. and M. Komilov (2000) Razvitie religioznoi situatsii v Ferganskoi doline: problemy i perspektivy izucheniia. In: *Obschestvennoe mnenie. Prava cheloveka,* Tashkent, No. 1–2, pp. 95–102.

Babajanov, B. and Komilov M. Domulla (2001) Hindustani and the Beginning of the "Great Schisme" among Moslems of Uzbekistan. In: Stephan Doudiangion and Hisao Komatzu (eds) *Politics and Islam in Russia and Central Asia.* London, New York and Bahrain: Routledge, pp. 195–220.

Bahtin, M.M. (1965) *The Work of Fransua Rable and Popular Culture of the Middle Ages,* Moscow: Khudozhestvennaya literature, p. 1.

Baiburin, A.K. (1988) *On Ethnographic Research of Etiquette: Etiquette of the Peoples of Asia Minor,* Moscow: Nauka.

Baldauf, Ingeborg (1984) *Zur Religiosen Praxis Ozbekisher Frauen in Nordafghanistan.* Religious and Lay Symbolism in the Altaic World, Germany, Wallberberg.

Basilov, Vladimir (1997) Chosen by the Spirits. In: Marjorie Mandelstam Balzer (ed.) *Shamanic Worlds: Rituals and Lore of Siberia and Central Asia,* A North Castle Book (originally published in New York: M.E. Sharp, 1990), p. 30.

Begmatov, Soibjon (1995) *Tradizyi Iskusstva Hafizov Ferganskoi Doliny.* Avtorefeerat dis na soiskanie uchenoi stepeni kanddiddata iskusstvovedeniya, Tashkent, UDK 78:03(09); 781, 7, p. 10.

Bertels, Evgenyi (1948) *Roman ob Alexandre,* M-L, Izd Ac Nauk SSR, p. 137.

Bertels, Evgenyi, Sufii (2002) *Voshoghdenie k istine* (Sufi: an assessment to the true), Moscow: EKSMO-Press, pp. 477–80.

Bodrogligeti, Andras J.E. (1987) The Impact of Ahmad Yasavi's Teaching on the Cultural and Political life of the Turks of Central Asia. In: *Turk Dili Arastirmalari Yilligi. Belleten (1992),* Ankara, pp. 35–41.

Bolshevik, Kazakhstana (The Bolshevik of Kazakhstan), Alma-Ata (1935) No. 3, p. 61.

Bolshevik, Kazakhstana (The Bolshevik of Kazakhstan), Alma-Ata (1938) No. 5, p. 55.

Bolshevik, Kazakhstana (The Bolshevik of Kazakhstan), Alma-Ata (1939) No. 4, p. 94.

Buhoriy, Sadriddin Salim (1993) *Dilda Yor,* Tashkent, G'afur G'ulom nashriyoti, p. 46.

Burke, Kenneth (1973) Definition of man. In *Language as Symbolic Action: Essays on Life, Literature, and Method,* Berkeley, CA: University of California Press.

Burney, Abbas Shemeem (2002) *The Female Voice in Sufi Ritual,* Austin: University of Texas Press.

CAR (Central Asian Review) (1957) *The Social Structure and Customs of the Kazakhs.* 5 (1): pp. 5–22.

CAR (1958) *The Survival of Religion and Social Customs in Uzbekistan.* 6 (1): pp. 5–15.

CAR (1959) *The People of Central Asia: Survival of Religion.* 7 (2): pp. 109–16.

Cagatay, Ergun (1996) *Once Upon a Time in Central Asia,* Tetragon Istanbul:

Cho'lpon (1991) *Kecha va Kunduz,* Tashkent: G'afur G'ulom.

Djumaev, Alexander (1995) K izucheniy ritualov 'arvohi pir' i 'kamarbardon' v gorodskyh tzehah muzykantov Srednei Azii. In: *Obshetvennye nauki v Uzbekistane.* Tashkent, No. 5–8, pp. 163–70.

Djumaev, Alexander (1996) Turkestanskij Starets Hodzha Akhmad Yassavi i musulmanskye dukhovnye pesnopenia. *Musykalnaja Akademija* 3–4, Moskva.

Djumaev, Alexander (2001) Hudojestvennye tendentsii i esteticheskie idealy v muzyke. In: *Amir Temur v mirovoi istorii.* Izdanie vtoroe, dop. i pererab. Tashkent, p. 179.

Djumaev, Alexander (2004) *Kambar-ata (Kambar, Baba-Gambar) I musykal'nye tradizyi narodov Srednei Azii,* Beshkek: Kurak, No. 6, p. 9.

Djumaev, Alexander (2004) Sredneaziatskaya hanaka, sufyiskie prepisaniya o slushanyii(sama') I tradiziya duhovnyh pesnopenyi (honakoi). V kn: Transoxiana. Istoriya I kul'tura. Sbornik nauchnyh statei. Tashkent (Seriya: Kul'tura Srednei Azyii v pis'mennyh istochnikah, dokumentah I materialah") s 314–21.

Dodkhudoeva, Larisa (2003) *Cultural Leadership in Central Asia: Ancient and Medieval Epoch.* Dushanbe: The Institute of History, Archaeology, Ethnography after A. Donish, the Academy of Science of Tajikistan, p. 60.

Edigen, Turkmen shygryetinin durdeneleri (1991) *Seven Volumes,* Ashgabat, Turan.

Eliade, Mircea (1972) *Shamanism:Archaic Techniques of Ecstasy,* Princeton, NY: Princeton University Press.

Esposito, John (ed.) (2004) *The Oxford Dictionary of Islam.* Oxford: Oxford University Press.

Farmer, Henry George (1925) *The Arabian Influence on Musical Theory.* London: H. Reeves.

Fathi, Habiba (1997) Otines: the Unknown Women Clerics of Central Asian Islam. *Central Asian Survey* 16 (1), pp. 27–43; Le pouvoir des *otin,* institutrices coraniques, dans l'Ouzbekistan independant. In: *Cahiers d'Asie Centrale* (1998) No. 5–6. Boukhara-la-Noble, Tashkent – Aix-en-Provence, pp. 313–333; Femmes d'autorite dans l'Asie centrale contemporaine (2004) *Quete des ancetres et recompositions identitaires dans l'islam postsovietique.* Paris: Maisonneuve & Larose, Institut Francais d'Etudes sur l'Asie Centrale.

Fierman, William (1994) Policy Toward Islam in Uzbekistan in the Gorbachev Era. *Nationalities Papers.* 22 (1), pp. 225–46.

Fitrat, Abdurauf (2000) *Tanlangan asarlar,* Toshkent, Ma'naviyat, 17, 82 betlar.

Friedman, Victor (1986), *Balkan Linguistics: Problems of Dialectology, Problems of Possessiveness,* Bucharest, p. 146.

Gavrilov, Ivan (1936) *The Tasks of the Young Communist League on the Cultural Front,* The Bolshevik of Kazakhstan No. 4.

Gennep,Van, Arnold (1960) *The Rites of Passage,* Chicago: The University of Chicago Press.

Gilberg, R. (1984) How to recognize a shaman among other religious specialists. In: Mihaly Hoppel (ed.) *Shamanism in Euroasia.* Partone, Germany, Horodot.pp. 21–7.

Gluschenko, Evgeniy (2001) *Geroi Imperii. Portrety rossiyskih kolonialnyh deiatelei.* Moscow: Izdatelskiy om XXI vek – Soglasie.

Gumilyev, L. N. (1967) Гумилев Л.Н. Древние тюрки, М, с 23.

Hajib, Yusuf Khass (1983) *Wisdom of Royal Glory (Kutadgu Bilig): A Turko-Islamic Mirror for Princes*, trans., with an introduction and notes, by Robert Dankoff. University of Chicago Press, p. 281.

Hajib,Yusuf Khass. (1985) *Qutadghu bilik* (Sogdian-based Old Uyghur script facsimile edition, Vienna manuscript). Urumchi: Xinjiang renmin.

Harshahi, M. (1897) *Tarifa Bukhoro*, Toshkent, 63 bet.

Heike, Owusu (2000) *Inca, Maya and Aztecs*, trans. R. Andreeva, Ilya, Izmir, p. 27.

Helminski and Adams, Camille (1994) *Women & Sufism*, Gnozis, No. 30.

Hultkrantz, Aks (1978) Ecological and phenomenological Aspects of Shamanism. In: Mihali. Hoppel (ed.) *Shamanism in Siberia*. Budapesht: Akademia Kiado, pp. 27–58.

Huccetul-Islam (1985) *Imam Gazali, Ihyau ulumid-din*, Bedir, Istanbul, cilt 2, bet 751.

Inoyat-khan, Pir-o-Murshid (1914) *A Sufi Message of Spiritual Liberty*, London, p. 47.

Ibragimov, Oqil (2006) *Ferghano-Tashkentskie Makomy*, Tashkent: UNESCO.

Ishakov, Faizulla (1997) *Natsional'naia politika tsarizma v Turkestane. 1867–1917.* Tashkent: FAN.

Ismailov, Esmagambet (1957) *The Akyns*, Alma-Ata, p. 187.

Ismailov, Hamid and Sultanova, Razia (1996) K poetike klassicheskoy uzbekskoy gazeli. In: Ismailov Hamid (ed.) *O'zbek ongi chizgilari*, Tashkent, p. 41.

Ismailov, Hamid and Sultanova, Razia (1990) *K metodologii izucheniya pyaterichnogo kanona v hudojestvennom tvorchestve Vostoka (na primere Hamsy i Shahshmakoma).* M, Izd. Nauka, p. 227.

Ismailov, Hamid (2006) *The Railway*, Harvill-Secker/Random House, p. 299.

Izvestia, 24 August issue (1932)

Jirmundskyi (1962) *Narodnyi Heroic epic*, M-L, p. 282.

Jomi, Abdurahmoni (1990) Osor. Dar hasht jild. Jildi hashtum. Nafahat al-Uns. Dushanbe.

Jung, Angelika (1989) *Quellen der traditionellen Kunstmusik der Usbeken und Tadshiken Mittelasiens. Untersuchungen zur Entstehung und Entwicklung des sasmaqam.* Beitrage zur Ethnomusikologie. Band 23. Hamburg: Verlag der Musikalienhandlung Karl Dieter Wagner, p. 14.

Kabulov, B. (1935) *On the Bolts of the Regional Cultural Congress.* The Bolshevik of Kazakhstan, No. 6, p. 39.

Kadyrova, Mahbuba (1980) *Svetoch vo t'me.* Tashkent: Izdatel'stvo FAN Uzbekskoi SSR.

Kandiyoty, Deniz (1998) Rural Livelihood and Social Networks in Uzbekistan: Perspectives from Andijan, *Central Asian Survey,* 17 (4), pp. 561–678.

Karomatov, Faizulla and Elsner, Jurgen (1984) *Maqam i maqom.* V knige: Muzyka narodov Azii i Afriki. Vypusk chetvertyi. M, p. 95.

Karimov, Naim (Dir.) (2005) *Ismoil Gasprinskiy va Turkiston.* Tashkent: Sharq.

al-Kashgari, Mahmud. Divan lugat at-turk (Compendium of the Turkic Dialects). Modern Uyghur edition (Xinjiang renmin, 1980); Chinese edition (Beijing: Minzu, 2002).

Kastren, M.A (1860) Trip to Lapland, North Siberia and Russia, *Journal of Geography and Travels: Geographical Compilation*, Moscow, vol. 6. part II Compilation of old and new travels, p. 388.

Keldysh, Georgyi (ed.) (1990) Музыкальный энциклопедический словарь (The music encyclopaedic dictionary) , Moskva, Sovetskaya encyklopedia.

Khalid, Adeeb (1998) *The Politics of Muslim Cultural Reforms. Jadidism in Central Asia.* Berkeley and Los Angeles: University of California Press.

Kharuzin, Aleksei (1988) Stepnye ocherki *kirgizskaĭ?a Bukeevskaĭ?a orda : stranichki iz zapisnoi? knigi s 13 fototipnymi tablĭt?s?ami* by Al Kharuzin, Tip. A.A. Levenson (Moskva).

Kleinmichel, Sigrid (2000) *Halpa in Choresm (Hwarazm) und atin ayi im Ferghanatal: Zur Geschichte des Lesens in Usbekistan im 20. Jahrhundert,* Das Arabische Buch, p. 363.

Komilov, Najmiddin (1996) Tasavvuf, Tashkent, Yozuvchi, 117 bet.

Koprulu, Fuad (1993) *Turk edebiyatinda ilk mutasavvifler,* Ankara, p. 98.

Koshifiy, Husayn Voiz (1991) XY century's Herat manuscript *On Ustad (Master) and his Conditions,* Dushanbe, Adib, translated from Persian by Futuvatnomai Sultoniy.

Krader, Lawrence (1963) *Peoples of Central Asia.* Bloomington: Univ. U.A., Uralic and Altaic Series, vol. 20.

Krader, Lawrence (1963) *Social Organization of the Mongol-Turkic Pastoral Nomads.* The Mouton: Hague.

Kuper, A. and Kuper, J. (1987) *The Social Science Encyclopaedia,* 2nd ed., London: Routledge.

Lambert, W.G. (1987) *Devotion: The Languages of Religion and Love.* In: *Figurative language in the Ancient Near East,* SOAS: University of London, p. 25.

Laufer, Berthold (1917) Origin of the Word Shaman. *American Anthropologist* 19: 361–71.

Levin, Theodore (1999) The Hundred Thousand Fools of God: Musical Travels in Central Asia (and Queens, New York), Indiana University Press.

Levin, Theodore and Sultanova, Razia (2001), The classical music of Uzbeks and Tajiks. In: *The Garland Encyclopedia of World Music,* Vol. 6, *The Middle East,* Routledge, pp. 913–14.

Liberated Kazakh Woman (1938) "Editorial". Bolshevik Kazakhstana (The Bolshevik of Kazakhstan), Alma-Ata, No. 3.

Lykoshin, Nikolay (1916) *A half of lifetime in Turkistan,* St Petersburg

Manas – geroicheskyi epos kyrgyzskogo naroda (1968) Frunze, p. 94.

Margoliouth, D.S. (1960) *Kâdiriyya. The Encylopaedia of Islam,* 2nd ed., vol. IV, p. 381.

Matyoqubov, Otanazar (2004) Maqomot, Tashkent, Musiqa, 92 bet.

Melik-Shahnazarova, N.G. (1988), *The National Tradition and Composition,* Doctor's Thesis syn., M, p. 31.

Mironov (1929) *Musyka Uzbekov* (Music of the Uzbeks), Samarkand, p. 9.

Musaev, Samar (1979) Epic Manas, Academy of Science of Kyrgyzstan, Frunze, Ilim, p. 47.

Musical Culture of Kazakhstan (1938) *Folk Art*, Vol. 12, p. 36.

Naroditskaya, Inna (2005) *Azerbaijani Mugham and Carpet: Cross-Domain Mapping*, Ethnomusicology Forum, Vol. 14, No. 1, Taylor and Francis Group Ltd.

Neergard, Soren (1999) *Oriental Carpet and Textiles Studies*, IV, Milan, p. 232.

Наливкин, В.П., Наливкина М.В. (1886) Очерк быта женщины оседлого населения Ферганы. – Казань.

Narodnoe Iskusstvo (*Folk Art*) (1939) Moscow, Pravda, Vol. 3, p. 17.

Narodnoe Iskusstvo (*Folk Art*) (1939) Moscow, Pravda, Vol. 4, p. 24.

Negria, Lev (ed.) (1991) *Islam: The Encyclopaedic Dictionary*, Moskva: Nauka, pp. 139–41.

Neubauer, Echard (1980) *Islamic Religious Music*, New Grove, vol. 9, pp. 342–49.

New York Times, 18 October 2000

Nishoti, Muhammadniyaz (1967) *Husnu Dil (Beauty and Heart)*, Tashkent: Gafura Gulyama.

Nodira She'riyatidan (1979) Tashkent 3-6 bet.

Nurnpeisov, J. (1935) *On Mass Political and Cultural Work in Villages*, The Bolshevik of Kazakhstan, No. 4, p. 18.

Olcott, Martha Brill (1999) *Russia After Communism*, Washington, DC: Carnegie Endowment for International Peace.

Olcott, Martha Brill (2005) *Central Asia's Second Chance*, Washington, DC: Carnegie Endowment for International Peace.

Owusu, Heike (2000) Inca, Maya and Aztecs, trans. R. Andreeva, Ilya, Izmir, p. 27.

Paksoy, H.B. (1992) The Sun is also Fire, In: *Central Asia Monuments*, ISIS Press: Istanbul, p. 3.

Pir-o-Murshid, Inayat Khan (1914) *A Sufi Message of Spiritual Liberty*, London, p. 47.

Popov, A.A. (1936, 1948, 1984) *Posthumous: Nganasany: sotsial'noe ustroistvo i verovaniya*, Leningrad: Nauka.

Popov, A.A. (1968) *How Sereptie Djaroukin of the Hganasans (Tavgi Samoyeds) became a Shaman*, Popular Beliefs and folklore tradition in Siberya, Utal-Altaic Series 57, Bloomington.

Pravda Vostoka (1933) 9 July.

Pravda Vostoka (1933) 24 June.

Pravda Vostoka (1934) 18 July.

Qosimov, Begali (2002) *Milliy Uigonish: Jasorat, ma'rifat, fidoyilik*, Tashkent: Ma'naviyat.

Qureshi, Regula (1972) Indo-Muslim Religious Music: An Overview, in *Asian Music*, No. 2, p. 16.

Qureshi, Regula (1992/1993) *Popular Religious Music*, New Grove, Muslim p. 145.

Rajabov, Ishoq (1976) *Maqomlar masalasiga doir*, Tashkent: Fan, bet 56.

Reichl, Karl (2003) The search for origins: Ritual aspects of the performance of epic, *Journal of Historical Pragmatics*, 4 (2), pp. 249–67(19).

Reinhardt, Ursula (1990) The Veils are Lifted. Music of Turkish Women. Intercultural Music Studies, In: Peter Baumann and Linda Fujie (eds) *Vol. 1, Music, Gender and Culture*. Wilhelmshaven: Florean Noetzel Verlag.

Religovedenie. Enziklopedicheskyi slovar (Theology, Encyclopaedic dictionary) (2006) A.P. Zabiyako, A.N. Krasnikova, E.S. Elbakyan (eds) Akademicheskyi Proekt, Moskva, p. 609.

Resolution of the Regional Communist party Committee (1935) *The Bolshevik of Kazakhstan*, No. 5, p. 94.

Reuel, Hanks (1994) The Islamic Factor in Nationalism and National-Building in Uzbekistan: Causative Agent or Inhibitor. *Nationalities Papers*, 22 (2) pp. 309-23.

Rossia, Zapad i musulmanskiy Vostok v kolonial'nuyu epohu. [Sbornik statei] (1996) St.Petersburg.

Sagalaev, A.M., Oktyabr'skaya, I.V. (1990) *Traditional World Outlook of Turkic Peoples of South Siberia. Sign and Ritual.* Novosibirsk, Ch: Laughter and Tears, p. 160.

Samoilovich, A. (1927) Kukol'nyi ustav – risola zeha artistov D340/341. Materialy po ethnografyi, T 3, vypusk vtoroi, Izdatel'stvo Gosudarstvennogo Russkogo Muzeya , Ethnograficheskogo otdela, Leningrad, s 115.

Sartori, Paolo (2003) *Altro che seta: Corano e progresso in Turkestan* (1865–1917). Pasian di Prato (UD).

Schimmel, Annemarie (1975) *Mystical Dimension of Islam*, Chapel Hill: University of North Carolina Press, p. 432.

Schurmann, H.F. (1962) The Mongols of Afghanistan: An ethnography of the Mongols and related peoples of Afghanistan. *Central Asiatic Studies no. 4.* 's-Gravenhage: Mouton.

Semyonov, A. (1950) *K istorii uzbekskoy klassicheskoy muzyki, Rukopis'*, Bib-ka Instituta iskusstvovedeniya im. Tashkent: Hamzy.

Sharipov, Rustam (2002) *Turkiston jadidchilik harakati tarihidan.* Tashkent: Uqituvchi.

Sidky, H. (1990) Malang, Sufis, and Mystics: An Ethnographic and Historical Study of Shamanism in Afghanistan. *Asian Folklore Studies*, 49, pp. 275–301.

Snesarev, Georgyi (1969) Реликты домусульманских верований и обрядов у Узбеков Хорезма (*Relicts of pre-Isiamic ritualsl and rites of Khorezm's Uzbeks*), Moscow.

Snesarev, Georgyi (1971) К вопросу о происхождении празднества суннат-тои в его среднеазиатском варианте // Занятия и быт народов Средне?? Азии. – Л, Vol. 3. – C, pp. 256–72.

Social'no-utopicheskie idei v Srednei Azii (1983) Tashkent, Fan, Uzbek SSR, p. 32.

Strauss, Neil (2000) The Pop Life: Uzbekistan Dreams Made of Music. *New York Times*, October 18.

Suhareva, Olga (1959). O nekotoryh elementah sufisma, geneticheski svyazannyh s shamanstvom // Materialy vtorogo soveshaniya arheologov I etnografov Srednei Azzi. Moskva-Leningrad, S 128–33.

Sultanova, Razia (1994) *Pojushchee Slovo Uzbekskikh Obrjadov.* Almaty: Konzhyk.

Sultanova, Razia (1998) *O vzaimosvyazi usulya I ritma melodidd v vocal#nyx chastyax Shahshmakoma.* Tashkent: Yana.

Sultanova, Razia (1998) Rhythm of Shahsmaqam, Tashkent: Yana, p. 28.

Sultanova, Razia (2005) *En soulevant le voile*, in *Cahiers de Musiques Traditionelles*, Volume 18, Ateliers d'ethnomusicologie, Geneva.

Sultanova, Razia (2005) Music and Identity in Central Asia: Introduction. In *Special Issue of Ethnomusicology Forum*, 14 (2) pp. 131–42.

Sultanova, Razia (2008) Female Celebrations in Uzbekistan and Afghanistan: The Power of Cosmology, In: Ursula Hemetek, Gerlinde Haid, Adelaide Reyes (eds). *Yearbook for Traditional Music*, Volume 40, International Council for Traditional Music: Australia.

Szuppe, Maria. (2003) Status, Knowledge and Politics: Women in Sixteenth Century Safavid Iran, In: Beck and G. Nashat (eds) *Women in Iran, vol. In: From the Rise of Islam to 1800*, University of Illinois Press: Urbana, Illinois, pp. 140–69.

The Oxford Dictionary of Islam. John L. Esposito (ed.), Oxford University Press: Sufism, pp. 302–03.

Troitskaya (1925). Lechenie bol'nyh izgnaniem duhov (kuchuruk) sredi osedlogo naselenia Turkestana // Byulleten' SAGU, No.10, s. 145–55.

Troitskaya (1928) *Zhenskyi zikr v Starom*, Tashkente, p. 174.

Ungvizkaya, M.A. (1972) Mainogasheva V.E *Hakassian Poetical Folk Creativity*, Abakan.

Upton, Charles (1988) *Doorkeeper of the Heart: Versions of Rabi'a* , Putney, VT: Threshold Books, p. 36.

Uspenskyi, Victor (1980) *Nauchnoe nasledie, vospominaniya sovremennikov, dokumanty, pis'ma.* Tashkent: Gafur Gulyama.

Uspenskyi, Vickor Belyaev Viktor (1979) *Turkmenskaya Musica*, Ashgabad Publisher, "Turkmenistan", pp. 61–2.

Uvaysiy, Jahonotin (1980) *Uvaysiy she'ritidan*, Tashkent, Izdatel'stvo ZK KP Uzbekistana.

Vakhidov (1976) *Uzbek Soviet Song*, Tashkent, pp. 50–1.

Verbitski, V.I. (1885) *World Perception and Folk Creativity of Siberian Indigenous Tribes* (Ethnographic materials). Literature compilation, SPB, p. 338.

Walker, Barbara G. (1988) *The Woman's Dictionary of Symbols and Sacred Objects*, Pandora, p. 176.

Yunusaliev, B. (1958) *Manas,* Kirish Sez, Frunze, c. IY.

Zeranska-Kominek, Slawomira with Lebeuf, Arnold (1997) *The Tale of Crazy Harman: The Musician and the Concept of Music in the Turkmen Epic Tale.* Warsaw: Harman Dali.

Zhainadarov, O. (2006) Мифы древнего Казахстана (Myths of ancient Kazakhstan), Almaty, Arona Ltd.

Ziyoev, H. (1998) *Turkistonda Rossia tajovuzi va hukmronligiga qarshi kurash* (XVIII–XX asr boshlari). Tashkent: Sharq.

For more evidence on medieval female Iranian female poets see: Szuppe, Maria (2003) Status, Knowledge and Politics: Women in Sixteenth Century Safavid Iran, In: Beck and G. Nashat (eds), *Women in Iran, Vol. I: From the Rise of Islam to 1800*, Urbana, Illinois: University of Illinois Press, pp. 140–69.

Index

Lightning Source UK Ltd.
Milton Keynes UK
UKHW020028150621
385531UK00006B/169

9 781780 766874